BRITISH LABOUR STRUGGLES:
CONTEMPORARY PAMPHLETS 1727-1850

THE AFTERMATH OF THE
"LAST LABOURERS' REVOLT"

Fourteen Pamphlets

1830-1831

Arno Press

A New York Times Company/New York 1972

Reprint Edition 1972 by Arno Press Inc.

Reprinted from copies in the Kress Library
Graduate School of Business Administration,
Harvard University

The imperfections found in this edition
reflect defects in the originals which
could not be eliminated.

BRITISH LABOUR STRUGGLES: CONTEMPORARY PAMPHLETS 1727-1850
ISBN for complete set: 0-405-04410-0

See last pages for complete listing.

Manufactured in the United States of America

Library of Congress Cataloging in Publication Data
Main entry under title:

The Aftermath of the "last labourers' revolt."

     (British labour struggles:
contemporary pamphlets 1727-1850)
     CONTENTS: An essay on the state of the country, in
respect to the condition and conduct of the husbandry
labourers, by F. Place [first published 1831?]--Swing
unmasked, by E. G. Wakefield [first published 1831]--
A letter to the Right Hon. Henry, Lord Brougham and
Vaux, Lord high chancellor of Great Britain, by J.
Richardson [first published 1831]. [etc.]
     1. Labor and laboring classes--Great Britain.
2. Poor--Great Britain. I. Series.
HD8389.A65   331.1'1'0942   72-2518
ISBN 0-405-04411-9

Contents

rates of profit in agriculture and in trade. By R. Torrens,
Esq. M.P.   2d ed. London, Longman & co., 1831.

Macqueen, Thomas Potter
The state of the nation, at the close of 1830 . . . London,
J. Ridgway, 1831.

Proposal for the establishment of village schools of industry,
submitted to the consideration of landowners and clergymen.
London, E. Bull, 1831

Farish, William Milner
A plan for immediately ameliorating the present distressed
condition of the agricultural poor, and permanently improving
their moral character: contained in a letter addressed to the
Right Hon. Viscount Melbourne, secretary of state for the
Home department . . . London, C. and J. Rivington
[etc., etc., 1830]

Postans, Thomas
Letter to Sir Thomas Baring, bart. M.P. &c. &c. &c. on the
causes which have produced the present state of the agricultural
labouring poor: to which are added practical hints for
bettering their condition. With a drawing and plan for a
double cottage . . . London, M. Staunton, 1831.

Gore, Montagu
Allotments of land. A letter to landed proprietors on the
advantages of giving the poor allotments of land . . .
London, J. Ridgway, 1831.

Demainbray, Rev., Stephen [George Francis Triboudet]
The poor man's best friend; or, Land to cultivate for his own
benefit: being the results of twenty-four years' experience.
In a letter to the Marquess of Salisbury, as given in evidence
before the House of lords' Committee on the poor laws. By the
Rev. S. Demainbray . . . London, J. Ridgway [etc., etc.] 1831.

Court, Major Henry
Tithes. Commutation versus composition: the rights of the
laity, and the rights of the church, illustrated, and proved not
to be the same; in a letter to the Lord Chancellor Brougham.
. . . London, J. Ridgway, 1831

AN
ESSAY

ON THE

STATE OF THE COUNTRY,

IN RESPECT TO THE

CONDITION AND CONDUCT

OF THE

HUSBANDRY LABOURERS,

AND TO THE

CONSEQUENCES
LIKELY TO RESULT THEREFROM.

NOT FOR SALE.

INNES, Printer, 61, Wells-street, Oxford-street, London.

AN investigation of this nature, to be complete, should consist of—

1. An exposition of the *actual condition* of the husbandry labourers.
2. An enquiry respecting the *causes* of their *condition*.
3. The *consequences* which have resulted, and are likely to result from their condition.
4. The *remedies*.

A detailed statement of the actual condition of the husbandry labourers would occupy a space incompatible with the limits prescribed to himself by the writer. It is agreed that the husbandry labourers are in a lamentable state of poverty: this has been shown in speeches in parliament; has been proved before committees of both houses, frequently exposed in the newspapers, and treated of more largely by respectable writers in books and pamphlets, and need not therefore be elucidated here.

The causes which have led to their distressed condition, and to the excesses they have committed, may all be traced to an increase of their number beyond the demand for their labour.

The causes of this increase could be stated without much difficulty; but this would also be going beyond the limits of the present Essay.

One case to show the increase, is as good as a thousand. Let us take the county of Kent. It has, in several instances, been proved before Committees of the Houses of Lord and Commons, that when as many labourers are employed as are sufficient to do all the work required to be done, there still remains many for whom no employment can be found. Every well-informed person, who has turned his attention to the subject, knows that there is a very large number of able-bodied persons in this county willing to work, but for whom no profitable employment can be found.

To enable those who have not given sufficient attention to the subject, clearly to comprehend the relative condition of farmers and labourers, it seems necessary to explain how the produce of the earth is obtained and distributed.

The farmer is a *capitalist,* that is, a man having property : he takes a farm, in the cultivation of which he expends his capital, or so much of it as is necessary to cultivate it. He lays out his capital thus : —

1. In providing necessary tools and implements, and in keeping them in repair; in horses, carts, &c.

2. In seed corn, and other seeds.

3. In stock, or cattle.

4. In the maintenance of servants and labourers, to cultivate the land and gather the produce, to tend the cattle, and assist in selling whatever the farm produces.

The produce the farmer has obtained, by having thus laid out his capital, is disposed of,—

1. To the Parson — he takes *one-tenth* of the produce as TITHE.

2. To the Landlord— he receives a certain sum raised by the sale of more or less of the produce, according to the market-price, in conformity to the agreement he has made with the farmer : this is RENT.

3. To the Parish as RATES, and to the State as TAXES.

4. To Himself, for the CAPITAL he advanced,

　　1. Wear and Tear of tools and implements.

　　2. Seeds.

　　3. Stock sold (in part).

　　4. Wages.

5. Profit. This is what *may* remain after all the before-mentioned claims on him have been paid : he cannot have any profit until they are paid.

It is reasonable to expect, that after the tithe has been drawn, the farmer should have the money he has advanced, returned to him; that is, he should have as much of his capital replaced as belongs to the preceding year's expenditure, and as much more as will enable him to pay—

1. Rent.

2. Taxes and rates.

3. Wages, and

4. To retain as much for himself as will enable him to maintain his family, and to lay by as much towards the settlement of his children in the world, as is usually obtained by persons engaged in other branches of business, who employ a like amount of capital, and give as much of their time to business as farmers give.

Under ordinary circumstances, farmers will be able to accomplish all these things. It is clear that when *tithes* have been drawn, *rent, taxes, rates,* and *wages* paid, what remains will be clear profit; including interest on the capital advanced; and that if the farmer be compelled to pay higher wages than he has been accustomed to pay, the difference must come from his clear profit.

If then any considerable increase of wages be taken from the farmer's profit, he must be ruined; and although neither farmers generally, nor labourers at all, are able thus to explain the operation, they all see, plainly enough, that the wages demanded cannot be paid unless the increase be deducted from *tithes* and *rent:* this has in many instances been anticipated by the husbandry labourers, who have promised to protect the farmers against the enforcement of every process to compel payment of the *tithe* first, and *rent* afterwards if necessary.

All the *profit* made from one end of the country to the other, may be represented by a certain sum; and any sum may be supposed to represent it. It must actually consist of the produce of the land, and of commodities, these being the only things with which business is or can be carried on*.

All the wages paid from one end of the country to the other, may be represented by a certain sum, and any sum may be supposed to represent them. *Wages must* actually consist of the produce of the land and of commodities, these being the only things the working people and husbandry labourers consume.

But some say—if wages rise, farmers, tradesmen, and manufacturers, can all raise the prices of the articles they deal in. This is so very absurd, that if it were not said by persons who ought to know better, and repeated by others who are led to conclusions without examining the premises from which they are drawn, the observation would not deserve to be noticed. As it is, it may be as well to say, that if the farmer could indemnify himself by raising the price of his produce, the labourer would be little benefitted by his increase of wages, and every-body else would be injured. Nothing can be more true, than that the price of farm produce, or of any commodity whatever, beyond the cost of production, does not depend

---

* If it be objected that money has been omitted, the answer is, that money would be useless without commodities, and that its use is merely to facilitate the exchange of commodities and farm produce.

on the will of farmers or manufacturers, but on the demand for the produce or manufactures; that is, the desire to exchange and the means of exchanging one sort of produce or manufactures for another sort of produce or manufactures. It therefore follows, as an inevitable consequence, that he who has nothing to give in exchange, or nothing which any body desires to have*, cannot be a purchaser, cannot be a consumer of any thing, unless it be given to him.

This includes the whole matter. It is not so much a question regarding the *price* of labour, as of the quantity of food and necessaries which a day's labour, or a year's labour, will procure for the working man, *when his labour is required;* in other words, when he is employed.

We may now suppose, that all the food and necessaries and conveniences which fall to the share of the farmers, the manufacturers, and others who employ husbandry labourers and working people, and also all that falls to the share of the working people and labourers, are brought to the same place; that the employers take their share, and the working people and labourers take their share. Each party have their share, and between them they have the whole quantity, all they can have for the ensuing year. In practice, the whole is not thus at once divided, but it is actually thus divided in the course of the year. It follows then, as certainly as the night does the day, that if one of the two parties demand more, and receive more, the other party must receive less. The reader who understands this, may proceed with its application to existing circumstances.

The working people who are employed in trades and manufactures, and are commonly called journeymen, are congregated together; they occasionally dispute with their employers; and sometimes strike, either to compel them to raise their wages, or to prevent them lowering their wages. These disputes and strikes enable them to decide pretty accurately on the actual power they have, either to raise their wages, or to prevent their falling: it leads them also to this just inference, namely, that the amount each workman does actually receive, is regulated by the number of hands, in each sort of employment respectively, being too few or too many. When for any considerable time the number of hands is too few, they compel their employers to raise their wages; and when the

---

* Labour is the only thing a poor man has to offer : it is subject to the same law as commodities.

number of hands has been for any considerable time too
many, their employers compel them to take lower wages.

Another important result of the combinations of workmen and their disputes with their employers is, the increase of useful knowledge, which prevents them doing
mischief to the property of their employers. Since workmen, by the repeal of the laws which forbade them to
combine either to raise their wages, or to regulate the
hours of working, have been repealed, they have generally abstained from doing mischief to the machines or
other property of their employers : very little mischief in
this way has been done since the final repeal of these laws
in 1826, and that little was done only by the most ignorant
of them.   No doubt need be entertained that, when
somewhat better informed, as workmen cannot fail to be,
all such unjustifiable proceedings will wholly cease *.

Vast numbers of working people are convinced that
destruction of machines and other property, must diminish,
and cannot increase, the quantity of employment, and this
conviction will become general.

Labourers in husbandry have not been able to associate
as workmen have done, and thus they have been debarred
the opportunities which workmen have had to instruct
one another. Workmen have been free agents in comparison with husbandry labourers, who have had no will of
their own. They have been interfered with in every possible way; they have been controlled and regulated in a
manner which tended to increase their number disropor-
tionately to employment, depressed them lower and lower,
and kept them in a state of ignorance, which deprived
them even of the hope of bettering their condition; it
prevented their understanding their relative situation, as
they might have been taught to understand it; and at
length *drove* them to commit enormities, by which they expected to draw attention to their condition; they resorted

---

* A very short time ago, in conversation with some
workmen who were complaining of the machinery used in
their trade, they were asked—" Why do you not, like the
husbandry labourers, break and burn the machinery ?"
The reply was—" NO, we will commit no violence :
" besides, some of the masters would be very much
" obliged to us for destroying their machines : many of
" them are almost out of date, in consequence of recent
" improvements : they would make the county pay as
" much money for their old machines as would enable
" them to replace them with the newest and most im-
" proved. No, no! we know better than that."

to intimidation in the only way which to them seemed likely even for a moment to be effectual; they knew that any attempt to intimidate by merely showing themselves in numbers would be useless; the time had long gone by, when such proceedings could have been of any use to them; and some, more desperate than others, set an example to all, which all could understand, and all were likely to follow, or to countenance; they set fire to stacks and barns; and yet when they commenced this course of proceeding, it was more from despair than hope, and probably (it may, indeed, almost be said certainly) without contemplating the increase of wages to which it led. The mischievous and lamentable example was followed; the intimidation it produced was at once apparent; advantage was taken of it, and increase of wages was demanded and obtained. Farmers have been compelled to sign agreements, and to promise to give wages which they cannot afford to pay. The labourers acknowledge this, but say they cannot afford to starve any longer, and starve they will not.

This, then, is the state of the case, wages are demanded and paid, which if they come from profit *must ruin* the farmers. Farmers must have a reasonable profit, or they must cease to carry on their business; they cannot have a reasonable profit, or any profit at all, if besides paying the wages demanded they pay TITHES, RENT, TAXES, and RATES.

Will intimidation cease? Will labourers desist from demanding wages which farmers cannot afford to pay? The answers are—No, they will not desist; intimidation will not cease. There may be, and most likely there will be, intervals of peace, or rather cessations of hostilities; but attempts to reduce wages, will again produce the burning of farm produce.

Much has been said of the efficacy of talking and writing to the husbandry labourers; but these at present would be utterly useless, as to any immediate effects to be produced on them. They should long since have been taught, it is too late to expect immediate good consequences from talking to men circumstanced as they are; their object is an increase of wages, and this to them, has become past, present, and future; they carry their reasoning no further. Talk to one of these men with the half-crown in his fist which he has received for his day's labour; tell him of the mischief of burning stacks and extorting wages; he knows the farmer cannot afford to pay, and the chances are ten to one, that he will show you the consequence of his conduct, by exhibiting the money, and reply to your arguments by laughing in your face.

To expect a *permanent* cessation of stack-burning, and a fall of the labourers' wages, which stack-burning has extorted, is unreasonable ; and he who does expect it will probably be disappointed.

What, then, may a reasonable man calculate upon as the result? Let us enquire.

1. Labourers obtain from farmers wages which they cannot afford to pay, if they are also to pay *Tithes, Rent, Taxes,* and *Rates.*

2. If farmers pay these wages, and pay them they must, they cannot long continue either to pay *Tithes* or *Rent** in full, if indeed they can pay much or any thing towards either; the deficiency must therefore fall on the Parsons and Landlords. The immediate terror from withholding tithes and rent, will be less than that which compels them to pay the increased wages and rates; add to which, that they will calculate on the protection of the labourers, to whom they pay good wages, against both Parsons and Landlords.

3. But if tithes and rents are not paid, or paid only in part, the incomes of Parsons and Landlords will either be wholly or partly destroyed, and they will be compelled to discharge servants, to purchase fewer articles from tradesmen, and to consume fewer manufactured goods.

4. The business of tradesmen and manufacturers must therefore fall off; and they, too, will discharge servants and working people: many of these must come upon the parish, for it will be impossible for them to procure employment, and the poor-rate will increase as the ability to pay it decreases †.

5. Thus poverty and misery will increase amongst servants and workpeople, the profits of their employers will fall, embarrassment will come on, and when this has proceeded to a certain length, the trading and manufacturing portion of the people will refuse to pay taxes.

---

* It has been concluded, from calculations made to ascertain the fact, that an increase of one shilling per head per day, to every husbandry labourer above 18 years of age, with a proportional rise to all below that age, and to women, and including only they who are actually employed, amounts to a sum greater than the whole rental received from land.

† If the condition of husbandry labourers should improve faster than servants, and work-people are compelled to come upon the parish, the poor-rate may for some time decrease, but it will soon again increase, and far exceed any amount it has hitherto reached.

6. Whenever any considerable portion of the people shall refuse to pay taxes, the example will be immediately followed, Government will be left without revenue, and be unable to maintain itself any longer.

7. If, then, husbandry labourers cannot be put back again to the pauper allowance, nor the number of the people be diminished to that for which profitable employment can be found, a REVOLUTION is inevitable.

Some of these statements may require elucidation.

The first and second need no comment; they will, it is concluded, be admitted.

The labourers have, in many places, learned them so well, that they have told the farmers not again to pay *tithes* in money, but to set them out, and leave the rest to them; and they have cautioned farmers not to pay rent beyond their means, and to rely on them for protection. It is fully admitted by intelligent persons, residing in the counties where burnings have been most frequent, that very many farmers and others, if they do not make common cause with the labourers, tolerate their proceedings, and look forward to the time when their assistance will be expected, to protect them from the consequences of omitting to pay *tithes* and *rent*.

To the matter contained in the remaining statements, many objections have been made : they may all, however, be resolved into this. That inasmuch as the husbandry labourers will, in consequence of increased wages, be enabled to purchase the goods which the Parsons and Landlords used to purchase, trade will not decline, as has been predicted ; and if trade does not decline, the consequences mentioned will not follow. This statement contains a fallacy. The labourers and their families will no longer be only half fed, whilst in employment. On the contrary, they and their families will be well fed, their number is very large, and the quantity of food they will consume must be very great; it will be an immense quantity, in addition to that which they have been accustomed to consume, and the increase of wages will be nearly all expended in food. They will no doubt purchase more articles of coarse clothing; but this, when compared with the quantity the Parsons and Landlords used, including, as ought to be done, their families, servants, and dependents of all sorts, will be but a small quantity; and the same may be said of traders and manufacturers, their servants and workpeople, who will be discharged, and reduced to abject poverty.

It has been shewn that all the farm produce, and all the commodities which can go to wages, without destroying profits and putting an end to business, is a certain proportionable quantity. This quantity is by no means sufficient, plentifully, to feed all the people who are employed, and are able and willing to work. All that is produced at home, and some which is procured from abroad, is consumed; and yet hundreds of thousands of persons have not enough.

The whole quantity of every thing eatable, which has been consumed by the labourers and workpeople, has been unequally divided—

 1. Amongst many who have had enough.

 2. Amongst a larger number who have not had enough.

 3. Amongst many more who have not had nearly enough.

 4. Amongst many who have been more than half-starved.

 5. Amongst many who have had such small quantities that they have died, either of starvation, or of the diseases which bad food, in small quantities, have either produced or rendered fatal.

From this statement, which will be denied by no observing man, it is plain, that if an equal distribution were made, *none* would have enough.

Husbandry labourers and their families, generally, have not had enough even whilst employed, if all of them were now to have enough; and if they, too, for whom no employment can be found are to have, as is demanded, an increased allowance, the whole of the difference of the additional quantity they will consume must be taken from others, and misery will spread all over the country. A different distribution, it must be remembered, is not an increase in the quantity to be distributed; * it can only be taken from one description of persons, from a vast number who cannot afford to have their usual quantity diminished,

---

* The distribution being altered as described, the price of food will rise, as the price of every thing else from decrease of demand falls; and this would put out of employment many who are retained by persons not engaged in business, who are neither Parsons nor Landlords. The fall in the price of commodities, under these circumstances, will not compensate the rise in the price of food. The different distribution of food will, to some extent, tend to increase the quantity of food imported; and this

to be given to another description of persons, who doubt-less very much need it.

As the increase of wages received by the husbandry labourers will be expended almost wholly in food, and as Parsons, Landlords, Tradesmen, and others, will be compelled to consume fewer commodities, the decrease in the demand for commodities will be very great*.

Let us endeavour, rapidly, to trace the consequences.

The demand for tradesmen's goods being on the whole diminished, the quantity of business done will be lessened; but tradesmen struggle hard under such circumstances; they exert themselves, to an extent scarcely to be conceived, to prevent a *decrease* in the *quantity* of business they have been accustomed to transact. Each will endeavour to supplant his neighbour by underselling him; but this can only be done by lessening profits; and the contention to retain old customers, and to procure new customers, will ruin a large number of tradesmen; and the same will be the result to manufacturers. As business continues to decline, and profits become less and less, tradesmen and manufacturers must discharge servants and work-people in great numbers, for whom no employment will be found. All persons employed in commerce, and dealers of all sorts, will be affected in the same way; and the consequences as they regard those persons will also be the same. Competition for employment amongst discharged servant and working people, will lower wages and produce a state of misery hitherto unknown. This appears to be a necessary and consequently an inevitable result. But this state would not be patiently endured by either the working people or their employers; and long before the misery of the working people became general, or their employers were ruined, an outcry would be heard, and the housekeepers, who have always had, and always must have, the power of the state in their hands, would refuse to pay taxes, and the government would come to its end.

---

is, as far as it goes, a mitigating circumstance; but as it does not at all invalidate the argument, it is therefore unnecessary to show how it would have this tendency, or to take any further notice of it.

* The price of food will rise, and the price of commodities will fall, and this will throw many out of employment who are now retained by persons who are neither parsons nor landlords, nor engaged in business. The fall in the price of commodities will not compensate the rise in the price of food.

This, too, may seem to require elucidation. It has been shewn how business will decrease, and profits become less and less. As these matters proceeded, the smaller trades-men and manufacturers would be ruined; many would descend into the class of work-people; and this too, it must be observed, as the demand for work-people decreased. This would aggravate their misfortunes, increase the mi-sery of the whole body of working people, and rapidly reduce the wages of those amongst them who were em-ployed, to the lowest sum on which a single man could keep soul and body together. All who had families would become paupers; to these would be added the large num-ber of discharged servants; and thus, when business had decreased and profits had fallen off, the number would be greatly increased, and the sum necessary for their mainte-nance become so great, that it would be impossible to raise it. But as this state approached, Tradesmen, Ma-nufacturers, Dealers, and Housekeepers generally, would conclude that struggling against such adverse circumstan-ces was useless, they would be satisfied that a continuance of efforts to overcome increasing difficulties would end in the loss of all the property they possessed, and they would make a stand in the hope of thus preventing total ruin, and this, they would conclude, could only be done by suspen-ding their occupations and refusing to pay taxes.

If the refusal to pay taxes were either to originate in London, or to be adopted there in consequence of its having commenced at some other place, so great would be the panic, that no one would take a Bank of England note in exchange for either food or commodities. Trade would cease at once, the shops would all be shut up, and neither a bullock, a sheep, nor a sack of flour, would be brought to market.

It will be useless to object, as many timid persons will be disposed to object, that the evils of bringing things to a stand-still, are too terrible to be contemplated. They must be contemplated; and if the condition of the hus-bandry labourers cannot be improved without taking the Rent from the Landlords, the Tithes from the Parsons, and the Food from the Working People, these terrible events must happen; and if they do, not only will the government be dissolved, but the very bonds of society will be in danger of being burst asunder. Men in business will not stand still looking on until all they possess has passed away from them; they will not, like the husbandry labourers, starve for a long time, and then commit out-rages on the persons and property of others; they will take what to them will seem the shortest remedy, and endeavour to preserve their property and possessions; they will form themselves into a national guard, to protect one another, and give confidence to those from whom supplies must come; and they will declare a government at the point of the bayonet, if such a course should to them appear necessary.

Many have been the proposals during the last thirty years to refuse paying taxes; but it was not until the autumn of last year that men of wealth and influence promulgated such proposals: they are now however doing so in several places, and the notion has spread far and wide; and steps have been taken by men of character and property towards forming associations for the purpose.

Soon after the opening of parliament in October, a proposal was made by a gentleman, who at the present moment possesses greater influence amongst the people than any other man in the kingdom, to obtain the signatures of the housekeepers in the Metropolis to a declaration, that in the event of, the then, ministers so conducting the government as to make war seem inevitable, it would be proper to refuse paying taxes. Change of ministers suspended proceedings; but it needs hardly be said, that the very contemplation of thus refusing to pay taxes by the householders, makes them familiar with the subject, and smooths the way to its adoption.

It seems as clear as that like causes produce like effects, that the results pointed out will follow the proceedings of the husbandry labourers, unless the causes can be removed.

REMEDIES. Here is *the* difficulty: men have been so reluctant to admit that the population was redundant, and so perverse in this respect has been their conduct, that instead of looking the evil in the face in its incipient state, and providing remedies in time, they have cherished it, and increased it to such an extent as to make its cure seem all but impossible.

Things might be restored to the condition they were in before the burnings commenced, if the husbandry labourers could be brought back to their deplorable state, and kept in it, but this seems impossible.

Either removing the redundant population, or increasing the *quantity* of produce, so that all may have food and other necessaries in sufficient quantities, would be effectual remedies. So would an increase of produce, and a considerable emigration, if both were carried on to a sufficient extent at the same time.

But can the produce be so increased as to enable every one to have enough? The answer must be, No. There are means, no doubt, by which, if they could be used, food for all might be produced in abundance; but then there must be a cessation to the production of conveniences and comforts, and the country must be brought into a state of barbarism, which would reduce the population to a much smaller amount than the present, and leave the smaller number in ignorance and misery. This then will not, we may be quite certain, be attempted.

Can the number of persons in Great Britain and Ireland, for whom there is no profitable employment, be emigrated, so that the condition of they who are thus removed shall be improved in other countries? This is a question which, notwithstanding all the pains which have been taken by individuals, by societies, and by parliament, remains undecided.

Can an increase of produce be obtained simultaneously with emigration, so as to lessen the number which it would otherwise be necessary to emigrate?

The answer is, NO. Farm produce cannot be increased without an outlay of capital, so large as to destroy all hope of obtaining any profit; and people will be no more disposed to expend capital in *manufacturing* corn and cattle, than in *manufacturing* cotton or woollen goods, when no profit can be obtained by the outlay.

In this Essay, care has been taken to exclude every thing which is not strictly pertinent to the subject.

No allusion has been made to unforeseen or fortuitous circumstances; and yet many may be expected to occur, and may accelerate the catastrophe.

The probable progress of events in all its ramifications has not been traced, as this would have extended the Essay to an undesirable length; and only such leading particulars have been noticed as seemed necessary to a right understanding of the case by persons desirous of information on the important matters treated of.

If, after all, the statements are incorrect, the reasonings erroneous, or the conclusions not warranted, no one will be better pleased than the writer to see them exposed and corrected.

26th February, 1831.

———————

DURING the three months preceding the above date, this Essay has been handed about in manuscript, and several persons capable of forming correct opinions on the subject have read it. The result has been, a confirmation in the writer that his notions are well founded. To the suggestions and remarks which several made, due attention has been paid. On some, a few words by way of remark will probably not be considered out of place, as they may lead others to examine the statements, and to elicit truth, should there be error in supposing that none of the remedies, nor all of them, are sufficient to stop the revolutionary march.

It was suggested, that if Tithes were at once abolished, a remedy would be found: it was admitted that the abolition all at once of tithes would spread ruin amongst a great many families; but that, as it would prevent a violent revolution, it would be a very small sacrifice to a great public advantage. It was said, there is much capital unemployed, or employed, at very low profits; that the abolition of tithes would induce capitalists, thus circumstanced, to apply their capital to the cultivation of the earth, and thus greatly increase the produce. When however the suggestion was examined, it did not appear to be founded on a correct view of all the circumstances of the case, and has not therefore been adopted. It seems also but reasonable to conclude, that if abolishing tithes would really have the effect suggested, government would *not* abolish them.

Other suggestions were also made, either as palliatives or remedies; such as—reduction of taxes; the sale of the crown lands; correction of the poor laws; preventing improvident marriages; a more general diffusion of knowledge; and by one gentleman, a " correction of the currency." The only observation which the several suggestions, not including the last, seem to require is, that every thing which can be made, in a very short period, to increase the quantity of farm produce, the free importation of corn, &c. and to decrease the rate at which the population has increased, would be *positive* benefits; but if all these suggestions could be adopted at once (and it is quite certain they will not be adopted), the question recurs— Would they be effectual for the purpose proposed? It is feared they would not. Very few men with sound understandings would, it may be concluded, consent to tamper again with the currency, now that it is in a wholesome state.

INNES, PRINTER, WELLS STREET, OXFORD STREET.

SWING UNMASKED.

SWING UNMASKED;

OR,

THE CAUSES OF

RURAL INCENDIARISM.

BY

EDWARD GIBBON WAKEFIELD, Esq.

———

LONDON:

EFFINGHAM WILSON, ROYAL EXCHANGE.

C. ADLARD, PRINTER, BARTHOLOMEW CLOSE.

SWING UNMASKED.

In the time of our wisest ancestor there was no new thing under the sun; but innovation is the order of these days. Amongst the novelties of modern times, new virtues, and, as if to keep the balance of good and evil, new vices occasionally spring up. Nations, by becoming tired of their laws, prepare for great political changes; and, whilst these are in progress, great political excitement brings forth good and bad actions without example. During periods of great political excitement, the weak have frequently devised new and secret modes of injuring the powerful: such periods, consequently, have produced unheard-of and mysterious crimes. A new crime requires a new name, and whatever is mysterious as well as original strikes the imagination with double force. Thus new crimes, attended with mystery, and productive of terror, have frequently been personified, and then named after the ideal beings who were supposed to commit them. Modern history furnishes many examples of this kind. The English *Swing* of 1830-1831 is the personification of a new and mysterious crime. Incendiarism, truly, is not a new crime; nor does England suffer for the first time from the wilful burning of farm produce; but never before was there so systematic and extensive a destruction of mere food lying in the midst of those whose labour produced it, and without injury to life or limb. The novelty of the *Swing* fires consists in the method with which they are conducted; in the perfect resemblance of each deed of destruction to all the others, which makes it appear as if there were but one destroyer; and in the great extent to which they were suddenly carried. The mystery attendant on these fires seems due, in part to the secrecy with which they are performed, in part to the pains that have been taken to invest them with a mysterious character, and partly to our neglect of the means by which truth is elicited.

Though the novel circumstances which belong to the *Swing* fires remain, the novelty of those circumstances is wearing off apace. Let us see whether, by collecting and comparing facts, we may not remove the mystery that yet attends on this new crime. *Swing*, though mysterious, will not be found inscrutable, if we search for him by the light of induction.

There are those who would object to any public discussion of the subject, saying, "Beware that you do not aggravate the evil by taking notice of it!" The first step towards the cure of most evils is a clear understanding of their nature; but allow that this is unlike all other evils, or like only to those which grow when they are mentioned, still, so long as the fires continue, the causes, objects, and probable effects of them will be constantly discussed by the press, in Parliament, under every roof, and most of all, perhaps, by those timid persons who talk of curing the evil by neglecting it. Whether or no discussion produce fires, fires will inevitably produce discussion. Besides, the evil is already so extensive as to seem past aggravation.

Who is *Swing?* One of our natural enemies, the French Jacobins, who has invented a wonderful fireball for the ruin of old England! This is the discovery of an ex-chancellor, who, on account of his capacity for great affairs, was, during the quarter of a century, chief director of the machinery by which the laws of England are made and administered.

Who is *Swing?* A rascally farmer, who destroys his crop to get an abatement of rent! So says the lord of many acres and boroughs, who was born to legislate in both houses of parliament.

Who is *Swing?* A disguised papist or methodist, bent on the destruction of our glorious church establishment!—or else a beer-shop! It is a revered Bishop that speaks, with thousands a year besides patronage.

Who is *Swing?* A well-dressed agent, either of Mark-lane,* or of the revolutionary spirit, who travels in a gig, and fires farm-yards, either to raise the price of wheat, or to promote reform of parliament. Doubt it not! whispers an electioneering alderman.

Turning from these creations of ignorance, hypocrisy, or fright, let us, with a view to the discovery of who *Swing* really is, see whether

---

* In some rural parts, Mark-lane is supposed to be a personage who regulates the price of bread; but I have been assured that a member of the present Cabinet used to attribute the *Swing* fires to some speculators in corn.

there be a portion, and but one portion of society, whose condition furnishes both the motive and the means for committing this extraordinary crime.

What is that defective being, with calfless legs and stooping shoulders, weak in body and mind, inert, pusillanimous, and stupid, whose premature wrinkles and furtive glance tell of misery and degradation? That is an English peasant or pauper; for the words are synonymous. His sire was a pauper, and his mother's milk wanted nourishment. From infancy his food has been bad as well as insufficient; and he now feels the pains of unsatisfied hunger nearly whenever he is awake. But half-clothed, and never supplied with more warmth than suffices to cook his scanty meals, cold and wet come to him, and stay by him, with the weather. He is married, of course; for to this he would have been driven by the poor laws, even if he had been, as he never was, sufficiently comfortable and prudent to dread the burden of a family. But, though instinct and the overseer have given him a wife, he has not tasted the highest joys of husband and father. His partner and his little ones being, like himself, often hungry, seldom warm, sometimes sick without aid, and always sorrowful without hope, are greedy, selfish, and vexing; so, to use his own expression, he " hates the sight of them," and resorts to his hovel only because a hedge affords less shelter from the wind and rain. Compelled by parish law to support his family, which means to join them in consuming an allowance from the parish, he frequently conspires with his wife to get that allowance increased, or prevent its being diminished. This brings begging, trickery, and quarrelling; and ends in settled craft. Though he have the inclination, he wants the courage to become, like more energetic men of his class, a poacher or smuggler on a large scale; but he pilfers occasionally, and teaches his children to lie and steal. His subdued and slavish manner towards his great neighbours shews that they treat him with suspicion and harshness. Consequently, he at once dreads and hates them; but he will never harm them by violent means. Too degraded to be desperate, he is only thoroughly depraved. His miserable career will be short: rheumatism and asthma are conducting him to the workhouse, where he will breathe his last without one pleasant recollection, and so make room for another wretch who may live and die in the same way.

This is a sample of one class of English peasants. Another class is composed of men, who, though paupers to the extent of being in part supported by the parish, were not bred and born in extreme destitution, and who, therefore, in so far as the moral depends on the physical man, are qualified to become wise, virtuous, and happy. They have large muscles, an upright mien, and a quick perception. With strength, energy, and skill, they would earn a comfortable subsistence as labourers, if the modern fashion of paying wages out of the poor-box did not interfere with the due course of things, and reduce all the labourers of a parish, the old and the young, the weak and the strong, the idle and the industrious, to that lowest rate of wages, or rather of weekly payment to each, which in each case is barely sufficient for the support of life. If there were no poor laws, or if the poor laws were such that labour was paid in proportion to the work performed, and not according to a scale founded on the power of gastric juice under various circumstances, these superior men would be employed in preference to the inferior beings described above, would earn twice as much as the others could earn, and would have every motive for industry, providence, and general good conduct. As it is, their superior capacity as labourers is of no advantage to them. They have no motive for being industrious or prudent. What they obtain between labour and the rate is but just enough to support them miserably. They are tempted to marry for the sake of an extra-allowance from the parish; and they would be sunk to the lowest point of degradation but for the energy of their minds, which they owe to their physical strength. Courage and tenderness are said to be allied: men of this class usually make good husbands and affectionate parents. Impelled by want of food, clothes, and warmth, for themselves and their families, they become poachers wherever game abounds, and smugglers when opportunity serves. By poaching or smuggling, or both, many of them are enabled to fill the bellies of their children, to put decent clothes on the backs of their wives, and to keep the cottage whole, with a good fire in it, from year's end to year's end. The villains! why are they not taken up? They are taken up sometimes, and are hunted always, by those who administer rural law. In this way they learn to consider two sets of laws,—those for the protection of game, and those for the protection of home manufactures,—as specially made for their injury. Be just to our unpaid magistrates! who perform their duty, even to the shedding of man's blood, in defence of pheasants and restrictions on trade. Thus the bolder sort of husbandry labourers, by engaging in murderous conflicts with gamekeepers and preventive men, become accustomed to deeds of violence, and, by living in jails, qualified for the most desperate courses. They also imbibe feelings of dislike, or, rather, of bitter hatred, towards the rural magistracy, whom they regard as oppressors and natural enemies; closely resembling, in this respect, the defective class of peasants from whom they differ in so many particulars.

Between these two descriptions of peasantry there is another, which partakes of the characteristics of both classes, but in a slighter degree, except as regards their fear and hatred of the rural aristocracy. In the districts where paupers and game abound, it would be difficult to find many labourers not coming under one of these descriptions. By courtesy, the entire body is called "the bold peasantry of England."

But is nothing done by the "nobility, clergy, and gentry," to conciliate the affection of the pauper mass by whose toil all their own wealth is produced? Charity! The charity of the poor laws, which paupers have been taught to consider a right, which operates as a curse to the able-bodied and well-disposed, whilst it but just enables the infirm of all ages to linger on in pain and sorrow. Soup! Dogs'-meat, the paupers call it. They are very ungrateful; but there is a way of relieving a man's necessities which will make him hate you; and it is in this way, generally, that soup is given to the poor. Books, good little books, which teach patience and submission to the powers that be! With which such paupers as obtain them usually boil their kettles, when not deterred by fear of the reverend donor. Of this gift the design is so plain and offensive, that its effect is contrary to what was intended, just as children from whom obedience is very strictly exacted are commonly rebels at heart. What else? is nothing else done by the rural rich to win the love of the rural poor?

Speaking generally, since all rules have exceptions, the privileged classes of our rural districts take infinite pains to be abhorred by their poorest neighbours. They inclose commons. They stop footpaths. They wall in their parks. They set spring-guns and man-traps. They spend on the keep of high bred dogs what would support half as many children, and yet persecute a labouring man for owning one friend in his cur. They make rates of wages, elaborately calculating the minimum of food that will keep together the soul and body of a clodhopper. They breed game in profusion for their own amusement, and having thus tempted the poor man to knock down a hare for his pot, they send him to the treadmill, or the antipodes, for that inexpiable offence. They build jails, and fill them. They make new crimes and new punishments for the poor. They interfere with the marriages of the poor, compelling some, and forbidding others to come together. They shut up paupers in workhouses, separating husband and wife, in pounds by day, and wards by night. They harness poor men to carts. They superintend alehouses, decry skittles, deprecate beer-shops, meddle with fairs, and otherwise curtail the already narrow amusements of the poor. Even in church, where some of them solemnly preach that all are equal, they sit on cushions, in pews, boarded, matted, and sheltered by curtains from the wind and the vulgar gaze, whilst the lower order must put up with a bare bench on a stone floor, which is good enough for them. Every where they are ostentatious in the display of wealth and enjoyment; whilst in their intercourse with the poor they are suspicious, quick at taking offence, vindictive when displeased, haughty, overbearing, tyrannical, and wolfish; as it seems in the nature of man to be towards such of his fellows as, like sheep, are without the power to resist.

But is this a new state of rural society in England? By no means. Those who have thought it worth while to ascertain what was the condition of our serfs in past times, know very well, that the misery of the rural poor is not greater now than it was fifty or a hundred years ago. A larger number, indeed, of husbandry labourers are now in a state of pauperism; because the application of more capital to old lands, and the cultivation of new lands, has increased the number of husbandry labourers; and because the payment of wages by a poor rate, in place of each man's selling his labour for what it was worth, has equalized the wages of labour, reducing what each labourer receives to that minimum which suffices for the support of life. But this difference of mere numbers or proportion is not very important. At all times of which any account is obtainable, the serfs of England were, like the poorest class of other countries (some new colonies alone excepted,) in a miserable condition. The important difference between past times and the present is, that whereas, in past times, the misery existed without being known,—we now know all about it. The modern press, with its myriads of eyes and tongues, penetrates into the hovel of the peasant, even pries into his heart, and every day disturbs the peace of fat warm men, by some fresh picture of physical want and mental suffering. In like manner, the press constantly supplies us with details of what takes place under our rural code; details which, however revolting to generous minds, differ from former crimes and cruelties of the same family, only in being published. This consideration deserves great weight.

Even those who reside in the country, and are familiar with the sufferings of the peasantry, obtain by means of the press, if not an increased knowledge of the subject, knowledge which disturbs them more; just as one who, living under St. Paul's church, hears not its great clock strike every hour, would be constantly reminded of the fact, if that fact were of sufficient importance to be daily laid before him in reviews, pamphlets, and newspapers. As for those who never see the country, or who, visiting it, see only its fields, woods, and streams, hear only the music of its groves, scent only its fragrance, feel only its pleasant freshness, and exhilarate their souls by dwelling only on the beauties of nature;—for these the busy press absolutely creates a new world of social evils, which when they contemplate, they bless their stars and wonder at the difference between past times and the present. In all times, and nearly all places, the weak have been wretched and the strong unmerciful: the

B

great novelty of these days is, that whatever happens becomes universally known.

Well then, if the peasantry of this day have no better right than their forefathers to the title of miserable slaves, why should they entertain towards their oppressors feelings of rancorous hatred such as we have no account of in the history of rural discontent? Why don't they bear their lot with resignation, as in duty bound, according to the Church-of-England catechism? These questions are easily answered. In some countries people are punished by law for teaching a slave to read; and our own West India planters have spared no pains to prevent the instruction of British blacks. About thirty years ago, the education of the poor became a fashion in England; but as the government did not adopt the fashion, as many of the ruling class violently condemned it, and as the bulk of the people had not leisure to take full advantage of it, its result to the poor has been only half-education,—a knowledge of their own debasement, a discovery that they are slaves. Twice as much education, assuredly, would not have taught the rural poor that they are free and happy; nor would it have reconciled them to hunger, cold and wet, the discipline of the workhouse, and breaking stones for sixpence a day; or made them fond of grinding overseers, reverend police-magistrates, and poacher-hunting squires. What a complete education of the poor might have done, in the way of mending their condition or rendering them satisfied with a bad one, is a question that does not belong to this inquiry. Here we have only to remark, that the poor have been taught (with what view, again, matters not,) to feel the depth of their own degradation. They no longer bear with patience, like that of the ass, the hardships of their lot. They draw painful comparisons between themselves and the rich. They perceive the proximate though not the remote causes of the evils that afflict them. The wealthy and powerful, whom formerly they reverenced, they now mistrust, and, though secretly, yet malignantly hate. In a word, by means of half-education, they have outgrown the bad old laws which were made for keeping them in order; and fear alone, in itself one of the most demoralising of sentiments, obtains from them an imperfect and gloomy submission to the arrangements of society.

From this brief review—of facts, which no sincere man will be disposed to question,—it appears, that rural society is divided (excluding the

B 2

farmers, who shall be noticed below,) into two classes, the rich and the poor, those who enjoy and those who produce, those who suffer and those who execute the law, proud lords of the soil and crawling or criminal paupers, oppressors and helots; the only novelty of the melancholy picture, being the newly acquired consciousness of the slaves.

But the class immediately above the peasantry are the farmers, towards whom, as with these the husbandry labourers have to contend upon the all-important point of wages, it might be expected that the latter would nourish a peculiar animosity. This, however, is not the case. Those who studied the details of the rural riots last year, must have remarked signs of sympathy, if not of concert, between the farmers and the peasantry,—indications of an unanimity of sentiment, which is quite new in the history of rural England. The few cases in which overseers were marked out for attack, must be considered as exceptions to the general rule of conduct pursued by the labourers; and if any one would satisfy himself that there still exists a general feeling of sympathy between farm tenants and farm labourers, he may do so at the small trouble of a visit to any of those parts in which the riots occurred. This novel and most important circumstance is the effect of many causes.

In the first place, since the time when, as during the late war, the farmers used to join the nobility, clergy, and gentry, in treating the peasantry as working cattle, there has occurred a great decrease in the profits of farming. Of late years, the hearts of the farmers have been softened by adversity. The farmers now know the meaning of the word *distress*. Many of them live in dread that the workhouse will be their own last home above-ground. Pauperism is a state to which they have seen some of their class reduced, and of which, by anticipation, they estimate all the evils. The body of farmers, therefore, with few exceptions, now look with compassion on the body of labour-ers; and the latter, who cannot but be aware of the new feeling on the part of their masters, repay it by a feeling of gratitude. Hence mutual sympathy.

Secondly: whilst the peasantry observe the dis-tress of the farmers, which they unjustly attribute to the individual greediness of landlords and par-sons, even their half-education enables them to see plainly, that their own distress is not owing to the greediness of the farmers. When the profits of farming were high, the labourer appeared to lose what his employer gained; but he must be stupid indeed, who cannot now perceive, that farming profits are reduced to the minimum,—to that point, namely, below which there would be no inducement to farm; and that, consequently, it is impossible for the farmer to raise the wages of his labourers without a corresponding abatement of his other outgoings, such as taxes, tithe, and rent. Whether wages might be permanently raised by the abolition of tithe and rent, is a question which will be asked by and by. From farmers' profits higher wages cannot come; and we may allow, that it is the half-education of the peasantry which enables them to perceive this, without giving much credit to the schoolmaster. Perceiving this, the husbandry labourers no longer regard the farmers as oppressors, but, on the contrary, lay the blame of low wages on the parsons and landlords. In this way, the old ground of dispute and animosity between farmers and their servants is removed.

Thirdly: the town spirit of fashion and being fine, which grew up amongst the ruling class with the advancement of the middle classes in knowledge, has been carried into the country, and has drawn a line of separation between the aristocracy and the farmers, far more offensive to the latter,

than the badges of sword and ruffles by which
a landlord used to be distinguished from his
tenant. Even so lately as in the time of our
fathers, there were frequent occasions on which
the gentry and tenantry of a district met upon
something like equal terms in pursuit of a common amusement. But nowadays, since, in respect of knowledge, the farmers have trodden
upon the heels of their superiors, the latter adopt
new modes of distinction, which, from similar
motives, were invented in the capital, and of which
the object and effect is to exclude the middle class
from all sympathy with the highest. Formerly,
a rural aristocrat used to pride himself on the art
with which he admitted his inferiors to good-fel-
lowship, without compromising his own dignity;
but now, forsooth, he would be degraded by the
least appearance of familiar intercourse with one
not of his own caste. The consequence is, that
the farmers, spoken of as a body, regard the rural
aristocracy with dislike; and this being known to
the peasantry, another ground of mutual sympathy is created.

Lastly: thirty years ago, agricultural capitalists
were little better instructed than agricultural
labourers are at this time. A great increase of
knowledge amongst the race of farmers has im-

proved their moral sentiments, awakened their intellectual powers, opened their eyes to the effects and causes of misgovernment, rendered them hostile to many laws, as well as any thing but friendly to the classes who execute the rural code, and above all, disposed them to pity, and, as far as in them lies, to serve, their unhappy labourers. Our farmers, like our peasants, have outgrown our laws and customs:—this is the grand point of agreement between the two classes.

Returning to the peasantry by themselves, it appears, that for some years back they have been in that state of misery, consciousness, and provocation, which amongst slaves announces the dawn of liberty. In fact, those who have watched them know, that so long as ten years ago they were in the mood to commence a servile war. I allude to the period of the queen's trial, when considerable political excitement prevailed, and when, on the defeat of the king, the peasantry generally found means to illuminate their cottages; not out of any particular dislike of George IV., or love of his spouse, but merely because the aristocracy, as a class, especially the landlords and beneficed clergy, took part with the king, and were anxious to prevent any demonstration of joy at the Queen's escape. Many an act of mean revenge followed that rural illumination: for this one it has not been found so easy to punish; but let us not anticipate. No doubt it was the political excitement attendant on the queen's trial which, acting on the established discontent of the peasantry, disposed them to fly in the face of the rural grandees.

Ever since that period rural · discontent has gone on increasing with the increase of knowledge; but until last year political excitement was wanting to put the combustible mass in a flame. Last year, a mere change of dynasty in France produced an instantaneous and profound effect on the public mind of this country. By the suddenness, the extent, and the intensity of that desire for political change which was manifested in these islands after three days' fighting in Paris, and by the extreme alarm which that short conflict occasioned to our dominant faction, we may measure the degree in which public opinion here had outgrown the laws. Even if the French had changed their whole system of government, still some years must have elapsed before any neighbouring people, then satisfied with its laws, would have imbibed from them the spirit of revolution. The people of France scarcely touched one of the institutions that were given to them by the holy alliance,—they only drove away a mischievous

Bourbon king to take a harmless Bourbon king; yet that small revolution electrified the people of this country, and all of a sudden caused them to demand radical political changes. Let us be sure, therefore, that, long before July of last year, there existed in this country a general and deep dissatisfaction with the existing laws. But, however this may be, with the Parisian affair of July 1830 there arose here, amongst the bulk of the nation, a loud cry for changes of the most important nature, and amongst the small minority in whose hands the powers of government rested, a degree of terror which would have been laughable if it had not been well founded. Between the two parties a struggle began instantly; and this, together with the violent hopes and fears that attended it, produced political excitement such as never, perhaps, was known in England before. The universal agitation is noticed, only for the purpose of explaining its effects on that class which had the greatest reason to long for change. The press, far more active than at any antecedent period, conveyed into the remotest parts a minute account of the "glorious French revolution," and represented, even to husbandry labourers, the agonies of hope and fear into which that event had thrown the middle and highest classes, as well as the whole population of the towns. The poor creatures received the news with delight. Here, in particular, I speak from personal observation. Being engaged, at the time, in a pursuit which had for its object an improvement in the condition of the poor, and especially of husbandry labourers, I was led to associate with many of that class; and, though there be not perhaps any class of men in any country more suspicious and secret than the bold peasantry of England, I could not fail to remark of those whom I had the means of observing, that a wild joy filled their minds, when they were led to think of the Parisian events, and of the effect of those events both on the population of the towns and on the rural aristocracy.

Of a truth, the immense importance which the educated classes here attached to the expulsion of Charles X. led our peasantry to believe, with the hungry rabble of the towns, that some mighty change had begun in the world, which was to banish misery from this land. They conceived also, that as "workmen," as belonging to the same class as the "heroes of the barricades," they were to be the chief instruments of effecting so happy a revolution; and I have always felt convinced, from what I saw of them in several counties, that if an insurrection had taken place in London, as seemed highly probable shortly before the Duke of Wellington's retirement, they would have risen in arms against the government. Indeed, we all know that some time before the Duke of Wellington's retirement, the peasantry of many counties were in a state not far removed from insurrection. But I allude to those partial riots, as well as to the graver events which I believe would have occurred if the Tories had remained in office, merely by way of illustrating the position,—that before July 1830 the peasantry of England were in a condition which rendered them peculiarly susceptible of political excitement, and that the Parisian revolution had the effect of violently inflaming them against those classes whom they most justly consider as their oppressors.

It is thus established that when the *Swing* fires began, the peasantry were disposed to adopt any course of proceeding, to commit any crime, which should gratify, at once, their revengeful feelings, and promise to mend their condition. Let us now see whether the destruction of farm produce was a crime of that description.

The injury done by the destruction of farm produce may appear to fall altogether on the farmers; a class with whom, as we have seen, the peasantry are inclined to sympathise.

But, in the first place, the property of most farmers is insured; so that the injury occasioned by most rural fires, falls immediately on the Insurance companies, about whom the peasantry take no thought. Secondly, ninety-nine out of a hundred farmers live so nearly from hand to mouth, that the loss of one year's crop would disable them from paying that year's rent. Consequently, whatever the amount of uninsured farm produce destroyed, a corresponding abatement of rent, whether more or less than the rent of a year, must follow in a great majority of cases : and this holds good of tithes not taken in kind ; so that when the uninsured stacks of a farm are burned, the loss almost inevitably is borne by the landlord and the parson, according to their respective shares in the gross produce of the farm. Thirdly, bearing in mind the small quantity of land from which tithes are taken in kind, and that tithes are but a tenth of the gross produce, it will appear that a very large proportion of *Swing* incendiarism has been directed against the property of beneficed clergymen. What that proportion may be I do not pretend to define; but every one, who reads the newspapers, will have remarked that tithe stacks have not been spared. The destruction of an uninsured tithe-stack produces immediate injury only to the parson; and it should be remembered both of farmer's stacks and of parson's stacks, that the men whose labour produces them, have little means of knowing, until the stacks be destroyed, whether or not an insurance have been effected. Fourthly, though some wiseacres have imagined that the Insurance companies are friendly to *Swing*, expecting to gain more by the increase of policies, than they will lose by the fires; still it must be plain, that there is an extent and duration of rural incendiarism which would put a stop to insurances of farm produce. What may be the maximum of loss to which the Insurance companies will submit before they close their books against stack owners, the state of their profits will decide; but meanwhile, it is evident, that every fire of insured stacks tends to the exhaustion of the Insurance companies' patience, and that when those useful bodies cry "enough!" the immediate losers by *Swing* fires, will be, for the most part, the peasant-hated rural aristocracy. Lastly, whatever the past or future effect of *Swing* fires, in the way of pecuniary injury, those fires produce great and manifest consternation amongst the class whom the peasantry detest, viz. noblemen, squires, and beneficed clergymen, who preserve game and act as magistrates. Fear is the most painful as well as the most depraving of sensations. A main cause of the revengeful inclinations of the peasantry is the constant fear in which they live. They know the pain of fear. If, then, they be the perpetrators of *Swing* incendiarism, that crime bestows on them a sweet revenge.

But, it is asked, if the motive of the peasantry be a desire of revenge, why do they burn stacks in particular? why do not they rather burn mansions and rectory houses, whereby they would still more effectually terrify the rural great? The question must be answered by another. Why do not the peasantry rise in open war against the government, and, as would not be difficult if they were all of one mind, divide the property of the rich amongst themselves? The reasons why they do not this are plain. They are not yet all of one mind. The most wretched of them,—those whose physical defects have been mentioned before,—are of a very cowardly disposition; and, though it be true that the present agitation of their minds is tending to bestow on them greater courage and energy, still their actual timidity and supineness prevent them from adopting any but the least dangerous mode of injuring the powerful. The cowardice, also, of these acts upon the others,— those better formed and braver men, who already engage in violent pursuits, and who, last year, showed shemselves inclined to fight with the rich,—

obliging them, since they are few as compared with the whole body of peasants, to abstain from a course of proceeding which could succeed only by dint of numbers. Noblemen's mansions and rectory houses could not be destroyed, any more than noblemen and rectors, without great risk to the destroyers; unless the latter were so numerous and so much of one mind as to be stronger than the government, in which case property would have changed hands, and somebody might write a pamphlet to shew that the present lords and rectors had become incendiaries. Therefore, if the burners of farm produce be peasants, we must admire their judgment in selecting for attack, the object which it is in their power to destroy with the least risk to themselves.

This last point requires elucidation. A husbandry labourer knows every path, hedge, bush, post, and dog, on his master's farm. His ordinary labour must take him every day close to his master's stacks, and he is thus enabled to reconnoitre, without exposing himself to suspicion, the spot on which we will suppose that he intends to act. Either as a poacher or a pilferer he is accustomed to prowl at night, and, like a cat, can see in the dark, besides being able to leave home at any hour of the night, without exciting the notice of his family or neighbours if they should happen to hear him on the move. He must be a great bungler indeed, unless he can put the tinder-box in his pocket without being observed. He can creep towards the devoted ricks, perfectly certain of not being seen, if it be a dark night, and yet nearly as sure of seeing any one who might be in the way accidentally. Arrived at the stack yard, his dog, or his master's dog, together with his own senses of sight and hearing, exercised on a spot with which they are familiar, will tell him that he is alone. With three blows of the flint and steel the tinder is alight: he touches it with a match, stuffs the match into a rick, shuts the box, pops it into his pocket, and shuffles away with the same caution as before. In five minutes the stack is in a blaze; and in thrice as much time, perhaps, he is either snoring, wide awake, by the side of his wife, or else bawling under his master's bedroom window,—"fire! help! lord's sake, sir, get up; help! fire!"

The supposable variations of this simple tale are few, and not very important: such as, when the labourer lights the stacks which he is set to watch, and, by dint of hard swearing to his own vigilance, leads the credulous to fancy that a fire-ball, placed when the watch was off, must have

c

done the business; or when he picks up, in the stack yard, before witnesses, having first laid it there, a paper partly burnt, but rolled up, and containing brimstone, grease, and soot, which curiosity, after every magistrate thereabouts has examined it, is carefully forwarded to his Majesty's principal secretary of state for the home department; or, lastly, when he imprudently gives notice of what is about to happen, by telling beforehand a circumstantial invention about "two well-dressed strangers in a gig, one of whom squinted and wore a white hat, being uncommon curious about master, and wanting to know if there was a watch kept." In any case the crime of burning farm produce may be performed by a farm servant, like genuine charity, the right not letting the left hand know what hath been done. It requires neither preparation nor assistance, and leaves no trace of guilt. Scarcely an incendiary has been discovered, who had kept his own counsel. Secrecy, by itself, assures impunity. This then is the easiest and safest mode of revenge ever devised.

Revenge is sweet, even among equals, and for a single provocation. Considering the temper of an English serf, the burning of a stack must bestow on him the most delightful emotions A *Swing* fire has taken place—what a commotion ensues in the parish! Is it credible that the paupers should not view with satisfaction the flurried steps and pale face of the rector, the assumed air of indifference, not half concealing the uneasiness of my lord, who owns the soil on which the stacks were burnt, and the violent rage of a neighbouring squire, mixed with nervous indications? A fire has taken place,—if it were lighted by a pauper, it confers on him not simple revenge alone, but revenge against the strong man whose foot had long been on his neck; and next a feeling of self-importance which must be grateful to one so abject; and, lastly, the pleasure of hope, which he never knew before. He has burnt, let us suppose, the produce of the farm on which he works. The powerful of his neighbourhood, before whom he used to tremble, now shake in their turn. He is anxiously noticed by well-dressed passers by, who, before, treated him as a beast of the field; but who now make kind inquiries about his wants, and take pains to become acquainted with his peasant's nature. What is yet more to the purpose, a new scale of wages becomes the topic of his parish, and is, probably, adopted after an understanding between the landlords, clergyman, and tenants, that rents and tithes shall be reduced in proportion as wages are raised. When his family ask for bread, they receive it; and at noon there is an

c 2

unusual smell of bacon about the cottage. He has now firing enough to dry his clothes, which, before the stack was burnt, he used to put on of a morning as wet as when he had taken them off at night. Moreover, his rustic vanity is gratified by reading, in the county paper, a minute account of the deed that he has done. Lastly, when he returns home, thinking of what he has also read in that paper, as coming from the lips of a Parliament man, about "the urgent necessity of some *permanent* improvement in the condition of the poor," he becomes fonder than usual of his wife and kinder to the children; and when they ask him why, he is prevented from speaking by what he would call a lump in the throat, but he answers, aside, with one great, rude, tear of joy. He has but burnt a stack; and his heart, (it has just been discovered that paupers have hearts,) his heart, lately so poor and pinched, is now swelling with the strange pleasure of hope.

In some cases, however, it seems probable that fires are lighted by persons, whose motives are not a desire of revenge and a longing to improve their condition. Occasionally the match may be applied in the way above described, but merely for fun, by a boy, who ever since the last fire has been laughing at his reverence's long face, and wants another piece of excitement;—the country lighted up for miles round, engines rattling, dogs barking, men swearing, women screaming, and the little children staring with wonder. Again, the incendiary may sometimes be a person of morbid imagination, not a peasant probably, but a weaver or pedlar, perhaps, who fancies himself inspired, and is three parts mad; resembling those eccentric beings, whom the French government was, not many years ago, obliged to protect from themselves, by forbidding the sale of a new drug, the use of which, as poison, had lately struck the vulgar mind. In such a case as this, it is not at all unlikely that a "fireball" should be used; but, as in both cases,—that of the boy and that of the madman,—it is likely that detection should follow, we may be sure that these are rare exceptions to the common character of *Swing* incendiarism.

Allowing for such exceptions, it is still clear that there exists a numerous portion of society having the strongest motives to commit the crime of incendiarism; and that those who have the strongest motives to commit the crime, possess, also, ample means of committing it with ease and impunity. The motives and the means brought home to one class, when there is no other class even open to reasonable suspicion,—when no other class has either the motives or the means possessed by that one class,—fixes the guilt upon those to whom it belongs. Three more facts corroborate this verdict. In a great number of instances, peasants have refused to assist in extinguishing fires: it is common for peasants to wink slyly at each other, whilst they assure the magistrates that farmer Smith is a good friend of the poor, and that the deed must have been done by some wicked stranger; and all the farm incendiaries yet discovered have, I believe, been farm servants. *Swing*, then, is a miserable serf, lately become conscious of his own debasement, and urged by political excitement to take the only way that he can see for gaining a place in the social system.

The problem that remains to be solved is—by what means may this new crime be repressed? Volumes, probably, will be written on the subject. Here I shall notice only the measures of prevention hitherto adopted or recommended.

Hanging would repress the crime, and prevent its recurrence, if that punishment were applied to *all* criminals *quickly after the offence*. But a preliminary of hanging is detection, which rarely happens, and which no conceivable device would render more frequent. Detect and hang one incendiary out of a hundred, the chances of impunity will still be ninety-nine to one; and so prone is man to believe in his own superior fortune, that the severity of a severe punishment, which is inflicted only in some of the cases to which it is awarded by law, disposes men to think of that punishment only as an evil which they are sure to escape. Hanging, also, besides being ineffectual, because we cannot apply it generally, has an irritating effect on those whom, by the force of example, it is intended to subdue. In towns, mere thieves are frequently converted into burglars and murderers, by witnessing the execution of burglars and murderers. As yet, the peasantry have spared life and limb. Considering the number of stacks burned, which were placed near to houses, it would appear that the burners must have watched the wind for the express purpose of preventing more destruction than was indispensable to the attainment of their object. By hanging a good many incendiaries, we might convert stack-burners into assassins. Harsh, barbarising laws are a main cause of the disposition of the peasantry to burn stacks. Is it desirable to make the peasantry all of one mind? By shedding peasant's blood profusely, we might drive the survivors to the possible, though more dangerous,

revenge of burning mansions and rectory houses.
The persons also of clergymen, squires, and even
lords, who reside in the country, are frequently
exposed to manifold modes of attack. Viewing
the subject in this light, it seems fortunate that
detections should have been so rare; but at all
events, hanging is plainly an inadequate method
of dealing with the rick-burners.

Exhortation has been, and will be, tried in vain.
You may talk to a pauper, or print for him, about
the wickedness of destroying the staff of life, and
the extreme folly of annihilating that which he
most wants—food; in his heart he will reply, that
bread is to him the staff of life so miserable as not
to be worth much care; and that, whatever may
be the scarcity and consequent dearness of food,
the parish must supply him with as much as usual.
He wants more food than the parish gives him;
and he knows that, come what may, he will not
have less. You preach to him, therefore, in vain;
more especially as what you say is contradicted by
two plain facts; viz. first, the increase of wages,
or parish allowance, which has in many places
been the immediate result of the fires; and, secondly, the new anxiety which those fires have produced amongst the ruling classes to serve the pauper herd.

Execration, also, has been, and probably will be, tried in vain. Exhaust on *Swing* the vocabulary of abuse—wretch, miscreant, monster, that he is! the pauper either points to the bacon in his pot, or tells you that he has expected such luxurious doings ever since the fires began.

An increase of wages is recommended by some. But out of what fund is it to come? and is it to be universal or partial? Whether universal or partial, the amount of the increase,—since from farmers' profits it cannot come,—must be levied as a tax on landlords and parsons. If only the landlords and parsons were concerned, many might not object to this most unjust plan, (such is the feeling which the injustice of landlords and parsons has raised up against them;) but a tax on landlords and parsons for the support of paupers, would diminish the expenditure of the aristocracy by so much, and, if the amount were large, would bring total ruin on a vast number of dealers and manufacturers of every rank. What the result of that would be, in the present state of political feeling, has been explained in a little tract, by Mr. Francis Place, to which I venture earnestly to direct the reader's attention.* But now, let us suppose that

---

* This tract, though not published for sale, is, I believe, obtainable by applying to the author.

the increase of wages, come from what fund it may, is but partial; that it takes place only in those parishes visited by fire. An excellent plan this for extinguishing fires in one spot, in order that they may break out in another! A premium on incendiarism! A new bounty for the production of a new tax! Who claims the discovery?

Subscriptions have been suggested. These would be a tax on the benevolent, and would, probably, like a partial increase of wages by means of a tax on landlords and parsons, be an incentive to fires. Besides, recollecting that few put more food into their mouths than they actually want, and that scarcely any food is thrown away, it becomes clear that we cannot give food to those who have not enough, without taking from others who have but just enough. Because he who possesses money easily obtains food, the unthinking talk of subscriptions to relieve distress, as if by these the quantity of food might be *increased* according to the amount of the fund subscribed.* It must be plain, however, to those who will reflect for a moment, that whenever food is artificially diverted from what may be called its natural course of consumption, a want of food is produced amongst one

* This vulgar error is very clearly exposed in the article "Colonies," in the *Encyclopedia Britannica*.

set of people, equal to the relief bestowed upon
another set. A subscription large enough to give
plenty of food to all the peasantry would, like the
abolition of rent and tithe, deprive of bread millions of dealers and manufacturers. But we need
not dwell on this mode of putting down *Swing* by
uproaring the universal peace. It has been noticed
mainly with the view of illustrating what would
be the effect of feeding the hungry peasantry by
a deduction from rent and tithes.

There is, however, a method of proceeding,
which would inevitably put a stop to the fires. I
allude to the manner in which such crimes of serfs
as peculiarly affect their lords, are repressed in
some of the United States, in our own West Indies, and in the dominions of our friendly ally, the
Emperor of Russia. *Send troops into the blazing*
districts; proclaim martial law; shoot, cut down,
and hang the peasants by wholesale, and without
discrimination. In this way we should be sure to
strike the guilty; and we might satisfy our con-
sciences afterwards by proving, what would be really
indisputable, that most of the innocent had been incendiaries at heart, and that we had spared them the
guilt of becoming actual burners. But this plan,
however justified by precedent, would be impracticable, by reason of the humanity of the middle

classes, which has lately grown to such a pitch,
that it would now be difficult to get up a second
Manchester massacre; much more an extermina-
ting war upon the peasantry. The very common
soldiers have learned to think and feel for others,
so far, at least, as to be no longer blind instruments of a strong bad government; whilst the
class of farmers, whose ignorant and brutal forefathers might have been easily incited to hunt down
the serfs, are intelligent, civilized, humane; and
bent on a reform of the government, as the best
means of improving both their own affairs, and the
condition of those whom they employ. Public
opinion, moreover, would not allow an evil disposed government to use the old Anglo-Irish
method of obtaining ease, by means of rebellion
and massacre. Were Sir Robert Peel minister, he
would acknowledge the "expediency" of abstain-
ing from harsh measures towards the peasantry.

I had almost forgotten to mention the specific
of his Majesty's present ministers, which, by their
partisans, was lately announced as a most valuable
discovery. If the bill for enabling farmers to set
spring-guns in their yards had become an act, it
would never, probably, have been put in force.
No farmer wishes to be burnt in his bed. Most
farmers know that the affection of our rural aris-

tocracy for spring-guns, is one cause of the savage
and revengeful feelings of the peasantry; but they
are not so generous as to draw upon themselves
the hatred of their labourers, in order to relieve
from it a class whom they love not overmuch.
Aware no doubt they must be, that spring-guns
set in their yards might kill or maim a few stray
children, cattle, or sportsmen; but they must also
be well convinced that, he who can, with perfect
ease and safety, burn stacks not protected by a
spring-gun, could remove, or avoid, with the same
facility, a spring-gun which, probably, he would be
employed to set. If the spring-gun suggestion
had come from the Tories, one might have supposed that its object was to sow dissention between
the peasantry and the farmers, and so to enlist the
latter on the side of our venerable constitution;
but, as the Whigs do not join the Tories in fore-
telling that reform of Parliament will ruin the
farmers, it is impossible even to conjecture what
they intended by their spring-gun bill.

Such, then, is the nature of *Swing* incendiarism,
that the crime is not to be stopped, either by hanging, or by exhortation, or by execration, or by a tax
on landlords and parsons, or by charitable subscriptions, or by martial law, or even by spring-guns.
The first main cause of the crime is misery. Par-

tial instruction, and great political excitement being added to misery, the effect is produced. Superficial statesmen will strive, though in vain, to remove the secondary causes. By no means can the peasantry be made to forget the little they have learned; and to confer on them such instruction as would much improve their moral sentiments, is evidently impossible whilst they constantly endure physical want. Political excitement, assuredly, will not subside until the nation, which has outgrown its laws, shall have obtained other laws in accordance with public opinion. A government, therefore, of comprehensive views and energetic purpose, would instantly seek to remove the original cause of the crime,—the misery of the unpunishable criminals. At present, we have no government; the attention of the legislature and executive being entirely absorbed by a question as to the mode in which governments ought to be created. When that question shall be settled, measures may be taken to suppress the *Swing* fires; which, meanwhile, promise to continue, and to produce consequences to the ruling classes far more disagreeable than any that have yet occurred.

December 17, 1831.

THE END.

C. Adlard, Printer, Bartholomew close.

RICHARDSON'S

LETTER

TO THE RIGHT HONOURABLE

LORD BROUGHAM AND VAUX.

PRICE TWO SHILLINGS.

BACON AND KINNEBROOK,

MERCURY OFFICE,

NORWICH.

A LETTER

TO THE

RIGHT HON. HENRY, LORD BROUGHAM AND VAUX,

Lord High Chancellor

OF GREAT BRITAIN,

ON

AN ALTERATION IN THE POOR LAWS,

The Employment of the People,

AND A

REDUCTION OF THE POOR RATE.

BY J. RICHARDSON,

OF HEYDON, NORFOLK.

SECOND EDITION,

WITH LARGE ADDITIONS.

London:

SOLD BY HATCHARD AND SON, PICCADILLY,
AND
BACON AND KINNEBROOK, NORWICH.

1831.

PRICE TWO SHILLINGS.

TO THE

RIGHT HONOURABLE

LORD BROUGHAM AND VAUX,

LORD HIGH CHANCELLOR

OF GREAT BRITAIN.

MY LORD,

I have been induced to address this Second Edition of a plan for the removal of the disorder of Pauperism, which now affects the land, to your Lordship, by the pledge which you have so lately given to lend your powerful aid to the subject. I am assured also by the Noble Lord to whom my first Essay was inscribed, that you are not unlikely, even amidst the never-ceasing calls upon your time, to give some portion of your attention to my design. This is all I either solicit or desire, for I write under a conviction, confirmed both by study and practice, that if the plan be fairly considered by such a mind as your own, its merits will be as fairly weighed; and being deeply impressed with its efficacy, I am led to hope it may present a means of rescuing the country from the misery which depresses the low, and the dangers which threaten the higher ranks. At all events I have done my utmost by thus placing my humble efforts under the direct observation of the personage most able to effect our deliverance.

I have the honour to be

Your Lordship's most obedient Servant,

J. RICHARDSON.

Heydon, Norfolk, August, 1831.

CONTENTS.

CONTENTS.

THE very favourable manner in which my former edition for an alteration of the Poor Laws has been received by the Public, and the paramount importance of the subject, has induced me to publish a second, with explanatory additions and facts, and also a subsidiary measure, calculated to effect much good under proper regulations. I have entered more into detail, in order that my design may be thoroughly comprehended and understood ; and I do this the more readily from an increased confidence and belief, that it is the only *plan* that has been published which embraces the *whole subject of the Poor Laws, and points out specific and practical remedies.*

Nothing is so much wanted upon this important subject, as a clear and concise illustration of principles and their effects. It seems to be the fate of mankind, to be most ignorant of the philosophy of those phenomena with which they are most familiar. The numerous projects for improving the condition of the poor in England, some of which have unfortunately found their way into our laws, sufficiently attest the interest the subject has always excited, while the inconsistent and often opposite directions the projectors have taken, furnish abundant proofs of the ignorance and prejudice in which it is still involved.

There is one point however on which all, or very nearly all, are now agreed, that in the system and practical operations of our poor laws, there exists a disorder of fatal tendency, which has long been preying upon the extremities, and daily progressing, and which must (unless speedily averted) seize the vitals of our body politic. Experience has proved that the very best of the remedies hitherto adopted have been but palliatives, retarding for awhile the progress, but of no efficacy to subdue the cause of the malady. Some indeed have only added to its malignity, and the most promising have been found in the end the most fallacious. In the meantime, every body knows, or thinks he can devise some improved scheme; but if upon a question of such grave and mighty importance, it were consistent with good taste or feeling to indulge a vein of levity, I might amuse the reader by stating the variety of projects I have read since this was first published, which have been so profusely suggested by the learned and the ignorant, of all classes and denominations. In short the diversity of views, the confusion of ideas, and the contradiction of opinions, which prevail on the subject of the poor laws, would astonish any man not accustomed to consider, that whatever is calculated to affect the imagination deeply, and in a great variety of forms, is for that very reason, more difficult to be mastered by the intellect, and more the subject of popular delusion and prejudice.

After much consideration I am still thoroughly satisfied that the real sources of the malady are to be found in the LAWS themselves, aggravated by their mal-administration, and the gross mismanagement and misappropriation of the poor rates in every parish, and that the only true and effectual remedy is to retrace our steps as rapidly as circumstances will permit.—

These laws form together an artificial code, in direct opposition to the liberty, the industry, the frugality, the morals, and the comforts of the labouring classes, and consequently, to the interests of the whole community. The principles on which this code is established, are chiefly, a restraint upon the free circulation and price of labour, an unlimited provision for poverty, an indiscriminate application of that provision to imprudence, to misfortune, to idleness, and to vice ; to one or to all of these sources may be traced the numerous forms of crime, of mischief, and of misery, which must strike the most superficial observer in the rapid increase of pauperism, in improvident marriages, in the hopeless indifference of the labourers as to the means of providing for their families in health, in sickness, or old age, in the discontent, the demoralization, the degradation, and the slavery of the poor. The object of the measure proposed is to meet these numerous evils in their sources, affecting neither existing rights nor vested interests.

The poor laws being therefore radically bad in themselves (except insofar only as they make a provision for the impotent and the sick) founded and framed for different times, and a different state of society, ought forthwith

to be repealed, and it should be our first care
and object, to establish and place them upon
true and *legitimate principles*, unerring in their
tendency and operation, such as provide for
and are adapted to the present wants and state
of society, giving to capital a more sure and profitable direction, through the medium of employment for the people, taking especial care above
all things, that industry and morality should be
encouraged and rewarded, and that the property
and happiness of the industrious man be protected. These essential remedies and objects of
immediate and indispensable necessity I assert,
and am prepared to establish by practical demonstration, may be easily and readily obtained,
and accomplished by an Act of Parliament, embracing and enforcing the following principles
and simple propositions :—

FIRST.—That each county shall constitute
and form *one entire parish*, expressly for the
purpose of employing, maintaining, and taking
care of its own labourers and poor, the repair of
roads and bridges.

SECOND.—That the present laws of parish
settlements, being twelve in number, should be
repealed, and reduced to *four*, viz. *birth, mar-*

riage, estate and renting of lands or tenements,
and those to be settlements on counties and not
on parishes.

THIRD.—That an equal rate of assessment
should be made upon all rateable property, in
each county, according to the natural, *intrinsic
value,* to be collected and paid into one fund, for
the general purposes of its own poor, and other
county rates ; such assessments to be conclusive
and binding upon all real property, lands and
farming premises, for a period of not less than
ten years,

FOURTH.—That a certain portion of labourers
belonging to the county, should be allotted to
the rate payers, according to the amount of their
respective assessments, say *three-fourths* of the
number considered to be fairly necessary for the
proper and *profitable* cultivation of the land—
the choice of labourers to be left to themselves ;
this number to be constantly employed, until
altered by the consent of the majority of rate
payers in the county. And every person having
less than the stipulated number, to pay two
shillings per day (or such other sum as may be
agreed upon) for every man so deficient, in aid
of and to the county fund.

FIFTH.—That each county should hire and have district farms of its own, of sufficient size, and convenient locality, for the beneficial and express purpose of always having profitable employment for all those labourers who did not obtain work elsewhere. The *maximum* of wages to be paid on those farms, to be *fixed* and altered as occasion may require. The produce to be sold to pay the labourers employed thereon; and every person to send a team of horses, one day in the year, to the district farm, for every forty acres they may occupy, at such times, and with such husbandry implements, as shall be required.

SIXTH.—That once a year or oftener, as may be necessary, the weekly rate of allowance and other relief to all the impotent and sick poor belonging to the county, should be fixed, according to their several wants and circumstances.

SEVENTH.—That an active and well qualified man should be appoined to superintend, and manage each district farm, the labourers, and roads.

EIGHTH.—That one person should be yearly chosen and appointed by the rate payers of each

parish (according to the Vestry Act, 58th and
59th Geo. III.) viz. That every one rated for the
relief of the poor, for any sum at or under fifty
pounds shall be entitled to give one vote, and
for every additional twenty-five pounds above
that sum, another vote (no one person however
to have in the whole more than six votes) in the
election of the person to represent them, at all
meetings that may be held, for the adoption,
regulation, and execution of this plan. These
parochial representatives when assembled to
have the whole and sole power of fixing and
altering (as occasion may require) the number of
labourers to be allotted to the respective rate
payers ; the maximum of wages to be paid on
the district farms, the weekly rate of allowance
and other relief to the impotent poor, and all
other matters connected therewith. And they
shall yearly appoint a committee from amongst
themselves, for conducting and carrying the plan
into practical operation.

LASTLY.—I would further recommend that a
certificate be given to each person belonging to
the county, to ensure them of employment at a
district farm, or relief if necessary ; that no payment should be made to any person from the
county fund, without a surgeon's order, stating

their illness and inability to work. That every rate payer should make a weekly return, in writing, to their representative, of the name and number of labourers employed by them— such returns to be entered in a book, to be kept at the district farms, once a month, where the representatives will attend to inspect the farm, superintendents' accounts, &c. and to enforce the regulations and prevent imposition, and always to report the particulars at the general meetings, and to the rate payers in the respective parishes. All minor details I shall for the present defer.

Having thus stated the several propositions, I submit them with due deference to the consideration of the public, in the hope, and with an earnest desire, that they may be thoroughly and rigidly examined by men of practical knowledge and experience, and tried by the test of the true and legitimate principles of legislation. I should entertain no fear as to the result, if I could but induce gentlemen to think and judge for themselves, upon an investigation of the entire subject. The hitherto imagined magnitude, importance and difficulties, that have surrounded this question, have deterred men of great learning and consummate abilities from encountering it ; as well as from an impression, that the malady was beyond the power of human redemption: we should not therefore be surprised at this sort of general feeling and understanding, when we have seen such men as Sir James Scarlett, with all his legal knowledge, acuteness, and immense experience, fail in an attempt at a remedy, and his very mind quail under the consideration of the subject. But his failure was not owing entirely to the magnitude of the question, nor the difficulties that beset it, but to a want of practical and a general knowledge of agricultural business. Sir James judiciously saw and pointed out the *first* and *principal cause* of the evils, viz. the laws of *parish settlements* and *maintenance* ; but unfortunately not possessing this requisite information, he was unable to apply or see the practical operation of the remedy he proposed, and consequently got confused and in despair gave it up. And while I briefly recite a part of what this plan proposes to effect, I most earnestly solicit the attention of those who are conversant with such matters, and who feel an interest and a desire to arrive at a correct conclusion upon the question of the poor laws, which far exceeds every other subject in importance under the present state of the country.

The first and second propositions are, that each county shall be, and form itself into, *one entire parish*, with but four laws of settlement, viz. birth, marriage, estate, and renting of land or tenements for a period of five years.

This will reduce the number of parishes from upwards of ten thousand to fifty-two, and the laws of settlement from twelve to four : It will remove all the adverse interests and causes of difference ; and will at once and for ever put an end to all litigations, expense and trouble between parishes on the subject of settlements, and its innumerable attendant evils, perjury, subornation of perjury, fraud, trickery, injustice, and cruelty, and save upwards of five hundred thousand pounds a-year to the parties concerned, on this point alone. It will also abolish all the arbitrary, oppressive, pernicious and unjust restraints imposed on the liberty, labour and industry, of the middle and lower orders of society, and the poor, by the unwise and destructive laws of parish settlements and maintenance. Consequently labour will circulate freely and unconstrained, without the possibility of controul from any one, to the entire extent of the county.

The third is, that an equal rate for the relief of the poor be made, upon true and beneficial principles, and to be permanent for a certain number number of years.

Thus will every description of property have to contribute its fair and just proportion towards the maintenance and support of the poor, and it will put an end to the present *law* and mode of rating, which are *based* upon vicious, unjust, and pernicious *principles.* Their effect is directly to impede and discourage the investment of capital in productive labour, by imposing an additional tax upon all kinds of *improvements* that are made, and which can only be accomplished by the *employment* of the people ; consequently they discourage and take away the very inducement for employing more hands on the land for its better cultiuation, by abstracting from the farmers the profits they would otherwise receive, but for the imposition of this increased poor rate. The rate being made according to the natural and intrinsic, and not the improved value, will give a wonderful stimulus to the investment of capital, enterprise, and industry, from the simple principle and fact, that it will secure to every man the fruits of his own capital, skill, industry, and improvements.

The fourth is, that a portion of labour, shall be allotted to property for its cultivation, amounting to only three-fourths of the number of hands that can be profitably employed, and which are indeed necessary. The choice of the labourers is to be left to the occupiers, and wages are to be settled between the masters and men.

This will provide permanent, beneficial, and remunerating employment for fully seven-eighths of the agricultural population ; it will establish the independence of the farmers, as to the men they will employ, the wages they will pay, and the time they choose to keep them ; by which means, it will increase their profits and capital, their farms will be improved, consequently more valuable ; it will create a principle of conciliation and respect between masters and men, making them independent of, though dependent on each other, thereby enforcing reciprocal duties and obligations which will encourage and promote their mutual interest, and unite them in social and friendly feelings, prosperity, and happiness.

The fifth is, that farms should be hired in proper districts of the county, for the profitable employment of the remainder of the labourers by spade husbandry, and at such a rate of wages as will support them, without any assistance or relief whatever from the poor rates.

This consummates and completes the principle and power of the entire project. These farms provide, regulate, and secure, both employment and wages to all that are able and willing to work, encourage and reward both industry and morality, at the same time discouraging idleness and vice, by throwing every man upon the resources of his own exertions, industry, and labour, for the support of himself and family, thus putting an end at once, to all parochial assistance and relief, either in the shape of making up wages for labour, imprudent marriages, or idleness. It will establish the independence of the labourers, not only in the choice of their masters, but in agreeing for the price of their work, and liberate them and their families from pauperism and parish controul, with a market always open to their wants, the competition, and the free circulation of their labour, to the full extent of the county; and by fixing the maximum rate of wages, to be paid upon those farms, will constitute the minimum rate of wages for labour throughout the county; and which the men

can always obtain and command. Thus an
important, elastic principle in the plan is provided, for wages can always be regulated thereby,
and being under the immediate controul of the
rate payers themselves, through their representatives, we may fairly assume, that the price of
labour will be governed by, and bear a fair
and true proportion to that of produce and the
necessaries of life.

This power and facility, which is innate in
the project, of contracting or extending, of increasing or reducing, the number of labourers
to be employed by the rate payers, or on the
district farms, and the general rate of wages for
labour, establishes this important consideration,
and proves the fact, that the plan is not only
calculated to provide for and meet the present,
but also the future wants, wishes, and state of
society, that can under all variations and circumstances arise or occur.

The sixth and seventh are, that the weekly relief to the poor should be fixed, as occasion may
require, and that practical superintendants be
appointed by the rate payers to manage the
farms. This gives them the entire power
over their own funds, and all parochial partiality

to the poor will be done away with, and imposition prevented; by the judicious management of the labourers on the district farms, they will earn that which they consume; and the produce will be more than sufficient to re-pay all the expences; thus will the hitherto idle labourers become a benefit instead of a burthen.

The eighth is, that each parish shall have and appoint its own representative; this will give to every person who contributes towards the employment, maintenance, and support of the poor, an interest and power in the appointment, according to their respective property, or the amount they pay towards the county fund. It constitutes virtual representation, and will be satisfactory to all. It places every part of the plan under the controul and direction of the parties interested and concerned, and will cause a wholesome distribution and application of labour in profitable employment, as well as the beneficial, and just appropriation of the poor's fund. Having thus enumerated a part of what the plan proposes to effect, I trust it will be found upon examination, that it is unnecessary for me here to enter into further argument or detail, to shew its practicability, for it must appear obvious to all, from the simplicity of the propositions, their daily occurrence and application in the common transactions of business, that there can exist no obstacles in effecting, and no difficulties in carrying them into immediate and practical operation. There will be no new capital required, no outlay for buildings, for stock, for horses, or husbandry implements, no new direction for labour, no confusion, no interference with personal rights, liberty, or any man's business. The means and materials are ready prepared and in our hands, it only wants the sanction of the Legislature to give it power and authority, to enable us to enforce the regulation, for it amounts to nothing more. It will not rob one man to enrich another. No, it will add to the wealth, to the liberty, to the comfort and happiness of all, and effectually secure the peace and prosperity of the nation, reducing at the same time the poor rates to one fourth their present amount, and saving at the very least four millions a year.

In order to illustrate the subject more clearly, and to bring the present destructive system completely before the public, I have taken eight parishes in Norfolk lying together, with which I am practically acquainted, and also connected, being of sufficient extent and population to con-

D

stitute one district of the county, with a farm, to shew the difference in the expence between the present parish system and the one proposed. To do this in the most correct way I have stated the quantity of land, the number of labourers, single and married, their children, the impotent poor, the rate of wages, &c. the valuation, and amount of poor's rates for one year in each parish, and how they were expended. And here I would beg leave to observe, that these accounts are correctly taken from the respective parish books and other documents by myself, and have been subsequently examined carefully with the parish officers, and their accuracy and truth are attested and signed by them respectively. I have thought it necessary to say thus much, from a belief that a reckless disregard of facts has been too manifest in many of the statements sent forth to the public, and which is not only very disreputable and mischievous in itself, but calculated to mislead, harass, and distract the judgment of those gentlemen who are desirous of providing a remedy and coming to a correct conclusion upon this momentous subject.

The names of the parishes and overseers are only withheld, in compliance with the request of the large proprietors, but should any person think it necessary either to know one or the other, for the purpose of making enquiries, my publishers are in possession of both, with the permission to give them upon the understanding above expressed.

PARISH of A.

CONTAINS 1500 ACRES. RATED AT £832. 13s. 3d.
POOR RATES £444. 3s. 2d. BEING 5s. 9d. PER ACRE.

Has 48 full-bodied labourers—7 are single and 43 married (4 of which are only half-men), and 147 children—56 are able to be employed—7 impotent poor, and 6 small tradesmen married, who have had occasional relief. Wages from 9s. to 10s. a week to a man with a wife and 3 children; all above that number are allowed meal money; in this parish there are 14.

This applies to all the other parishes, and meal money means making up wages for all the children above three. £25 a year sufficient to keep the roads in repair. The poor rate was expended thus:—

	£	s.	d.
Paid to widows, old men, and those unable to work	64	5	4
to labourers and their families in sickness	22	17	6
for medicine and attendance on the poor	24	15	9
for cloathing to the poor	62	14	4
Workhouse rent	7	10	0
Constable and carpenter's bills, coffins, barrows, &c.	5	11	10
County rate	24	0	6
Overseer's expences	8	3	3
to able-bodied labourers out of employment, on the roads, and meal money	224	4	8
	£444	3	2

June, 1830.—We, the under-signed Overseers of this Parish, do hereby certify the above statement to be correct in every particular.

W. I. ⎫ Churchwardens
J. K. ⎬ and
W. K. ⎭ Overseers.

D 2

PARISH of B.

CONTAINS 1500 ACRES. RATED AT £1300.

POOR RATES £712. 2s. 3d. BEING 9s. 5d. PER ACRE.

Has 48 full-bodied men—11 single and 42 married (4 of those only half-men), and 128 children—17 capable to be employed— 7 impotent poor—10 weavers married, have had occasional relief—18 extra children. Wages 9s. a week. £25. a year sufficient to keep the roads in repair. The poor rate was expended thus :—

	£.	s.	d.
Paid to widows, old men, and all those unable to work, and children	116	8	0
to labourers and their families in sickness	15	0	0
for medical aid	5	4	0
for cloathing to the poor	9	16	9
Rent for workhouse	10	16	0
Overseer and guardian's expences	8	14	0
Constable's bill and expences	2	0	4
County rate	57	13	6
to labourers out of employment on the roads, and meal money	486	9	8
	£712	2	3

June, 1830.—We, the Guardian and Overseer of this Parish, do hereby certify the above account to be correct in every particular,

M. A. Guardian.
R. K. Overseer.

PARISH of C.

CONTAINS 650 ACRES.   RATED AT £167. 10s. 0d.

POOR RATES £111. 13s. 2d. BEING 3s. 5d. PER ACRE.

Has 15 full-bodied labourers, 11 married and 4 single, and 27 children—10 able to be employed ; three widows and 1 extra child. £5. a year sufficient to keep the roads in repair. Wages 10s. a week. The poor rate was expended thus :—

	£.	s.	d.
Paid to widows and old people	15	0	0
for cloathing for the poor	10	18	0
County rate	11	13	4
Overseer and constable's expences	4	3	10
for labour on roads, sickness, and meal money....	69	18	0
	£111	13	2

N. B.—Only two houses in the parish, and not one cottage for labourers. This parish is thought to be as well off in regard to poor rates, as any in the county.

June, 1830.—I, the Overseer of this Parish, do hereby certify the above acoount to be correct in every particular.

R. G. Overseer.

PARISH of D.

Contains 948 Acres. Rated at £714. 0s. 0d.

Poor Rates £366. 13s. 3d. being 7s. 8½d. per Acre.

Has 36 full-bodied labourers, 8 single and 31 married (6 of those only half-men), and 102 children—40 able to be employed—8 impotent—9 tradesmen married, had occasional relief; 6 extra children. Wages 9s. a week. £8. a year sufficient to keep roads in repair. The poor rate was expended thus:—

	£.	s.	d.
Paid to widows, old men unable to work, and children	60	0	0
to labourers and their families in sickness........	21	5	10
for medical aid	19	9	0
Cloathing for the poor	17	6	6
County rate...................................	9	10	0
Carpenter for barrows and coffins, and Constable's expences	5	4	6
Overseer's expences	4	5	0
House rent	10	0	0
to labourers out of work, on the roads, and meal money for children	219	12	5
	£366	13	3

June, 1830.—*We, the Overseer and Assistant Overseer of this Parish, do hereby certify the above account to be correct in every particular.*

H. J. Overseer.
J. R. Assistant.

PARISH of E.

CONTAINS 2000 ACRES. RATED AT £921. 0s. 0d.

POOR RATES £800. BEING 8s. PER ACRE.

Has 94 full-bodied labourers—40 are single and 58 married (8 of these only half-men), and 201 children—65 are able to be employed—16 extra children—12 impotent poor—6 tradesmen married, had occasional relief. Wages from 9s. to 10s. a week. £30. a year sufficient to keep the roads in repair. The poor rate was expended thus:—

	£.	s.	d.
Paid to widows and those unable to work	166	9	0
to labourers and their families in sickness........	52	10	0
to surgeon for attendance on the poor	14	14	0
for cloathing for the poor	83	15	4
Workhouse rent and repairs	54	18	5
Carpenter's and constable's bills	3	6	0
County rate	34	13	4
Overseers' expences	8	5	6
Churchwarden's bill	15	13	18
Gravel for roads	7	1	0
to labourers out of work, on the roads, and meal money	858	13	6
	£800	0	0

June, 1830.—*We, the Overseers of this Parish, do hereby certify the above account to be correct in every particular.*

A. W. I.
 J. B. R. } Overseers.

PARISH of F.

CONTAINS 2034 ACRES. RATED AT £1400. 0s. 0d.

POOR RATES £922. 11s. 4d. BEING 9s. PER ACRE.

Has 49 full-bodied labourers—6 are single and 45 married (4 of these only half-men), and 150 children—34 able to be employed—18 extra children—35 impotent poor. Wages 9s. a week. £30 a year sufficient to keep the roads in repair. The poor rate was expended thus :—

	£.	s.	d.
Paid widows, old men, and those not able to work... ...	140	18	10
Labourers and their families in sickness	23	0	0
Doctors attending the poor	8	15	0
for clothing the poor...........................	39	14	1
County rate....................................	10	12	0
Churchwarden's bill	9	3	2
Carpenter for coffins, barrows, &c...............	4	4	4
Overseer's expences and constable	3	8	0
Ablebodied labourers out of work on the roads, and meal money.................................	682	16	11
	£922	11	4

June, 1830.—I, the Overseer of the above Parish, do hereby certify the above account to be correct in every particular.

R. N. Overseer.

PARISH of G.

CONTAINS 4833 ACRES. RATED AT £2727. 0s. 0d

POOR RATES £1,609. 13s. BEING 8s. 0½d. PER ACRE.

Has 86 full-bodied labourers—16 are single and 74 married (8 of whom are only half-men), and 215 children—66 able to be employed—24 extra children—8 old impotent married men. Wages about 9s. a week. 28 weavers—6 single and 22 married men, having 51 children—11 able to work, and all of whom have had relief occasionally; and also for standing out against the masters for wages. £70 a year sufficient to keep the roads in repair. The poor rate was expended thus :—

	£.	s.	d.
Paid to widows and those unable to work	277	0	0
to labourers and families in sickness	61	0	0
to doctor for attending the poor	18	2	0
cloathing for the poor	38	19	5
Rent of workhouse	14	11	0
to constable's expences	2	0	3
County rate	64	0	0
to guardian, workhouse governor salary and expences	64	17	5
for gravel and marl to the roads	14	8	0
to carpenter for coffins, barrows, &c. and blacksmith's bill	8	12	7
Law expences for trying the settlement of one pauper	46	2	4
to labourers out of work on the roads, the heath, and meal money	1000	0	0
	£1609	13	0

June, 1830.—We, the Guardian and Overseer of this Parish, do certify the above statement to be correct in every particular.

J. D. Guardian.
M. F. Overseer.

E

PARISH of H.

CONTAINS 1550 ACRES. RATED AT £1210. 0s. 0d.

POOR RATES £857. 14s. 1d. BEING 11s. PER ACRE.

Has 60 full-bodied labourers—15 are single and 47 married (4 of whom are only half-men), and 123 children—47 able to be employed—6 extra children—81 impotent poor—11 married men, weavers, who have had occasional relief. Wages 9s. a week. £20 a year sufficient to keep roads in repair. The poor rate was expended thus :—

	£.	s.	d.
Paid to widows and those unable to work	306	17	0
labourers and families in sickness	11	0	6
to doctors for medicine and attendance	6	6	0
cloathing to the poor	67	3	1
Carpenter for coffin	1	0	0
Constable, bill and expences	2	1	0
county rate	24	11	3
rent of workhouse, salary of governor, guardian, treasurer, and overseer's expences, and sundries at workhouse	120	16	6
to able-bodied labourers out of work on the roads, and meal money	317	18	8
	£857	14	1

June, 1830.—*We, the Overseers of this Parish, do hereby certify the above account to be correct in every particular.*

R. G. Overseer.
T. K. Assistant.

Summary of tne eight parishes, shewing the amount paid under each head of expenditure for one year, the number of labourers (married and single), and children able to be employed: the quantity of land, the valuation, and the amount of poor rates in each parish per acre.

Parishes.	No. of Married Men.	No. of Single Men.	No. of Children.	No. of Acres.	Amount of Valuation.	Amount of Poor Rates.			Rate per Acre.*	
Parish of					£.	£.	s.	d.	s.	d.
A	48½	7	56	1500	832	444	2	11	5	9
B	37½	11	17	1500	1300	712	2	3	9	5
C	11	4	10	650	167	111	13	2	3	5
D	28	8	40	948	714	366	13	3	7	8½
E	54	40	65	2000	921	800	0	0	8	0
F	43	6	34	2034	1400	922	11	4	9	0
G	70	16	66	4833	2727	1609	13	0	8	0½
H	45	15	54	1550	1210	857	14	1	11	0
Total 8	337	107	342	15015	9271	5824	10	0	62	4

* Average per Acre 7s. 9½d.

Of these 15,015 acres, 13,000 are arable, 1,900 pasture, 665 woods, and 350 acres waste, roads, houses, &c. &c.

£5,824. 10s. 0d.   One year's Poor Rates, and expended thus :—

	£.	s.	d.
Paid to widows, old men, and all unable to work	1156	19	2
to labourers and their families in sickness	202	16	0
to doctors for medicine and attendance	99	14	9
for cloathing	330	14	4
Overseers, guardians, governors, salaries & expences	200	15	7
for rent, for work and other houses	118	16	6
County rate	236	13	7
Churchwardens' bills	24	17	1
for gravel and marl for roads	21	0	0
Carpenters for coffins and barrows; and constables' expences	31	19	10
Law expences, trying the settlement of one pauper	46	2	4
to able-bodied labourers for want of work, on the roads, and meal money	3354	1	9
	£5824	10	0

Here then we have a true exposition of the present destructive and demoralizing system and practice, exemplified in these parishes, and it establishes this fact, that upwards of three thousand pounds have been paid yearly out of the poor rates, to labourers out of employment, in a state of idleness, pauperism, and discontent, when at the same time we had plenty of profitable and remunerating employment for them upon the land. This wasteful system has been going on for the last ten or fifteen years. Is it therefore to be wondered at, that farmers complain for want of capital? How can it, let me ask, be otherwise? Was there ever such folly! This large expenditure and practice has been productive of nothing but mischief, misery, crime, and poverty, exciting a spirit of strife, discord, and dislike, between the employers and the employed, making all parties equally dissatisfied with the other, and equally complaining of oppression, injustice, imposition, and want; producing neither respect, security, or profit to the farmers, nor giving satisfaction, comfort, or employment to the men; its tendency is to widen and perpetuate the breach and unfriendly feeling that unfortunately subsists between the parties, which, if not speedily put an end to, must bring on general poverty, destruction, and confusion. I foresaw the consequences that would inevitably follow therefrom, and pointed them out, and they have been verified by the proceedings of last autumn and winter. That warning was disregarded. Let us not suppose that we are now in a state of greater security— we are still standing as it were upon a barrel of gunpowder, and it wants but the igniting spark to cause general confusion and destruction. *But do justice and fear not.*

This then puts us into possession of one material cause, which tends to impoverish the farmers, and pauperise and degrade the labourers. Many suppose that a remedy can only be obtained by taking off taxes. This is a fallacy and mistake, for Government by such *means* will not be able to do any such thing. If a third of the taxes were remitted to-morrow, it would not prove a remedy, although it would give some relief, but it could not remove a hundredth part of the evils that oppress society. No, we *must* rely upon ourselves, after a proper revision of the poor laws. All is not yet rotten in the state of Denmark, as some believe. And why should we attempt to disguise the fact, and blame others for losses which have been mainly occasioned by gross mismanagement and selfishness, at least since 1822? For if we had acted fairly and honestly by each other, and applied and expended these immense sums upon labour on the land, (which is very much wanted) instead of throwing them away, as we have done for years, in paying able-bodied labourers for idleness, they would have returned to us again, and accompanied with profits. To assert that we neither have or can obtain the means, nor the field for the profitable employment *of all the labourers*, is to assert that which is not correct, and contrary to the fact, which I shall presently shew. But let me not be misunderstood, nor underrate the benefit and importance of taking off taxes, for off they must come, but especially those that press upon the productions of our own soil, and the springs of productive capital and industry. And I may be excused in remarking, that none would give greater satisfaction, and relief, than the remission of the tax upon malt, and an equitable commutation of tithes, which is not only very desirable, but has become indispensably *necessary*.

In order to justify my opinion as to the evil, extent and expense occasioned by the laws of parish settlement, I here insert an authenticated statement, received from the Clerk of the Peace, which shews the number of appeals to the Sessions, and upon what grounds.

Appeals entered and tried at the Quarter Sessions held in the county of Norfolk, in the Years 1828, 1829, *and* 1830.

		Appeals entered.		Appeals tried.
In 1828, against	Removal Orders	51	..	31
	Poor's Rates	4	..	3
	Accounts, &c. of Overseers .	1	..	0
1829........	Removal Orders	77	..	56
	Poor's Rates	5	..	2
	Accounts, &c. of Overseers .	1	..	1
1830........	Removal Orders	96	..	66
	Poor's Rates	8	..	6
	Maintenance of pauper during suspension of removal order	1	..	0
		244		165

COPEMAN, CLERK OF THE PEACE.

Aylsham, 14th July, 1131.

From this, it is evident that the removal of paupers and litigation is rapidly increasing (they will necessarily increase in the ratio of population), which must occasion a corresponding increase in the amount of the poor rates, and other expences as well as inflict great and cruel hardships upon the poor and unoffending. That we may form some notion of the immense sums wasted upon this point alone, I beg to refer to the parish of G. where it is proved that the law expences in trying the settlement of one pauper at the sessions cost £46. 2s. 4d. and which was determined in their favour ; the order of Sessions was appealed against and quashed by the Court of King's Bench, the pauper was returned upon their hands, and they removed him to another parish ; this order was also appealed against—they had to stand another trial at the Sessions, and were again successful ; this cost them £25. in addition to the £46. 2s. 4d. making £71. 2s. 4d. As the other parishes were the losing parties, and incurred an additional expense by the application to the Court of King's Bench, we may fairly conclude that it cost them not less than £80. making together the sum of one hundred and fifty-one pounds. This immense expenditure and trouble, attended with no small exercise of cruelty to the pauper, has been occasioned *merely* in order to determine whether it shall be the parish of A. B. or C. that is to maintain or find employment for this poor wretch, who, whichever way it goes, be it remembered, must still be maintained by the public. This man, I have learned, has maintained himself and family by his labour ever since, not costing the parish he was fixed upon, one farthing. Was there ever such waste and such folly ? and does it not at once prove, beyond the possibility of a doubt, that such a law and practice should be put an end to ?

Taking the 105 appeals that were brought to the Sessions last year, and supposing the 72 tried cost only two-thirds as much each, as the one stated, and the 33 settled out of Court one-third, the law expences alone would stand thus :

$$
\begin{array}{lrr}
72 \text{ at } \pounds100 & \ldots\ldots & \pounds7200 \\
33 \text{ at } 50 & \ldots\ldots & 1650 \\
\hline
& & \pounds8850
\end{array}
$$

And when we consider that this is scarcely a moiety of the expences which must necessarily fall upon parishes, and which we have a right to compute, but as it has been my desire throughout to under-state rather than over-state, I shall take it at only one-half of that sum, and if the county of Norfolk approximate to any thing like an average of the other counties, the yearly expense for litigation will stand thus :

$$
\begin{array}{lr}
\text{Law expences} \ldots\ldots & \pounds8850 \\
\text{Other unavoidable expences which fall on} & \\
\quad \text{parishes} \ldots\ldots & 4425 \\
\hline
\text{Total expenses for Norfolk per a.} & 13275 \\
\text{This sum multiplied by} \ldots & 52 \\
\hline
& 26550 \\
& 66375 \\
\hline
\end{array}
$$

Gives a total expence for the 52 counties of 690300 a year.

From this we may form some conjecture of the immense sums taken from the diminished means of the farmers by this arbitrary and unjust law of parish *settlements*, and which operates to the injury and oppression of every one, producing NOTHING but pauperism, immorality, discontent, expense, crime, strife, contention, and hostility, amongst and between the hundreds of parishes, the tens of thousands of masters, and the millions of labourers and poor who are perpetually annoyed and goaded into acts of desperation and crime, by the severity and cruelty of its operation. *Rely upon it*, without we first *remove* the *demarkation of parishes*, all other atte.npts at a remedy will prove nugatory. Can we then, let me ask, wonder at the complaints of the farmers, and the uncomfortable circumstances in which they are placed by these laws.

It remains only to shew what would be the expence and amount of poor rates under the practical operation of the plan I propose, and this is done by taking from the present parish accounts all the unnecessary sums paid for idleness, &c. I beg the reader to remark the magnitude of the saving in each parish.

PARISH of A.

	£.	s.	d.
To be paid to widows, old men, and all those who are unable to work	64	5	4
to doctors for attendance and medicine	24	15	9
to labourers and families in sickness	22	17	6
Constable's bills and expences	2	10	0
County rate	24	0	6
to labourers to keep the roads in repair....	25	0	0
Total expences of A.	£163	9	1

PARISH of B.

	£.	s.	d.
To be paid to widows and all unable to work	116	8	0
to labourers and families in sickness	15	0	0
to doctors for medicine and attendance	5	4	0
Constable's expences	2	10	0
County rates	57	13	6
to labourers to keep the roads in repair	25	0	0
Total expences of B.	£221	15	6

PARISH of C.

	£.	s.	d.
To be paid to widows and all unable to work, and in sickness	20	0	0
to doctor for medicine aud attendance	2	10	0
Constable's expences	1	10	0
County rate	11	13	0
for labourers to keep the roads in repair ..	5	0	0
Total expences of C.	£40	13	0

PARISH of D.

	£.	s	d.
To be paid to widows, old men, and all unable to work	65	0	0
to labourers and families in sickness	16	5	10
to doctors for medicine and attendance	19	9	0
Constable for expences	1	10	0
County rate	9	10	0
to labourers on the roads to keep them in repair	8	0	0

Total expences of D £119 14 10

PARISH of E.

	£.	s.	d.
'o be paid to widows, old men, and all unable to work	166	9	0
to labourers and their families in sickness ..	52	10	0
to doctors for medicine and attendance	14	14	0
for gravel for road, and constable's expences	7	0	0
Churchwarden's bill	15	13	4
County rates	34	13	4
for labour on the roads	30	0	0

£320 19 8

PARISH of F.

	£.	s.	d.
To be paid to widows, old men, and all unable to work	140	18	10
to labourers and their families in sickness	23	0	0
to doctor for medicine and attendance	8	14	0
County rate	10	12	0
Churchwarden's bill	9	3	2
Constable's expences	2	0	0
for labour on the roads	30	0	0

Total expences of F. £224 8 0

PARISH of G.

	£.	s.	d.
To be paid to widows, old men, and all unable to work	277	0	0
to labourers and their families in illness	61	0	0
to doctor for medicine and attendance ..	18	2	0
Constable's expences	2	0	3
County rate	64	0	0
for gravel and marl for roads	14	8	0
for labour on the roads	70	0	0
Total expences of G.	£506	10	3

PARISH OF H.

	£.	s.	d.
To be paid to widows, old men, and all those unable to work	306	17	0
to labourers and their families in illness	11	0	6
to doctors for medicine and attendance	6	6	0
Constable's expenses	2	1	1
County rate	24	11	3
for labour on the roads	20	0	0
Total expences of H.	£350	15	10

SUMMARY OF NECESSARY EXPENCES

Under new Plan and present System of the Eight Parishes.

	New Plan.			Present System.			Yearly Saving.		
	£.	s.	d.	£.	s.	d.	£.	s.	d.
The Parish of A.	163	9	i	444	2	11	280	13	10
—————— B.	221	15	6	712	2	3	490	6	9
—————— C.	40	13	0	111	13	2	71	0	2
—————— D.	119	14	10	366	13	3	246	18	5
—————— E.	320	19	8	800	0	0	479	0	4
—————— F.	224	8	0	922	11	4	698	3	4
—————— G.	506	10	3	1609	13	0	1103	2	9
—————— H.	350	15	10	857	14	1	506	18	3
Total	1948	6	2	5824	10	0	3876	3	10

Thus it is evident that a yearly saving may be made of £3876. 3s. 2d. in these eight parishes, and which amounts to two-thirds of the entire poor rates. And should they approximate to any thing like an average of the other parishes, it must appear obvious that a saving might be made of upwards of £200,000 a year in this county alone, as the entire amount of poor rates are £320,000 per anuum, a greater sum than is raised in the whole principality of Wales.

These parishes, be it remembered, contain 15,015 acres, 444 full-bodied labourers, and 342 children of different ages, all of whom want employment and wages sufficient to support themselves and families without parish relief.

I propose to take 200 acres for a district farm, allowing for waste, &c. 815, which leaves 14,000 in the hands of the occupiers. It is intended that the rate payers shall only employ three-fourths as much labour as is necessary for the proper and profitable cultivation of the land. Upon this proposition I have come to the conclusion, with the advice and assistance of practical men, that this proportion should be one able-bodied man to 36 and one boy to every 45 acres, classing the parishes together;

this arrangement will take and employ 388 men and 311 children. Ten men and five boys will be constantly employed to keep the roads in repair, and eight more and ten children by rate payers not occupying any land. Thus we have disposed of 406 of the labourers and 326 children, which leaves 38 men and 16 children to go for employment to the district farm, if they do not find work elsewhere. But assuming that they all resort thither, the expences will stand thus :—

	£.	s.	d.
Rent of 200 acres, 21s. per acre	210	0	0
Tithe of ditto	40	0	0
Artificial manure	60	0	0
Manager's salary and expences	100	0	0
38 men, 10s. a week for 52 weeks	988	0	0
16 children from 1s. 6d. to 3s. per week	93	12	0
Additional expences, harvest	40	0	0
Seed wheat, barley, clover, potatoes, and turnips	130	0	0
Total expence of the district farm	£1661	12	0

Although I am fully satisfied, as well from experience as from the various opinions of numbers of men who have tried the effects of spade husbandry, that the district farms will, under such culture, produce more than sufficient to repay all the expences; still to remove all doubts upon that point, I shall charge the rent and superintendent's salary, £310, to the necessary expences; which brings the entire cost of the farm, men's wages, seed, &c. to £1351 a year.

It having been stated that the produce would not cover this expence, I here give the estimated produce and value; it must be remembered all is to be sold off.

Estimated produce of 200 Acres of Arable Land, of an average quality.

	£.	s.	d.
50 Acres of wheat, 28 bushels per acre, at 7s. 6d. per bus. 525	525	0	0
Straw of ditto, chaff, colder, &c.	60	0	0
50 Acres of barley, 40 bushels per acre, at 4s. per bushel	400	0	0
Straw of ditto, chaff, colder, &c.	30	0	0
25 Acres of Swedish turnips, at £5 per acre	125	0	0
25 Acres of potatoes, 350 bushels per acre, at 15d. per bus.	437	10	0
50 Acres of hay, at £4. 10s. per acre	225	0	0
Feed upon the whole farm	30	0	0
Total produce	1832	0	0
I have charged the farm with only	1351	0	0
	£481	0	0

which leaves a surplus of nearly £500 a year. I hope this will set the point at rest—the produce and price are both underlaid, and there is a much more advantageous mode of farming than this, but I have adhered as near as possible to the usual custom, to obviate objections.

Thus will stand the total of necessary ex-

pences of these eight parishes, and the amount
of poor rates required.

	£.	s.	d.
Brought forward from page 37	1948	6	2
Rent of the district farm, as per other side	210	0	4
Salary and expences of manager of ditto	100	0	0
	£2258	6	6

Brought forward, from page 37, the amount of one year's poor rates and expenditure under present system	5824	10	0
Do. required under new plan	2258	6	6
Difference . £3566	3	6

which makes a yearly saving of three thousand, five hundred, and
sixty-six pounds in favour of the plan proposed.

From the perusal of these documents I trust
it will appear that £2258. 6s. 6d. is all that can
be required to be raised as poor rates for one year,
and which will be amply sufficient to meet
every charge for the maintenance and support
of the impotent poor, or sick in those parishes,
and may be raised in the following manner:

	£.	s.	d.
Poor rate, at 2s. 7½d. per acre, on 14,000 acres, amounts to	1836	9	4
Poor rate on the tithe for ditto	367	0	0
Poor rate on houses and capital in trade	54	17	2
	2258	6	6

It will be necessary to bear in mind that
labour will not be allotted by the acre, but

according to the assessment ; nor can we exactly tell what the poors' rate would be in each parish per acre, as that can only be determined by the natural value of the land. I merely mention this to avoid being misunderstood, and which is the best, and most correct method I at present can adopt. From the above statements it will be seen that the highest poor rate per acre is now 11s. and the lowest 3s. 5d. in these parishes, the average being 7s. 9½d. Under the plan proposed the average will be 2s. 7½d. per acre, which is considerably lower than the very lowest; and as the parish of C. does not come up to the average of the others in quality, it will still be less per acre.

As these statements are founded upon authenticated facts, there can be no question that these parishes have paid £3354. 1s. 9d. to labourers out of employment and on the roads, and from which they have received no benefit except keeping the roads in repair, which is estimated at £213 a year. The loss of this sum forms but a small part of that which they ultimately sustain, and but a minor consideration in the greater loss, that inevitably follows from such a practice and system, the full effect of which I now intend to shew.

It has often been asserted and generally believed that we have more labourers than can be profitably employed, or are under any circumstances necessary ; let us examine and see how the fact stands with regard to these eight parishes. They contain 15,015 acres, 444 able-bodied labourers, and 342 children of various ages, all of whom are capable of and want employment. I have shewn that 18 of these men and 15 children will be required to keep the roads in repair, and be employed by rate payers that do not occupy any land. This leaves 424 men and 326 children for all agricultural purposes, which if divided between the occupiers of the soil, there would be three men and two boys to every 100 acres, or more correctly speaking, one man to 35 and one boy to every 45 acres. Surely this number is not more than is necessary for the proper and profitable cultivation of the land ? Supposing then they are all to be employed, and the men are paid 10s. per week for 48 weeks, and £5 for the harvest month, and the children 3s. 4d. and 36s. for harvest each, the whole expence for labour would amount to £15,370 a year, or about 20s. 6d. per acre—a sum not exceeding the computation which every farmer *should* make for necessary labour. The able-bodied labourers would earn £31 a year each, independent of their children. The next consideration and question is, can the farmers afford to pay this sum, and rate of wages, according to the present price of farm produce, assuming they have their farms at fair and reasonable rents? and is it a sum sufficient for the maintenance of a man and his, family without parochial relief? Both of these questions I should answer in the affirmative. I believe that these parishes may be considered and taken as constituting a fair proportion to the others of this county in all the essential particulars; Norfolk contains 1,338,880 acres—has 722 parishes, which if divided, gives to each parish 1855 acres. The eight I have taken on a division contain 1876 acres each, so that in point of extent they form a very accurate *average* of this county ; and I believe also of both quality and population ? I therefore cannot see where the superabundance of labourers is to be found; indeed so thoroughly convinced am I of the very contrary being the fact, I would hazard any wager that if the plan I have suggested be adopted, labourers will be scarce, and the district farms will have to be cultivated by the plough, or considerably reduced. I have been in the habit for a great number of years of being practically concerned in agriculture, and seeing and observing the cultivation of land generally, in several counties in

England, but more especially of late in this, and I have regretted to perceive how great has been the falling off in the cultivation and produce, generally owing in a great measure to the want of more hands being employed to keep the lands clean, dry, and in a better state of tillage, and to have them always in a proper state, and ready in time, to take advantage of favourable opportunities of the seasons, for putting in seed, and getting in the crops. I have made numerous enquiries amongst the old, steady, best informed, and expe- rienced labourers, who have been mostly employed in thrashing both by the flail and machine, as to the produce of land now and what it was ten or fifteen years ago, and they all agree in opinion that there has been a considerable falling off from *one* to *two* quarters of barley, and better than *one* of *wheat* per acre generally, the turnips and hay crops being neither so good nor so heavy. The farmers most to be relied upon in an inquiry of this sort, themselves admit, that the falling off is about *half* of what the labourers have stated. My own opinion is that neither the one or the other is correct, but for the sake of illustration, and to keep on the safe side, I will take it at the lowest estimate, viz. four bushels of wheat and eight of barley per acre. After deducting all the pasture land, and allowing for waste, hedge rows, &c. there remains 12,000 acres of arable land, which being farmed generally on the four years' course of husbandry, there will be 3000 acres of wheat, 3000 acres of barley, 3000 acres of turnips, and 3000 acres of grass.

Thus will the account stand, taking the average price of wheat at 7s. 6d. and barley 4s. per bushel :—

	£.
Wheat 3,000 acres, deficient 4 bushels per acre, 7s. 6d. per bushel	4,500
Barley 3,000 acres, 8 bushels per acre, 4s. per bushel . .	4,500
Turnips 3,000 acres, 10s. per acre, at the very least . . .	1,500
Grass, 3,000 acres, 10s. per acre	1,500
	£12,000

Here then there is a yearly loss, at the most moderate computation, of £12,000 a year to the farmers in these parishes, but the real truth goes far beyond this sum. At first view this statement will be scarcely credited or believed, but remember such things creep upon us, year after year, so gradually and imperceptibly, that we are not aware of the extent and consequences, till it is almost too late to remedy them; for when land is once let down in cultivation and overrun with weeds and poverty, it not only requires time, but much capital and labour, to restore it. Farmers, generally speaking, are slow in discovering the decrease of their property—

few of them keep any thing like proper and regular accounts—so that at the end of the year, it is very doubtful, if one in ten, if he farms to any extent, can tell within one or two hundred pounds whether he is so much richer or poorer. But this £12,000 is not all, for on reference to the disbursements of the poor rates, it will be seen that £3,344 1s. 9d. have been paid away to labourers for idleness and out of employment, for which the rate payers have received no advantage in return whatever ; we therefore shall be justified in adding this sum to the other, which makes a total loss of £15,354 1s. 9d. a year, a sum equal to the rental of the whole land, and sufficient to pay and keep in constant employment, at a fair rate of wages, the whole of the labourers belonging to these respective parishes. In justice I must say that there are some as good farmers in these parishes as can be found in any part of the kingdom.

This statement, has been submitted to many of the best practical farmers ; men well versed in business, and they cordially coincide in opinion with me, both as to the cause and the extent of the loss, as well as there *not* being more labourers than can be profitably employed, provided there was a regular distribution of labour according to each person's assessment. They all complain of limited means, but still believe, that under the operation of this or a similar plan, they either have or could procure the necessary capital. This also further proves, that had those immense sums, which have been entirely wasted, and paid to the unemployed, been judiciously expended for their labour upon the land, we should at this very moment have been able to maintain double the number of labourers we now have, without any person being a single sixpence the poorer or the worse off. Such facts, surely must dispel the erroneous and mischievous notions about super-abundance of labourers, and that no profitable employment can be found, while they prove that neither emigration nor home colonization is absolutely necessary. Population has increased considerably, I admit, and the causes are very apparent, viz. vaccination, a state of peace, and giving a premium for improvident and early marriages; and the last has been promoted by as gross acts of injustice as ever was committed—by compelling the single men to do the same quantity of work as the married, for one half the wages; but we are very far as yet from being overstocked. If ever that period arrives, and such a necessity exists, then resort to the culti-

vation and planting of waste lands, for they
contain great sources of wealth and employment
for the people ; but at present no such necessity
does exist. It is generally now admitted on all
hands, by those most conversant with the subject,
that we have plenty of profitable employment for
all the people upon the lands under cultivation,
provided there was more available capital in the
hands of the farmers ; but to adopt, under existing circumstances, either emigration or home
colonization, would only add to and aggravate
the evils we so much deplore, besides crippling
the productive industry of the county the more by
abstracting from the farmers a part of that available capital which they now complain so much of
wanting to enable them to do justice to their
families, their farms, and the labouring population. This would not only occasion individual
but national loss, arising from the profit on that
portion of the labour we should lose. But it
is said, the money can be borrowed—true, and it
must be repaid, and with interest. This brings
with it another expence ; it would therefore
operate to our loss and disadvantage in *three*
ways—first, by losing for ever the sum necessary
for carrying them abroad—in the second, by the
loss of profit on their labour—and the third, by
increasing our expences, by borrowing money

to repay it, and with interest. These temporising plans will not do ; resort to a national measure such as I have pointed out, which requires no advance of capital, but will daily add to it, and increase the farmers' means and the wealth and comforts of all.

They who have attentively perused these several documents and considered the project, can but admit, that under its operation, every able-bodied man will have it in his power to procure (and indeed *must*) the necessaries of life for himself and family, by his own labour, without parish relief. Yet I would earnestly recommend that small allotments of land be let to the labourers as a *subsidiary* measure, to give them the *comforts of life*, derived from their own industry, and to enable those with large families to bring them up, without experiencing too many miseries and deprivations. But according to the present system, and as the law now stands, it is a doubtful question whether such a measure would prove a benefit or not. Many that have had small pieces of land have not been *permitted* to derive the least advantage from them. I can speak to many such instances myself where that has been the case. I will merely relate one of an industrious labourer

with four children, who rents a cottage of me.
I let him half an acre at the rent the tenant
paid, and lent him four pounds, to enable
him to cultivate it well ; he worked early and
late, and it produced him 7 bushels of wheat
and 85 of potatoes. After harvest, work became
slack ; he could scarcely ever get a day's employment, the farmers alledging that as he had
had a very good crop he could not be in want;
this went on for some weeks ; he then applied to the overseer for relief, as all refused
him work, and he gave him a similar answer ;
at last he went to the magistrates, and
stated his case ; the overseer was summoned ;
he told them he had found in this man's house 3
bushels of wheat and about 30 of potatoes; he was
not therefore in any want ; and he was bound to
maintain himself and family, and he must do so,
as he had the means. The magistrates declared
under these circumstances, they had no power to
interfere ; so that this poor man was actually
obliged to remain out of work till the whole of
his little crop was consumed. He came with tears
in his eyes to me to say he must give the land up ;
that instead of doing him good, it did him a
great injury, for he had done every thing he
could in hopes of bettering himself, but he was
not allowed to derive any advantage from all his

extra trouble and care. Since then he has been principally sent on the roads, as a sort of revenge. I am afraid this is and would be too often the consequence under the present system and laws, unless the labourers could be protected by the landlords, and this can only be partially done by large proprietors using influence with their tenants. To give the poor man the full benefit from its general adoption, he should be made perfectly *independent*, and *secure* of the *profits* arising from his industry and land, without the protection or intervention of any man. It is this very principle of security and self-interest, that has produced such beneficial consequences in the colony of Frederick's Oord, in the Netherlands. As a subsidiary measure the allotment of small portions of land is calculated to produce benefits unspeakable. With a view to make it better understood, and the advantages to be derived therefrom, I shall state the expence of cultivation and the value of the produce. I should recommend half an acre as being sufficient for one person, and cropped thus: 40 rods of wheat, 30 potatoes, and 10 barley.

THE EXPENSE AND PRODUCE OF HALF AN ACRE OF LAND,

CULTIVATED BY SPADE HUSBANDRY.

Dr.	£	s.	d.
Oct. To 3 cart loads of manure for 40 rods of wheat	0	13	6
To labour in barrowing on manure	0	3	6
To digging 40 rods, at 4d. per rod	0	13	4
To 3 pecks of wheat for seed	0	6	6
To dibbling and covering in the seed	0	3	6
To digging 40 rods, preparatory for potatoes and barley—4d. per rod	0	13	4
Mar. To one day's labour, croming over the land to get out weeds	0	2	0
Apr. To 4 cart loads of manure for 30 rods of potatoes	0	18	0
To labour, barrowing on ditto	0	4	0
To digging 30 rods and planting potatoes	0	14	0
To 7 bushels of potatoes for seed	0	10	6
To digging 10 rods for barley	0	3	4
To barley for seed, sowing, &c.	0	3	6
To labour in weeding, harvesting, and getting in the crops	1	0	0
To threshing wheat and barley, dressing, &c.	0	5	6
To one year's rent . . . 12s. 0d. tithe. . . . 2s. 6d. poor rate 1s. 6d. }	0	16	0
Total expence	7	10	6

Cr.	£	s.	d.
Aug. By 7½ bushels of wheat, 8s. per bushel	3	0	0
By 80 bushels of potatoes, 1s. 6d. per bushel	6	0	0
By 3 bushels of barley	0	13	0
By straw, chaff, and colder	0	8	0
	10	1	0
Expences	7	10	6
Profit	2	10	6

The great benefit to be contemplated to the labourers is, the expectation, that after a little assistance for the first crop, himself and family will be able to do all the labour at spare times, whereby they will reap a profit of upwards of eight pounds a year, being more than one-fourth of their yearly earnings : this sum, in addition, will make them comparatively independent and happy. I advise this mode of cropping, which will enable them to keep and fat a pig, which, if killed about Christmas, salted, and dried for bacon, and the lard put into bladders, will support them for many months. If the malt tax was taken off, they could malt their barley and brew, which would still make it considerably more beneficial. This system would have a great influence in improving the morals of the people; they would have a stake in the country, and an interest in the general welfare; it would attach them to their superiors, and make them good and useful members of society. I should advise as many allotments to be laid together as possible, as I have found from experience that it excites a spirit of competition and emulation amongst the men to try which can grow the best crops, and have their land in the best order ; but more especially so where gentlemen will take the troubleof occasionally inspecting them; nothing shames them more than to be told that their land is in a worse state than their neighbours. Great care should be taken to lay the allotments as near as possible to the cottages; *this point is of essential importance*, not only as to getting on the manure, but to enable the labourer if he has but ten minutes to spare to turn it to good account, by slipping out to his allotment. The land should be tolerably good, and let at the same rent as paid by the farmers generally. Most of the farmers are much prejudiced against the measure, which shews how necessary it is that the labourers should hire the land from the landlords themselves. But as I have before shewn, as the law now stands, and while the overseers and occupiers of the soil have the *power*, either directly or indirectly, of depriving the poor man of the profits arising from his industry and produce of his land, by withholding employment, the plan will fail in producing the benefits we expect, and will seldom be found of any service to them. Many have refused pieces of land on this very account, and I think very justly. It should only be considered as a subsidiary measure.

In confirmation of the instance I have related

of my own tenant, comes a still more extensive case, stated (upon oath) by the Rev. Charles
Wetherell, a very benevolent clergyman, the
Rector of Byfield, in Northamptonshire, before
the late Committee of the House of Lords. This
gentleman let small allotments to the poor, and
the following extract from his evidence will shew
how his kind intentions were frustrated.

Is there any land in your parish occupied by the poor for their
own benefit?—There is.

By whom is it let to them, and in what quantities?—It is let by
myself, and in quarter and half acres.

At what rents?—At a rent of 50s. per acre, which was the rent
the farmer paid.

How long have the cottagers held it?—Since the commencement
of the year 1825.

What results have you experienced from those lettings?—The
results have not been exactly what I had anticipated. I had hoped
to see a considerable reduction in the poor rates; but the letting
of land to the poor does not thoroughly satisfy me; let in that
manner, at least.

To what cause do you attribute that?—In a great measure to an
attempt on the part of the farmers to take advantage of every act of
charity, so that I find them disposed to say to a poor man who
wants employment, "Go to the Rector." When I first let the
land to the poor, an understanding took place between the farmers
and myself, that they would employ a labourer who took a quarter
or half an acre of land from me, to benefit himself, before they
employed another labourer, in order to encourage a man who
was attempting by extra industry to benefit himself.

Have they not done so?—They have not done so to the extent I
expected. They have not employed them in preference, but have
rather endeavoured to say to a poor man, "As you have this
advantage, you are not in such great need of employment; go
work in your garden plot." It is sometimes a source of reproach
to them.

Do you mean to say that they have refused parish employment,
or that they have refused to employ them on their own farms, in
consequence of their holding those plots?—They have refused to
employ them on their own farms in some instances; and, because
there was a necessity of relief, they have compelled the men to
go to work upon the roads. There is an enormous evil in that
permission, which I believe is a portion of the poor law at present,
that labourers may be employed upon the Roads.

This precisely bears out my opinion and the case I have cited, and shews that even to effect so partial a benefit as the allotment supposes, an alteration in the laws must be previously made.

When this project was first laid before the public in 1830, I was represented to have advanced opinions that appertained to myself alone, and in direct opposition to the general belief, consequently considered to be fallacious. With a view to ascertain how far the opinions I have entertained are supported by those of the persons thought to be best versed in the theory and practice, I have looked through the evidence given before the Committee of the House of Lords. The two great and leading principles I then laid down—first, that there is no EXCESS of the agricultural population—and secondly, that whatever surplus there might appear to be, may *be profitably employed upon the land now under cultivation*, are confirmed by most of the gentlemen examined, persons of apparently great practical knowledge and judgment; indeed so common is this belief, that it may truly be said to be universal. In order to enable the public to judge for themselves, I shall introduce a few short extracts from a part of the evidence on these points, and I can but regret that the disso-

I

lution of Parliament, and that *alone* prevented me from adding my testimony on oath to those already stated, and giving a more comprehensive and practical explanation before the Committee of the plan I have proposed, than can be done in a publication of this sort. I was summoned for the 25th day of April, the Parliament being dissolved on the 23d, therefore it was purely accidental that I was not examined.

Minutes of Evidence taken before the Select Committee of the House of Lords, appointed to consider of the Poor Laws, in 1830—1.

The Rev. James Beard.

You are a clergyman and magistrate of the county of Bedford.—I am.

How many labourers were unemployed ten years ago?—I cannot charge my memory with that.

Are more employed now than then?—Now, far less.

Is not your opinion, that if the occupiers throughout Bedfordshire had capital and means to apply the labour to the cultivation of the land, that would not exhaust the entire disposable labour even at this moment?—I have not the least doubt of that.

Are you of opinion, that having sufficient capital, the farmers could use that capital profitably in the employment of all those labourers?—Certainly I have never found the parish in which the whole of the labourers could not be employed beneficially, if the farmers had capital, and the labour were rightly distributed.

You mean that it could be so employed as to produce to the farmer a sum equivalent to the increased cost of employing so many more labourers.—Yes, certainly ; a profitable application of capital.

Thos. Law Hodges, Esq. M.P. for Kent.

Are the lands so well cultivated as they were some years ago?—Not half so well ; and that I have remarked in many counties in England ; that the state of agriculture is getting much worse, and the country getting out of cultivation generally.

Is the produce in corn less than it was 15 years ago?—In the Weald of Kent much less.

Do farmers keep less stock than they used to do ?—Much less in that district.

You say that the produce of corn is considerably less in the district in which you reside than formerly; to what do you attribute that ?—To the loss of capital on the part of the farmer.

And to the employment of fewer labourers.—The employment of fewer labourers follows the loss of capital.

Mr. Richard Holloway, Overseer of the Parish of Shipley, in the Weald of Sussex.

Are you a farmer yourself ?—Yes.

What land do you occupy ?—About 350 acres.

Do the farmers in general in your parish employ as many as they used to do ?—There is a difference; some are not able to employ the men.

Is the land in a worse condition now than it was 15 years ago ?—I think the land is driven harder than it was.

How many men do you employ constantly ?—About nine or ten; sometimes ten or eleven.

Richard Pollen, Esq. Chairman of the Quarter Sessions of Hampshire.

There are a great many more labourers in the parish now than there is employment for among the farmers.—I think there is not, in my tithing, more than ought to be employed, provided the farmer was in good case; if the times were good for the farmer, I think he would employ all that there are.

Has there been any reduction of rent within your parish ?—A very considerable reduction, speaking of my own experience; I have reduced from ten to thirty per cent.

Has that enabled the farmers to employ a greater quantity of labourers upon their farms ?—It ought to have done so; but I should say it has not made a great deal of difference. I have reduced my rents this moment twenty per cent. Probably there is not a single man employed now more than there was four years ago.

You have said that the farmers do not drain so much as they did formerly, and might with advantage. Do you conceive that the agriculture in that part of the country is deteriorating ?—I should say, on my own estate, from the three very wet seasons we have had, the land is materially deteriorated, and that can be cured only by extensive draining.

Mr. Robert Chick, Mitcham, Surrey, Drysalter and Agent.

Have you had any particular acquaintance with the poor laws ?—I have paid very great attention to them, and attended vestries.

Are there more labourers to be employed in your parish than can find profitable employment ?—Probably not, if properly managed; but as circumstances are, it is so.

You say that persons employ less hands than they used to do; what is the reason of that ?—The fall in the price of produce.

The Rev. Henry Fowlis, a Magistrate of Lincolnshire.

Are there any labourers out of employment in the winter months?—Yes.

Are you aware of any cause that has produced it ?—The farmers have not capital to employ labourers, although I have no doubt there are not so many labourers there as could be profitably employed; because when you consider a population of 1000 as compared with 5000 acres, it is only one person to five acres, which is certainly not too great a proportion.

Do you think that more labourers might be profitably employed for the purpose of cultivating the land?—I have no doubt of it.

Thomas Walker, Esq. a Magistrate at Lambeth Street.

Have you turned your attention to the state of the poor in London?—I have.

Are there many men out of employment in your division now that come to you as a magistrate to apply for work or money?—Very few come to me.

Do you conceive that there is more population in your division than can be employed?—I have no doubt but that all the people could maintain themselves if they were prudent.

Do you think the law (poor law) sufficient for the object?—I think it would be better if there were no law at all. I act as if there were none; entirely according to my own discretion, and my aim is to abolish pauperism altogether.

Mr. Francis Sherborn, Farmer, Bedfont, near Hounslow.

Have you any persons out of employment in the parish?—None at all. Myself and my brother occupy in this and the adjoining parishes (about 900 acres), and we have about 17 persons that do not belong to the parish in our employ, and generally every man, woman, and child that can work and is willing to work are employed.

Does it appear to you to be your interest to employ the large portion of labourers that you do upon that land rather than suffer them to be paid out of the poor's rates?—Certainly. We think the principle a bad one to drive the men to the poor's rates, and the additional outlay is made with a view to repay us.

You say you now employ 17 persons who do not belong to the parish: why do you employ those persons?—Because there are not persons enough in our parish to do the work.

How many able-bodied men do you employ per 100 acres?—There are such a variety of classes that it is difficult to answer the question, but I think about 10 persons of all classes. We have about 60

And it is your opinion that you can profitably employ as many as that?—Yes; we employ them with that view.

Mr. Thomas Turner, Farmer, Sompting, Sussex.

In what proportion do you agree to employ them?—Taking the whole population, we were to have one man to every 30l. that we stood rated in the poor books.

How many men do you employ to 100 acres of arable land in your parish?—My farm is called 486 acres. I have classed the land under three heads—195 acres of very good and middling land—

80 acres of inferior land that we occasionally farm, but it is principally used for sheep, and there are 211 acres of Down.

You now employ 11 men upon your farm; do you conceive that to be a greater strength than you can profitably employ upon your land?—I think I could employ all those hands if I had the means of paying them. Do you mean that if you had more capital you could employ them, or if the prices were more remunerating? Since I have been there I have been unfortunately a loser in times when things have been against me, therefore I have been trying to do it as cheap as I could.

Would the land be capable of improvement by the application of so much additional labour?—I think it would.

Mr. G. Harrison, Farmer, Lenham, Kent.

Has any land gone out of cultivation in your parish?—Yes, a great deal.

What extent of land do you hold?—300 acres, my own property. I have occupied 900 acres in the parish, and my ancestors did the same for many years; but now I have declined a little more than a year ago.

What number of labourers do you employ now upon the 300 acres?—Eight.

What proportion of it is arable?—About 100 acres, and the rest sheep-walk and wood-land.

Do the other farmers in the parish employ the same number of labourers in proportion to their land?—No; I am sorry to say there are a great many occupiers very poor, and who cannot do justice to their land. When the proprietors hold it they employ more than the occupiers.

Do you think they could employ more labour profitably, under existing circumstances, if they had capital?—They could improve the property; but as to whether they could realize enough to pay interest upon the capital, I think not upon the poorer part of the parish.

Mr. John Cameron, steward to Mr. Poyntz, Midhurst, Sussex.

Do you think there are more men in that parish than can be profitably employed?—No; there is a great deal of the land that is in cultivation, which, in consequence of the poverty of the occupiers, has never had the labour employed upon it that ought to be employed in order to make it produce. If a proper proportion of labour were bestowed upon the whole of that parish as it ought to be, the produce of the parish would be three times what it is now; and therefore if the men were allotted to the farms in proper proportions, I am satisfied that there is not a labourer too much in the parish. I have not only my own opinion for that, but I have the opinion of two industrious farmers of the place, who do farm their land well, that if every one would take their proportion of labour, we should not have at this time, and we never should have had, hands out of employment.

Do you mean to say, that they have not employed the quantity of labour which they ought to have done in order to have their farms in the best possible cultivation?—I do not mean to say the best possible cultivation, so as to have the farms extraordinarily neat, but merely so far as advantage goes.

Do you conceive that if the amount paid to the labourer from the poor rate, in addition to the payment that is made to him for labour now performed, were paid in the shape of payment for labour, that it would produce a profitable application of that money to the payer?—No doubt it would.

Have you ever known any parish in which the land was so well cultivated that it would not produce such a return for an additional outlay of capital?—I have never seen such land.

Rev. George Wells, Weston, Sussex.

How many acres do you occupy?—I believe I may have in occupation at this moment about 200 acres, besides Down.

Is it arable land?—Partly; a fair proportion of both arable and pasture; the pasture, perhaps, rather exceeds the arable in proportion.

How many labourers do you employ upon that farm during the winter months?—I believe at present I have seven men and four boys, and occasionally women.

Do you conceive there are more people in your parish than could be profitably employed in the winter?—I think not, provided the means were in the possession of the tenant to pay them.

Do you think farmers in general employ as much labour as they ought to employ in the cultivation of their farms at present?—No I think not.

Is there not, on that account, a considerable diminution in the produce of those farms?—Undoubtedly the farms are less productive.

John Grey, Esq. a Magistrate, Milfield Hill, Northumberland.

What is the average number of men to a tillage farm?—I conceive there is one regularly-employed man hired through the year to 35 or 40 acres, exclusive of extra hands employed on other work.

Have you very few persons out of employment?—Very few.

Is the quantity of corn produced lessened?—Yes, I should apprehend it is lessened; as the farmer gets into difficulties he applies more severely to the productive powers of his land, and does less for it in return.

Has the capital of the farmer been, by these means, so much diminished as to prevent his farming the land in as good a manner as he was used to do?—Yes, in many instances; and in some instances to ruin him altogether : but before a farmer gives up a farm he takes all he can out of it, generally.

You have stated that you employ extra hands; are those your own population, or not?—Generally our own population, except in the time of harvest; in the harvest we have Irish and Scotch labourers generally; but those are not employed until all the people of the county are taken up.

RICHARD SPOONER, ESQ. Worcester.

Are you acquainted with the state of the labourers in
Warwickshire and Worcestershire ?—I am.

The agricultural as well as the manufacturing labourers ?—I am.

Are you of opinion that more labourers could be profitably
employed than are employed at present ?—Certainly ; I am not
aware of any farm—I have seen a great many—where the farm
itself is not now suffering in point of cultivation from the smallness
of the number of labourers employed upon that farm, and where
the returns of the tenant are not very greatly diminished by that
same circumstance.

Would not the number of labourers be deficient in time of
harvest were it not for the Irish labourers who resort to that
county ?—Certainly ; in the midland counties we have by no means
population enough to get in our harvest without the Irish and
the Welch, both of which flock into the midland counties at
the time of harvest.

If gentlemen before this committee have stated their opinion
that there are in the south-west counties of England many labourers
who cannot be profitably employed, what remedy would you
propose ?—I cannot propose a remedy to a fact which I cannot
believe to exist. I come to a very different conclusion : I believe
there is, when I say no land—I believe, with very few exceptions—
there is no spot in England where, if a labourer was set to work,
the result of that labour would not be a larger product than that
labourer, with an average number of family, would consume.

And therefore a gain to the community ?—And therefore a gain
to the community.

Your opinion is founded upon this, that there are no more
labourers in England than might be profitably employed ?—My
opinion is so founded upon the principle I have stated, that a
labourer set to work on a certain quantity of soil will find that
soil produce more than he and the average number of his family
would consume. The want of profit upon the employment of that
labour may arise from different circumstances ; the tenant may be
burdened with engagements which have brought him into a state in
which he may not have the means of employing labour ; not having
the means of employing labour—not having the capital nor ability
to wait 'till its return—he is disabled from doing so, not being able
to maintain the labourer 'till a profitable return can be made.

You have stated that you think there is no excess of population in
this country ?—I have.

If there are one hundred labourers in a parish, and funds only
properly to support eighty, if the surplus could be removed without
any expence would it not be a benefit ?—I even doubt whether
there would be any benefit arising from that in the present state of
the country ; if the state of the country was such that we had one
fifth more population than could by a proper application of capital
be profitably employed at home, that would be correct ; but I deny
that position altogether. I say that this country is not in that
position but that by a judicious employment of capital all the

labourers of this country may be profitably employed, and would cause a corresponding increase to the wealth of the country, by employment at home.

Are you yourself an agriculturist?—I have been all my life very fond of it, and have always practised it.

EARL STANHOPE.

Is your Lordship acquainted with any parish in which the population is too great for the present means of employment?—That is less the case in the parish I inhabit, of Chevening, near Seven Oaks, than it is in some parishes adjoining, in which there appears to be a surplus of labour, arising, as I conceive, from the poverty of the farmers.

Does not your Lordship believe that in many districts in England there are more men seeking for employment than can be profitably employed?—I believe that such is the case in the present situation of the country, but solely in consequence of legislative measures; and that if the country were to be replaced in a state of prosperity, full and constant employment and adequate wages might be provided for every labourer.

If there is an excess of population at present, would a pauper settlement at home remedy that excess?—I am not of opinion that there is generally an excess of population; though undoubtedly there may appear to be such in certain districts, and from particular causes.

Those causes being legislative enactments?—Those causes may not in all cases arise from legislative enactments. The failure of a manufactory may throw upon a parish an immense number of persons for support; an undue extension of machinery may also throw a great number of persons out of employment; but in those districts which are entirely agricultural I do not believe that there is a greater number of persons than could be profitably employed, or than are actually requisite, taking the average of the year.

From the perusal of this evidence, I trust it will appear I am fully borne out in my original opinion as to these matters. There are also many other striking facts which establish my conclusions relative to the productive powers of land, and its great falling off in point of produce for want of better cultivation and a more enlarged application of labour to the soil. From its great length it is impossible for me to introduce it more fully, and I must therefore content myself with referring gentlemen to the evidence itself.

I shall now endeavour to state and to obviate the objections to the plan I propose, which have been made to it by a few intelligent persons, who have done me the honour to read and consider it in the first edition. I shall neither underrate nor exaggerate the arguments for or against, but leave both to their natural weight.

It is objected,

FIRST.—That to compel any one to employ a given number of men, is to interfere with the conduct of his business, and is alike contradictory to the free exercise of personal rights, and to the law of political economy, which declares that the interests of the individual are best left to his own care and protection.

This objection appears to me purely visionary, for this simple reason, that every farmer *must* of necessity employ labour, and can *profitably* employ considerably *more* than is even proposed by my division ; it consequently follows that no restraint is imposed, nor the conduct of his business interfered with. And when we consider the very large sums he is now compelled

K

to pay in the shape of poor rates towards the maintenance of labourers in idleness *will be saved*, the alledged grievance not only ceases, but is converted into a positive benefit.

If it be imputed that the payment he might be obliged to make to the county fund, for not employing his stipulated quantity of labour, operates like a tax, which I cannot admit, that tax he is now compelled to pay in a more extensive and grievous form. So much for the personal right and the economical assumption. And here I must point out, that this law of the old writers will no longer hold. Individual care it is obvious will not go far enough ; the entire labour is not absorbed by individual interest and enterprise, although it is evident from the various proofs I have adduced that it might be, and with considerable advantage to the occupier, as the land now under cultivation is capable of and might be made to produce ample means for that purpose. It therefore becomes the imperative duty of the Legislature to enact more efficient laws for calling this apparent surplus into profitable action. It is to meet this very postulate that the mind of the country is now turned, and I merely fall in with what is required by the measure I suggest.

SECONDLY.—It is objected, that making counties as it were into parishes would indeed equalize the rate, but it would at the same time relieve one parish at the expence of another—that it might reduce rates in the highest, but it would raise them in the lowest.

Here again I plead the practical benefit. It has been seen that the most favourable poor rate of the eight parishes the accounts of which I have produced, is that of Parish C. and which stands at three shillings and five pence per acre. There will scarcely be found any parish in the county of Norfolk more advantageously situated, the poor being so few. But under the plan I propose, the average rate would be reduced to *two shillings and seven pence halfpenny per acre.* The highest at present is no less than eleven shillings, and the average *seven shillings and ninepence.* The inference that may be justly drawn from these facts with regard to those parishes is, that the very lowest would be much lower, and have *cause* to rejoice, whilst the very highest would be reduced several hundred per cent. No evil could be inflicted, but much benefit accrue, especially by entirely removing all cause of litigation and expense about settlements.

K 2

THIRDLY.—It is objected that the district farm would not be productive, upon the common principle, that the business of the public is never conducted with sufficient care to make it profitable.

To this very general assumption I reply, that, in this case, a competent steward would be appointed, with sufficient capital, under the supervision of persons who are themselves practical men, and who have not only a personal interest, but a delegated trust to whet their diligent observation. It is no speculation—no new experiment, but a very common process—land, it is well known, when properly tilled, does remunerate the cost. And in confirmation of this I must refer the public to the accounts of the expenditure and produce of the district farm. Upon those accounts I rely, and have a right to consider them conclusive until they are proved to be erroneous. But were I to give every possible latitude to this assumption, still compare it with the loss sustained for want of better cultivation, compare it with the loss of £3257 15s. 10d. which at this moment is paid as poor rates for the maintenance of idle and discontented labourers, kept in a state of pauperism. It must be evident that whatever portion of this sum can be earned is all so much clear gain. In the one case the loss is certain—nor in the other is the gain less sure, whatever be its amount. This mode of employment differs in its constitution from all others that have ever yet been tried of a public nature. It gives personal liberty and personal choice. Labourers can resort thither for work, and leave when they think proper, without the controul or interference of any person.

FOURTHLY.—It is objected that a difficulty might arise in obtaining land for the district farms. To this I reply, that no fewer than three proprietors within these eight parishes are willing to let land, convenient for such purposes ; and there can be no doubt that other land owners would be equally desirous to grant land for such a benevolent object, producing such important benefits to themselves and their tenants, as well as having a good rent regularly paid and the land well cultivated. But to guard against any such difficulty, the committee ought to be empowered by act of Parliament, according to the general principle laid down by the Legislature in all cases of public or national improvement, to select land convenient for that purpose, occasioning no loss to the owner, and as little inconvenience as possible.

A minor objection is, the distance that the labourer will have to go to his work on the district farm ; but this will disappear before a very little calculation. This district farm is proposed for the relief of 15,000 acres. Now five square miles contains an area of 16,000—therefore, if at all centrally situated, the radius of the circle could extend at the utmost no more than two miles and a half, the average distance being only one mile and a quarter.

Another is, that the machinery for its practical operation is complicated. Upon investigation I am sure it will be found, that nothing can be more simple or more easily performed. There is not a tenth part of the duty or difficulty that besets the office of a single overseer. Such cavils are indeed scarcely worth notice, but they may perhaps seem formidable to gentlemen whose practical knowledge is limited.

To those who shall have attentively examined and considered these documents there needs no recapitulation, but that I may leave nothing unexplained, I will briefly recite what the plan promises to effect, and point out some of the benefits to be derived from its adoption.

The plan proposes
To repeal the laws of parish settlements, remove their demarcation, and reduce the number from upwards of 10,000 to 52, thereby forming each county into one parish, with four modes of settlement. To make an equal rate for the relief of the poor upon the intrinsic value—to allot to each rate-payer a portion of profitable labour—to hire land for the beneficial employment of the remainder; and to place the whole project under the immediate direction and controul of those who contribute towards the maintenance and support of the poor.

And promises
To put an end to all litigation, expence, and trouble, occasioned between parishes on the subject of settlement, removals of paupers, &c. amounting to between £6 and 800,000 a-year.

To remove those arbitrary, unjust and perni-

cious restraints imposed on the liberty, industry and labour of the people, by the unwise
laws of parish settlements.

To make the farmers independent of the men in
their own parishes, employing whom they
please, provided they belong to the county,
and agree with them as to wages. They can
thus change their labourers as often as they
find it necessary, without inconvenience or
loss to themselves.

To liberate the labouring man from parish controul and pauperism, with the privilege of
choosing his own master, agreeing for his own
wages, and to create for him a market to the
extent of the county for the competition and
free circulation of his labour.

To put the law of rating property upon true and
beneficial principles—to encourage the investment of capital in improving the cultivation
of the land, by securing to every man the
fruits arising from his own skill, industry,
and enterprise.

To provide permanent employment for all the

able-bodied labourers, with wages sufficient
for the maintenance of themselves and families
without parish relief.

To compel every man that is able, to earn that
which he and his family consumes—to encourage and reward industry and morality—thus
discouraging imprudent marriages and putting an end to all parochial relief and assistance in the shape of making up wages, meal-
money, or for idleness—thus saving to the rate-
payers those immense sums, computed at no
less than four millions a-year, expended upon
able and willing labourers kept in a state of
idleness, pauperism and discontent, and to prevent the destructive and demoralizing system
of sending men to congregate on the roads
and in gravel pits, for no other purpose than
to hatch and practise all kinds of mischief,
corrupting each other by evil example, and
uniting to plan and perpetrate every species
of fraud and crime.

And lastly—To increase the means of the
farmer, to add to his respect and security, as
well as to the value of his land, by making it
more productive ; to ensure the labourers independence, regard, and comfort through their

own industry, and to unite all parties in one general, benevolent, humane, and just purpose.

I hope I have not over-stated the beneficial results that will accrue from the measure, and that upon examination it will be found I am fully warranted in the conclusions I have drawn. It therefore only remains to refer to the facts, and in so doing I must especially direct the attention of the reader to the exposition of the eight parishes, not only as to the amount of the poor rates and their appropriation, but to the immense loss that is occasioned by the present system, a loss ulti-ultimately amounting to the incredible sum of £15,000 per annum, or about 20s. per acre, a sum sufficient to pay a full rate of wages to all the labourers in them respectively. Compare this with what it will be under the operation of the plan proposed, the expense and general result which is accurately stated, drawn from experience and supported by the opinions of practical men—and then judge of the advantage.

I think it is now clearly established, that we have not more labourers than is requisite for the proper and profitable cultivation of the soil:

and that they can all be advantageously employed upon the lands now under cultivation,
giving to the farmer, over and above the expense
of the labour, a fair and remunerating profit for
his capital, skill, and enterprize. It consequently only remains to remove the cause of all
this mischief, misery, and loss, by enacting a
better code of poor laws, enforcing a more
general and just distribution of labour in its
application to the soil, and compelling every
one to pay a full rate of wages to those he
employs. It is the opinion of every man that
has either written or considered the subject, that
no effectual remedy can be obtained without a
compulsory measure, and indeed this is so clearly
proved and supported by the fact, that although
labour is remunerating, still it is left stagnant in
the market, and maintained in idleness. The
first and great cause is the laws of parish settlement and maintenance, and until we remove
the demarcation of parishes, by consolidating
them into counties, all our efforts, either to
relieve the poor or the farmer, will prove nugatory. In confirmation of this opinion, and
to shew the progress of the public mind upon
this momentous question, I beg to observe
that at the period this project was first published, I took the liberty of sending a copy to Mr.

Weyland, one of the chairmen of the quarter sessions for this county, and a member of the legislature, soliciting the favour of his sentiments upon the plan. Mr. W. possessing great theoretical knowledge, and being much versed in all the laws of political economy, aided by a portion of practical information, and prompted by a laudable desire to render a public good, made his opinion a matter of interest and solicitude to me, and I am much obliged to the Hon. Member for his kind expression as to the value of my exertions. Having denounced the evils arising from the laws of settlement in strong terms, the Hon. Member in his reply observes, " I have the misfortune to differ from you in the tone of feeling expressed on this point, and hope to convince you of the inexpediency of speaking in a slighting or bitter spirit concerning the *Law of Settlement*, and with the exception of practically simplifying them, I do not think that much more good can be done by legislation directly applied to the system of the poor laws." In July last I find Mr. Weyland in the House of Commons introducing a bill upon this very question, and he so fully and so clearly confirms and supports me, in what I then expressed on the subject, that I shall introduce his speech, which is a clear, comprehensive, and judicious exposition of the evils arising from this villainous law. The Hon. Member, in rising to address the House on the occasion of moving for leave to bring in a bill to alter and amend the laws of settlement by hiring and service, observed,

" I may venture to express my conviction, that any Member, however humble his pretensions, who proposes a measure for the moral and political improvement of the labouring classes, will be received with favour, and that his proposition will be entertained with candour and patience. This, indeed, I apprehend will be the case at all times ; for there can be no Hon. Gentleman present who is not fully convinced that no country can be safe and prosperous while the numerous and useful class to which I have alluded is in a debased and degraded condition. The moral structure of society, framed by preceding legislatures, can no more afford secure and permanent shelter to the several classes who take refuge under its roof, unless based upon the happiness of the people, than the material structure of wood and stone could withstand the assault of time and tempest, unless it rest upon a solid and well cemented foundation. And it may be said of the works of the moral, as well as of the material architect—
Si monumentum quæris, circumspice.
Now, if we look around us and above us, upon the present condition of society, we find the higher and the middle classes in the possession of a fair and reasonable portion of comfort and prosperity. There may be intervals and fluctuations, but such is their fair and average condition ; but, if we look below us, to the state of the labouring classes, we behold a prospect any thing but satisfactory. In Ireland, we see a great portion of the people starving in the midst of plenty ; in England, we see an appalling and rapid increase of crime, chiefly to be ascribed to the difficulty of obtaining an honest livelihood by labour; and we perceive also, what is the natural result of such a state of things—a growing spirit of discontent and disorder, and outrage, not fomented by the infamous publications alluded to in the early part of the evening, but in parishes too remote for this influence, and plainly arising from a sense of unrequited toil, of hopeless destitution, and a corroding conviction that, as a class, they are deprived of that fair participation in the general improvement of the country, which is, in every respect, so justly their due.
It is not my intention, Sir, to enter at large into all the causes which have produced this dangerous and calamitous result. I will confine myself to that one, which the measure I recommend proposes to remedy—I mean the impediments which the laws of settlement impose upon the free interchange and circulation of labour. By this means a wall of brass is, as it were, erected round every village of the land, which its inhabitants can neither penetrate nor

overleap, imprisoning the active and enterprising youth of the country each within its narrow limits—precluding them from expatiating in the fair field of competition which busy society offers—and condemning them from youth to age, to a miserable alternation of ill-paid labour, at the expense of the parish, and an eleemosynary subsistence reluctantly wrung from the overseer. This, Sir, is the result of my own observation and reflection as an impartial spectator. But I hold in my hand a more convincing proof of the truth of the proposition. Here are two petitions from parishes in the county of Bucks, actually labouring under an aggravated degree of the evil, and setting forth, in language more just and forcible than I can use, some of the causes to which they ascribe it. The petitioners declare—

That they feel themselves justified in stating that the laws of settlement are opposed to such free circulation of labour as is essential to the peace and lasting prosperity of the country, because, amongst other pernicious results, they congregate indefinite numbers of people able to work in spots where frequently no work is to be obtained; and the result therefore is, that the property of the inhabitants of such parishes is sacrificed to provide an unearned maintenance for the idle and dissolute.

They further state that—

Their experience proves that the law of settlement is fatally opposed to that unrestrained circulation of labour which ought to be admitted in every free country, as being essential to its prosperity.

And they further say—

That they believe that the late alarming disturbances in this kingdom were occasioned (at least in part) by the operation of the poor laws, by which an undue accumulation of the working classes is concentrated in many of our towns and villages, and which also unreasonably decree the performance of what is morally and physically impossible—namely, that an indefinite and rapidly increasing population should for ever be provided with work and maintenance within certain fixed parochial boundaries.

Now, Sir, to remedy, in some degree, these evils, so acutely felt and so forcibly expressed, is the main object of the Bill, which I have now the honour to submit to the consideration of the House. At present the fear of conferring a settlement prevents the employers of labour from hiring servants out of the parishes where they reside; they, therefore, either confine themselves to the youths of their own parish, or endeavour to evade the law by some problematical agreement, which is sure to give rise to litigation, and to all the perjury, trickery, expense, and low parochial diplomacy, which are so conspicuous in cases of appeal upon the laws of settlement by hiring and service. The Bill, therefore, which goes to abolish those laws, as between agricultural parishes, will, I trust, work the double benefit; first, of opening a free interchange of labour, and next, of cutting off, probably, three-fourths of that litigation which, both in itself and its consequences, is a hardship and a disgrace to the country.

I hope, Sir, however, that the time may come, and I do fully anticipate its arrival, when these distinctions may be all done away—when it may be safe to enact, that every poor and destitute person may be relieved where he happens to be found; or that, at least, a few years' residence, and industrious labour, shall confer upon him that right. In the meantime we must do what we can, and the measure which I humbly submit to the House, is a step, though I regret it is so short and inadequate, yet still, I trust, it is a step in the right course.

Sir, I have only one word more to add. This is a measure which has for its object to remove the one great blot, and to diminish the one great danger which defaces and puts to risk the present structure of our Commonwealth—at least, it is the greatest blot, and the most imminent danger—I mean the unfortunate and unjustifiable condition of our labouring classes. But, Sir, there is also a cheerful side of this question which may well encourage us to spare no pains in the search and prosecution of the remedy. Those classes are not only a very acute and sensible, but they are also a very grateful race. Any measure disinterestedly entered upon for their benefit, they duly appreciate, and are ready to respond to it by their own best exertions. I do trust, Sir, that we shall all join in united and earnest consultation upon this vital question of the moral and political condition of the labouring classes. It can neither be neglected or delayed with any chance of safety to the Commonwealth; and I am sure that a successful issue of our deliberations upon it (if it can but be attained,) will open to the country a prospect through a long vista of happiness and prosperity;—solid, because it will rest upon the eternal principles of justice and humanity—and permanent, because it may well be expected to draw down upon it the blessing and protection of Providence."

I can but express my pleasure at this happy conviction of the Hon. Member to my original opinion upon the subject, and of now having him as an able and discreet advocate in the same cause, to which he was formerly opposed, as appears from his own letter. Mr. Weyland observes— " If I am asked why I do not open the door more widely, and include the commercial and manufacturing, as well as the agricultural districts, I answer, that the time is so little ripe for such a proceeding, that I am sure the whole

measure would be defeated by such an attempt."
To this I reply, rather than *stop here, be it so ;*
for it is evident that it can be of no service, or
accomplish the least good, and for this very
reason, that every parish has adopted the resolution of *not* employing any labourers but those
legally belonging to them.   This practice not
only clinches the parish fetters on the poor man,
but at once renders this attempt of Mr. W.
nugatory.   It *must* go much further, even to the
extent I have marked out.   Only consider what
must be the state of feeling, confusion, expence,
degradation and misery, caused by parish settlements, when this county alone contains upwards
of seven hundred such prisons and colonies of
task-masters and slaves, armed with twelve distinct laws, operating to the disadvantage of each
other, and prompted by upwards of one hundred
inducements of supposed interest for litigation,
every one of which tends to set parish against
parish, landlord against tenant, & tenant against
landlord—the master against the labourer, and
the labourer against the master—the rich against
the poor, and the poor against the rich.   Can we
then wonder at the state of society, and the danger in which the country is now involved ?

I hail this conversion of Mr. W. with the greater

delight, because it proves the principles I have laid down are progressing rapidly towards consummation, and a further evidence of this fact was exemplified in the House of Lords. When the Earl of Winchelsea proposed to introduce a Labour Rate Bill, it was characterized as arbitrary and unjust, and cruelly oppressive in its operation upon the poor man, without containing a single redeeming quality to recommend it. During the debate, the Right Rev. the Bishop of London, who is highly esteemed for his benevolence and liberality, and possessed of extraordinary talents and judgment, observed, " I am of opinion a great deal of the evils which unhappily exists, are occasioned by our adhering to the demarcation of parishes, without considering the alteration that is daily taking place in the number of the inhabitants." *True*, my Lord, this is the first *cause*, and *must be removed*.

The present system and poor laws are made to bear most unjustly upon the honest and able-bodied labourers ; there is neither hope nor inducement held out to them whereby they can better their condition, however industrious or well behaved. They are doomed to endure all kinds of privations, insult, and oppression, without the possibility of escape. They have no

M

voice in the sale of their labour, nor choice of masters, but compelled to accept the price offered, if not half its value, and must serve those who require them, however obnoxious. They are driven as a last resource to the poor's fund, and sent to the overseers as suppliants of charity, to eke out the miserable means of subsistence, and then characterized as paupers. This treatment breaks down their spirits, degrades and demoralizes them, they become reckless as to character and consequences, inspired with feelings of hostility and dislike, and looking upon all those who are above them as tyrants and task masters, who have conspired to deprive them of their liberty and their rights.

This is a true and just representation of their situation and feelings. We cannot therefore be surprised at the spirit that is abroad, and the disordered state of the public mind.

The period has arrived that justice must be done, or the reaction may not only shake the very foundations of society, but bring on a general convulsion. This danger, so immediate, may be easily averted and removed, if we do but act fairly and honestly to the people ; the only thing required is work, and fair and reasonable wages—they want nothing more ; they will honestly and richly repay it, and it may easily be accomplished in the manner proposed. In fact, it is only obliging a man to do that which his interest and advantage ought to have prompted him to do, and however parodoxical this may appear to theorists, still in practice it is not the less true. It will be invariably received and acknowledged by the suffering poor with expressions of the most ardent gratitude and satisfaction. Upon consideration it must be evident the labourers are unfairly dealt with, and deprived of their indisputable right. They are entitled both by the common and statute law, as well as by the first principles of justice, to a reasonable maintenance from the land, in return for their labour, which is now denied them, although it is the general opinion, that it will not only repay the cost, but leave a remunerating profit. It is urged there is a deficiency of capital—admitting that it is so to a certain extent, it forms the exception, not the rule ; but as far as the labourers are concerned, it is entirely out of the question, and it ought not to be permitted to affect them, for the reasons above stated. And further, the labourers have not occasioned the want or the disgraceful waste of capital that has gone on for years, but have suffered in consequence. They have not occasioned farmers to pay too high rents and tithes, but have suffered in consequence. They have not occasioned farmers to take more land than they ever had capital for, but have suffered in consequence. They have not occasioned parishes to expend those large sums about litigations of settlements, but have suffered in consequence. They have not occasioned the falling off in the produce of land for want of better cultivation, but have suffered in consequence. They have not occasioned their being sent upon the roads and kept in idleness, but have suffered in consequence. They have not occasioned land-owners to accept ignorant tenants without capital, and at too high rents, but have suffered in consequence. They have not occasioned farmers to send the men they employ to have their wages made up out of the poor rates, to enable them to pay high rents, high tithes, high taxes, and for want of capital, but have suffered most severely in consequence. They have not occasioned a fifth of the produce to be taken away by the tithe owners, without paying a sixpence towards the cultivation of the land, but have suffered in consequence. They have not occasioned the imposition of the malt and other taxes, but have suffered in consequence. In short, there is no end to it, but surely I have shewn enough, if not more than may be agreeable, to convince the most sceptical, that *self* always stands first, and the weakest must go to the wall. That such things should be permitted in a free country is most cruel, unjust and ungenerous ; and I would ask what trade, what business, or what description of farms, can support and stand against such an expensive system and practice as this ?

And can there be a heart so hard as not to feel, on considering the miserable situation of such a large part of his fellow citizens, and, on feeling, not to wish for the power of relieving them ? But it is not from the want of humanity and feeling that I apprehend danger to this my proposal. Humanity and feeling are large ingredients in the composition of the English people. I alone dread danger from the want of exertion and enterprise, which, regarding difficulties through the deceitful vapour of long habituated national apathy and indolence, sees it in the dreadful form of a chimera, or a lion in the way. And yet I entertain hope, that having brought them so near, that they may be viewed in their true and real forms, the pungent stimulus of

present hard *national necessity*, with the chearing
cry of hope, and the pity-moving voice of
humanity, will, by their united power, spirit up
the national energies to encounter them.

It is morally impossible as the law now stands,
to guard against the foolish, disreputable, and
wicked conduct of those persons who hire land,
knowing that they have not adequate capital, and give higher rents than the present
and probable price of produce, will under any
circumstances justify—and then to secure themselves against the loss, resort to the mean and
disgraceful alternative of neither employing a
sufficient number of hands for its proper cultivation, nor paying them full wages, but sending
them to the overseers to have their wages made
up out of the poor rates at the expense of others,
and are perpetually grinding down the earnings
of the poor to make it a matter of greater advantage to themselves. This occasions a spirit of
dissatisfaction throughout the parish amongst
the farmers, and from a mistaken notion of self-
interest and protection, most of them resort to
the same sort of unjustifiable means, which
not only tends to impoverish themselves, but
immediately falls npon the poor, who are made
to suffer FIRST.

It is to put a stop to and remedy the
evils originating from conduct and practices
like these I have mentioned, that renders an
obligatory measure absolutely necessary, not
only to make every occupier pay for the cultivation of his own farm, and employ an equitable portion of the labour, which he can profitably
do, but to compel him to bear the consequences
of his own ignorance, want of capital, imprudence and folly, and to protect the poor man
from such grinding oppression, and secure to
him employment when he choses to work, with
a fair rate of wages ; thus securing to all parties
their property, and rights, and privileges.

Since the days of Elizabeth the Government
has been legislating only for particular circumstances and temporary purposes, without either
considering the foundation on which they framed
their enactments, applicability to the circumstances of the times, or the general state of society. The Legislature has never taken, since that
period, an enlarged and comprehensive view of
the subject, nor treated it as a national measure.
All that has been since accomplished has been
mere patch-work of the most despicable kind,
making confusion worse confounded. How the
laws of settlement could be permitted to exist

for such a length of time, to me is a matter of surprise, unless it is, that the severity of their operation always falls upon the weak and unprotected. For I believe the ingenuity of man could not devise laws more destructive to the liberty of the subject, more arbitrary, tyrannical, and cruel in their operation and consequences than they are, to say nothing of the perjury, fraud, and expence, to which they give rise and entail upon the public. There are besides other causes, but it is not my intention to attack individuals or parishes, trusting that the documents and calculations that are now submitted to the public will sufficiently speak for themselves, and prove to the satisfaction of the thinking part of the community, that by a proper application of the labour and the poor rates, in the way recommended, the condition of every individual will be improved, from the highest to the lowest ; that an entire change for the better will be made in the character of the lower class of people, and that there will not be required above one-third of that enormous tax which at present is collected under the title of poor rates, and applied towards maintaining and holding the poor in that abject and slavish dependent state of existence on the charity of others, thereby rendering them useless in every respect, and a heavy burden to the public as well as to themslves, but it will put them in the way of earning an honest, independent, and comfortable subsistence on the value of their own labour and industry, and of becoming useful members of society.

Such, my Lord, is the design and the *course* I have the honour to submit to your Lordship and the public. I hope it is true alike in theory and in practice. If upon the examination I thus invite, it shall be thought worthy the trial, it belongs to persons of rank and power to give it that impulse which can alone raise it to the importance and benefit of a county or national measure. And here I may be allowed to remark, that the accomplishment of this scheme would do no violence to individual or national feeling, aloof entirely as it is from all political consideration, with no spoliation of property, destruction of vested rights, rescinding of contracts, interference with charitable bequests, or taking away any privileges that may belong to individuals or parishes.

I think an experiment may be as effectually made in this county (if it be not adopted as a national measure) and more so than any other, because a somewhat extensive observation of the industry and character of other counties bears me out in the belief I entertain, that those who are interested and employed in the agriculture of Norfolk, are at least equal in intelligence, skill, and perseverance to the inhabitants of any other part of his Majesty's dominions. I speak alike of landlord, tenant, and labourer. If then the plan should be approved upon examination by your Lordship, I am sure it will meet with that attention and support it deserves, from the paramount importance of the subject.

I have the honour to be, my Lord,

With great respect,

Your Lordship's most obedient humble servant,

JOHN RICHARDSON.

Heydon, August, 1831,
Norfolk.

BACON AND KINNEBROOK,

MERCURY OFFICE, NORWICH.

PLAIN SENSE AND REASON.

LETTERS

TO

𝕿𝖍𝖊 𝕻𝖗𝖊𝖘𝖊𝖓𝖙 𝕲𝖊𝖓𝖊𝖗𝖆𝖙𝖎𝖔𝖓

ON THE

UNRESTRAINED USE

OF

MODERN MACHINERY,

PARTICULARLY ADDRESSED

TO MY COUNTRYMEN, AND FELLOW CITIZENS.

If it is the earth on which we tread,—if this earth is fruitful,—if its fruits are for the use and benefit of mankind,—if it produces enough of these fruits for the use of man,—then it is not Taxation, nor Rent, nor Tithe, nor the Currency, nor Over Production of the fruits of the earth, nor Over Population, nor Competition among Labourers or Farmers, nor Free Trade, nor High nor Low Prices, nor Fire, nor Sword, nor Pestilence, nor Famine in the land, have caused Starvation. It is Machinery! for let the produce of the earth be reduced to the lowest possible value; let there be but coin, and labor paid in that coin; let that coin be essential to procure the necessaries of life, so long will labour, the means of procuring that coin, be warred against by unrestrained Machinery, compared to the workings of which, the great questions of Reform and the National Debt itself are mere bubbles. Machinery is a many-headed reptile, born of Ambition, her Fosterchild is

STARVATION;

Monstrum horrendum informe ingens cui lumen ademptum.

Let the poor petition against it, deprived thereby of their daily bread;—Let the middle class, for by it they are daily sinking into poverty;—Let the philanthropist, that he may render the human race more service;—Let the religionist, that he may assist in purging the community of the prolific source of immorality;—And let the rich, that they may retain their possessions.

NORWICH:

PRINTED AND PUBLISHED BY WILKIN AND FLETCHER,

EAST ANGLIAN OFFICE; SOLD ALSO

BY SIMPKIN AND MARSHALL, STATIONER'S COURT, LONDON.

Price Sixpence.

The following paragraphs should have been introduced in Letter IV. line 15, page 11.

The French carried on their last war by the assistance of English merchants. Even the battle of Waterloo was fought with money borrowed in England.

Napoleon Buonaparte said, *" Bills were discounted by merchants in London, to whom ten per cent., and sometimes a premium, was paid as their reward. Bills were then given by them upon different bankers in Europe for the greatest part of the amount, and the remainder in gold, which last was brought over to France by the smugglers. Even for the equipping my last expedition, a great part of the money was raised in London."*—See Voice from St. Helena, vol. 2, *p.* 21.

ENGLISH MONEY LENT BY ENGLISHMEN TO FOREIGNERS, TO SLAUGHTER ENGLISHMEN AND RUIN ENGLAND ! ! !

DEDICATION.

TO BENJAMIN DRAKE, M. D.

NEW YORK.

From the respect I bear you as a friend—from the knowledge I gained through the courtesy of your countrymen during my stay on your side of the Atlantic,—and the interest I can but feel in your welfare, witnessing as I do the idleness, immorality, wretchedness, and starvation, of one part of this community, most industriously inclined had they but employment, and witnessing the imminent danger to which the other is at this moment exposed, on whom rests the burden of their maintenance,—knowing your countrymen are gifted with quick penetration, yet that they are subject to like frailties with the rest of the family of Adam,—knowing that they, aided by machinery, are pushing their manufactures to rival us with the ardour of men determined to succeed,—knowing that in this densely peopled country the want of employment has been mainly occasioned by machinery superseding the necessity for manual labour, reducing those employed by it to the lowest pittance on which human nature can subsist, robbing the others of their earnings, and throwing them a burden on the community,—knowing your people are as yet fully employed, well paid, and that machinery will soon arrive at maturity with you, but that it is a many headed monster, and requires constant watching;—I beg to dedicate to you the following letters; and, connected with them, an object of enquiry and great interest on both sides of the Atlantic, I have subjoined a comparative meteorological table; shewing the points of difference in climate between the two countries.

The last summer here was called wet and cold, and the winter months were more severe than is usual; during the year the thermometer ranged higher and lower by about 10 degrees on the days marked in the table than for very many years preceding; yet I think, with the exception of the excess of heat and cold on the days mentioned, it averaged a fair specimen of this climate, and it is here selected for the present purpose. The account was kept by myself; my thermometer was placed on the north side of my house in the midst of a populous city, twenty miles from the ocean; its altitude was about twenty feet above the level of the ocean, and twelve feet above the surface of the earth; it faced due north; and as these observations were always made from it in the same situation, they are, perhaps, as correct as any thing of the sort can well be. The observations on your side were made by officers under your government, and published as authentic. Boston, New York, and Philadelphia, being the places most known here, I have taken an average between the three, and that gives you a great excess of heat and cold; but had any particular place alone been selected, or had I

B

noted my own experience, the excess must have been much greater; for at St. Peter's, in the western territory, situated about the latitude of Boston, it is remarked that the thermometer has been 30 degrees below zero; that at Council Bluffs, also in the western territory, and in about the same latitude, it has ascended to 105°. I have seen it stand at 96° at midnight; yet these are extremes of which little conception can be here formed, and cannot fairly be taken into the present comparison.

The table shews the same winds prevail in both countries; that the number of fine and rainy days differ less than is generally supposed. I have noted fair, foggy, and frosty days, and by arranging the fine and fair days together, there are here most fine days; and by arranging the foggy with the rainy, there is here also an excess of rainy days—an excess of snowy days—but of frosty days, could I have met with any account of them, you would in them exceed us infinitely: it will be seen also in the summer some of your days exceed any here in heat 22°, and in the winter 20° in cold; that in May, June, July, and August, here are many days many degrees cooler than any of yours during those months, and that here many days in October, November, December, and February, are warmer than with you; that in December the thermometer stood here at 8°; that it stood the same at Boston; but taking the average of Boston, New York, and Philadelphia, here was an excess of cold on the 26th of December of 9°: from this view, the climate of this country appears subject to less vicissitudes, and to be decidedly preferable if moderate temperature gives a preference; a day without a breeze is scarcely known here, the absence of a breeze renders the heat with you almost insupportable. Here musquitos and other noxious insects or reptiles are unknown, with you they add in no small degree to the miseries of human life; not with you only, but to the inhabitants of all countries subject to extreme heat. Here spring, summer, autumn, and winter, seed time and harvest, duly succeed each other, as with you; but here are longer days for the enjoyment of the summer, and shorter in the winter, when daylight has less enchantment. I have asserted that this country and climate ensure to the inhabitants as great, if not greater power of animal enjoyment than any other, and I think no foreigner who ever visited these shores, divested of prejudice, will refuse to award the claim I make in their behalf, of possessing the most favourable situation on the face of the globe; and the inhabitants, on that account, the most favoured of all the nations of the earth; I speak as an Englishman, and as every one ought who loves his country; and in addressing you I know that I address one equally devoted to the place of his birth, yet of candour to admit it has some disadvantages, of liberality to allow others to speak well of their own, of charity to excuse me if *amor patriæ* has betrayed me into any expression of too favourable an opinion, or undue praise of my own.

NORWICH, OLD ENGLAND,   THE AUTHOR.
   January, 17th, 1831.

INTRODUCTION.

In the following Letters I feel it unnecessary to enter upon a lengthy disquisition, or to search, had I the inclination, into deeply concealed mysteries. Suffice it therefore that mankind inhabit a globe whose surface is fertile, whose inhabitants are numerous, whose wants the spontaneous fruits of the earth will not support; that we live on islands situated in a happy climate, unannoyed by excessive heat, excessive cold, pestilential vapours, noxious insects, or hideous reptiles, whose shores are fertile and of extent sufficient to maintain their population for many generations; that we are associated into a community capable of enjoying the greatest blessings allotted to human nature, but that we are victims of false philosophy, ignorant of, or unable to enjoy these transcendent blessings, of intense intellect, the phantasies of which are in direct opposition to common sense and the wise dispensations of Providence.

It may be said these letters are a mass of plagiarism—assertion without proof; if so, let it pass, good may arise from evil;—whole volumes have been written and may be again to prove 't is taxation, rent, tithes, currency, over production of the fruits of the earth, over population, competition, free trade, high and low prices, the national debt, and national corruption; each writer advocating that as the cause which most affects his own particular interest; but these are effects whose pressure is but relative and subject to local remedies, the effect of machinery is *universal*. To those who espouse the opposite side of the question, I say, let them prove 't is not the earth on which we exist—that the earth is not fruitful, that its fruits are not for the enjoyment of mankind, or that it does not yield to the industry of man a bountiful return. Let them prove the belly has no craving and that food is unnecessary, let them prove raiment is more than food, that the cultivation of the earth is useless, let them prove that one nation cannot rival another, let them prove that the burden of this rivalry is not thrown on the labouring population, let them prove that starvation is the effect of plenty, and I have done. To those who say the mind must progress, I ask, where is Babylon and where the cities of the East?—Were they built without heads and hands? To those who urge that machinery will find its level, I answer, so does every mountain torrent. To those who heap abuse on our country, our soil, our climate, let them leave it— 't is too good for them. To those who love it, I say, let them petition against machinery; for while the creation exists in its present form, while day and night, summer and winter, seed time and harvest remain, so long will the unrestrained use of machinery produce

STARVATION.

LETTER I.

THAT the want of food creates more of the difficulties and dangers that surround us than aught else, is not disputed ; and a little consideration convinces, that of the many conflicting opinions as to the cause, none can be right in the extreme, if any in a degree ; and as there is no famine, the natural enquiry is, how is it ?—That 'tis the earth on which we tread no one denies, nor yet its fruitfulness, nor that its fruits are for the use and benefit of mankind, nor that enough for all his wants it can and does produce by man's industry; this granted, why or how is it, that starvation stalks among us while plenty stares us in the face? How can it be or what is it that so perverts dame nature's laws that so it is? Is it taxation, rent or tithe, competition or free trade, high or low prices, or the currency, or the national debt, or national corruption? If 'tis all these, 'tis not dame nature's fault, these are the works of man. Dame nature says the earth is good, increase and multiply is her first law; the Deity made man the Lord of the creation, gave him plain sense and reason, and to his use ordained the earth and its productions. Nature has no hand in this starvation—'tis man; his intellect has wrought this strange fatality, excessively civilized men, whose exalted minds have marched clean over common minds, all common sense, and left the vile crowd to wonder and admire, not that they are immortal, but that they can't reach the moon. 'T is that queer thing the belly keeps common minds to common sense, 'tis that convinces us men are but mortals. Yes!—the back may be clothed, the head may be sheltered, but unless this belly be fed, pestilence, or famine, or sword will devastate the face of this fair land.   In the sweat of his face shall man eat bread, without the sweat of his brow he cannot exist, such is the lot of the human race, but the earth does yield abundantly to his industry, and shall not the labourer be worthy of his hire, when it is said muzzle not the ox that treadeth out the corn? It is not rent, nor tithe, nor taxes, nor the national debt, nor national corruption, nor the currency, nor over population, nor free trade, nor high nor low prices, nor competition, nor fire, nor sword, nor pestilence, nor famine; 'tis not all these combined, nor any one, though of sufficient import to plunge a state in difficulty, has caused this unnatural starvation. 'Tis the march of mind pursuing folly's phantom—universal peace and brotherhood; it is this forgets that nations are but men, each obstinately bent on its own real or fancied prosperity,—that its votaries are men whose schemes and principles war with the philanthropy they teach,—that their own dogmas must let loose a torrent to which they can oppose no barrier, and to which they themselves must fall a sacrifice ; is not this march of mind Ambition?—one of nature's ills,—the stumbling block of kings,—the rock on which men, princes, priests, rulers, kings, kingdoms, all have split,—which caused the fall of angels? But is not reason also a gift of Providence, raising man lord of the creation? Does reason guide this march of mind? Does reason teach that all the nations of the earth are one community of universal brotherhood, that Britain shall be the head to whom all the earth must bow? Is it not Ambition, whose mighty engine is in war the sword, in peace machinery? And is machinery her darling offspring? 'England's machinery in the competition shall put down all other;' 'cheap, cheap' is the cry; 'buy where you can buy cheapest,' the order of the day; to attain which end, one portion of the human race must be reduced to the lowest pittance on which it can exist, the other unemployed, beings quite useless in this new creation, are thrown a burden on the vitals of the country, on which they will prey till human nature driven past endurance, breaking through all bonds, sweeps the monster from the earth, its progeny and projectors, and gives good sense her sway. Is this philanthropy,—is this the march of reason,—is this that march of mind and common sense,—or has the march so many routes so near alike? Have reason and folly such close resemblance, that the goal must be possessed ere wrong or right is known? It is not so with common minds; 'tis exquisite refinement, 'tis the march of intellect past common sense, disdaining to look down on common things, on human nature, on human frailty, to consider man as man.

Machinery is the hydra of the present day, starvation is her offspring, and as long as the land is cursed with unrestrained machinery, machinery vying with itself, the inhabitants of the whole earth cannot consume the produce. Every market must be glutted, the industry of the human race be of no avail; and let tithes, taxation, rent, national debt, and extra population be all swept off; free trade and competition have full sway; let there be but currency, let the produce of the earth be reduced to the lowest particle of price, let just one farthing support a family one whole day, let there be but coin, and labour paid in that coin, let that coin be essential to procure the necessaries of life, so long will labour, the means of getting that coin, be warred against by unrestrained machinery, so long must the human race be sacrificed; and the projectors themselves, however they may have grown rich for a time, must be involved in the general ruin, most certainly awaiting the unnatural yet universal competition that must emanate from the unrestrained production and unending power of machinery.

Machinery is a many headed reptile, the hydra of the present day, born of ambition, her foster child is

STARVATION,

Monstrum horrendum, informe ingens cui lumen ademptum.

LETTER II.

IF industry be wealth, so then it may be said must machinery be, rendering industry infinitely more productive; but what is wealth? —to the great bulk of mankind it is the source from which must flow their food, their raiment, shelter, all that rewards their industry and renders life desirable. Nations *may* be rich in learning, comforts, and conveniences of life; *must* be populous, and as long as there is coin *must* be rich in that. Gold is the precious metal which the unceasing industry of ages has sought to acquire and increase. Gold cannot be sown or mown; it is one of nature's products of so rare occurrence that by its own value in labour is it alone to be procured. What is trade to nations, but to get gold or that they have not? And to this end the mind of man has called machinery to his aid, to multiply the produce of his industry to get this gold. Machinery cannot make gold, and where gold grows not, it must make goods of various sorts, and having made them, change them for gold. But all nations scrambling for gold go to the same market; all nations having their machines, their population, their surplus produce, all striving to get and keep some gold, the earth cannot supply their want, and that nation which can give most goods, *while goods are wanted,* (for there is a limit to consumption,) will get most gold. Nations compete with nations, machinery with machinery; to get this gold mankind are slaves to things inanimate; their industry and invention urged to the utmost pitch of human capability; their sustenance, to make cheap goods to meet this competition, reduced to just starvation's point. But gold is wealth, gives power, without it nations cannot move, and trade is only barter, barter in surplus produce. Who changes gold for gold? No nation parts with gold but by mischance or war. War scatters gold; all want the gold; if not, to grow rich might nations increase their surplus produce for sake of barter, barter in useless or surplus produce, *ad infinitum;* for so must all produce be when the supply exceeds the need of the consumers; and where is the limit to the produce of the earth, aided by this machinery?

Man cannot outstrip the purpose of his existence, but by the aid of this machinery he may so exceed the power of consumption in hundred and hundred fold degrees as to render its production useless, and it must rot. Population may increase but nature will have its course.

Industry, to be wealth, must be productively employed; not paralized and pauperised. If literature, if comforts and conveniences be wealth, then are they the effect of social industry actively employed,—but how can industry exist without a population? Then must population be a source of wealth, and as gold is wealth, there must be population to keep it safe, and if gold gives power there must be population to support its dignity. Social industry actively employed gives power to population — population to a nation, and such a nation can command its share of gold infinitely more easily than by stooping to pauper making and degrading competition, to satisfy the caprice of dealing gold diggers, thereby sacrificing population, social industry, national happiness, comfort, and convenience, to the market glutting power of machinery.

LETTER III.

By political writers here, the United States of America are frequently alluded to by way of comparison. They are externally and internally in a flourishing condition,—they, politically speaking, enjoy the greatest possible happiness, yet they live not without labour. They have their independence, but they have their debt, their taxes, their paper money. They as well as other nations *have seen* England's machinery; they too have England's mechanics, but had they not, they have heads to invent as well as other nations, though invention proceeds more slowly than imitation. They have their machinery, manufactures, and factories. They have a vast capital in land, rivers, mountains, forests, Indians, and buffaloes; in civilized people, houses, mines, canals, corn, cotton, ships, and steam-boats; the estimated value of them all set down in dollars, and in a supply for all the essential wants in common with other nations;—if not in all the luxuries, causes of effeminacy, 'tis no great loss;—the Americans are but men, and they will have them, but they have not heaps of gold. What Yankees think of gold?—they scarce ever saw it. Their very dollars are all paper, circulating at every degree of discount from par to zero. Their Dr. Franklin knew gold was not paper, but he also knew paper or credit could well supply the place of gold for their domestic wants, and leave the gold for other uses. Their debt has made them independent, but their debt is not in gold, nor is it paid in gold, 'tis paid in paper, circulating at par with their own currency; and those who will have gold, must make the sacrifice. But for internal purposes, paper is of equal use with gold; with paper they buy land, clear forests, grow cotton, build houses, bridges, banks, ships, cities, churches, make machinery, and canals; paper is their very life and soul, the spring to their industry; their fleet owes its creation to paper money. Though all these are classed as capital they cannot well trade with them, and they make the necessary distinction between capital of intrinsic value, whether fixed or moveable, paper or credit capital, and specie capital. Their people know the difference well; never could they have cleared the forest, never could they have raised these houses, churches, bridges, cities, banks, ships, and machinery with specie; they know this well, the government knows it too, and whatever the fate of this local paper, the improvements remain, the people remain, these cities &c. remain; the land grows corn, and cattle, and cotton; machinery clothes the people, the houses give them shelter. Though there are many who regret *the paper currency is not monopolised for the benefit of the nation,* the government, knowing its power to do so, yet wanting not the income derived from the issue of this paper, leaves it to individuals, and risking nothing, is content with the increase of national strength, every where accumulating thereby. They rival every nation in power by the force of this paper, and as they know its power, they will use it till they have accumulated sufficient stock of gold, and having redeemed their debt, will redeem the paper also, and need its use no longer. Without it centuries must have passed ere they could have ranked with independent nations; but paper money is worthless, rotten printed rags, too frail for nature's meanest office, yet such its power, the independence of the Union its fruit; and let its end be what it may, (for be it remembered gold will wear as well as paper) there it is across the Atlantic in power, in men, in ships, in lands, in cities, in cotton, in looms; and their own wants supplied, will beat the world in the cheapness of their commodities. They have no starvation, no poor rates, no surplus population, their land produces plenty, and they will share it, each according to his industry; but will they bear the existence of machinery, when its increase of power shall so far exceed their wants, that they must ferret the whole globe nor find its produce vent, throwing the population encouraged to its use, a burden on the rest of the community?

The Americans are a moral and religious people, their elegant churches, conspicuously placed in·every rising village, gratify the passers by, but the Americans are but men, they have their laws and punishments, the country abounds with gaols crowded .with classed criminals, gaols like castles, and they encrease with their population. They have their taxes too, a tax on all the land they occupy, 'tis very light, but must be paid in currency, ('tis paper certainly,) but so small a quantity of land is tilled upon each farm, that it weighs heavily even in paper on the Americans; but in the prosperity of their country, they see a limit to the grievance, still even in paper 'tis a heavy grievance, and many of their people to escape this tax, emigrate to Canada. For taxes, seizures there are just as common as seizures here for rent, and press heavily or lightly in proportion to the price of produce: what taxes can that man pay who sends his produce 1000 miles to market? what taxes can that man pay whose fat ducks are sold for 6 cents each, York currency? for the tax is just the same let the market be near or distant. The Americans can by their industry live well, but not in idleness.—They cannot grow rich in gold, but by the natural course of saving industry; the Americans are poor in gold, because they have no gold mines within their grasp.—Their government is rich, because its income far exceeds its expenditure; but to raise their taxes in gold! to pay their debt in gold! perish the thought! impossible! and they well know for the attempt they would be branded madmen.

The Americans from necessity have cherished agriculture, bread the staff of life their first object; that attained, they turn their thoughts to the less needful but more delicate pursuits of commerce and manufactures. They have, too, their political economists, one of whom addressing his fellow citizens on that subject, says, " your country is finely skirted with seas and traversed by noble navigable rivers. Your climate is peculiarly favourable for raising the choicest fruits of the earth. Your government, your own choice, is probably the most frugal on earth, but can be modified and amended to suit existing circumstances. Your rulers are appointed by yourselves and with *due attention* to their selection, your government cannot fail to lead to happiness and felicity. You have 140 acres to every individual; and to use the words of a celebrated statesman, you have

'room for your descendants to the thousandth and thousandth gene-
'ration.'" After enumerating many of their difficulties he says, " I
shall endeavour to lay before you the true cause of the great difficulties you have had to contend with, under a conviction that a
clear view is the best method of pointing towards a permanent remedy." To that end, after giving many statistical tables, and proving that " they have about 28 persons in every 100 actively employed,
that of the 28, *only the proportion of 3 are engaged in manufactures;*
that as Britain, (whose inhabitants are the most industrious on the
earth,) has 33, in every 100 actively employed, he concludes that number would apply to the United States, and of that number 20 should
be employed in agriculture, 10 *in manufactures, and 3 in commerce.*"
"That *England had* 17 *employed in commerce and manufactures,* and
16 in agriculture, that England aided by machinery must be an ex-
porting country of manufactured goods; and the United States an
importing country, while such is the relative condition of both countries;" he goes on to state, " That their national policy ought to be
changed by legislative provision. That the nations of Europe for years
having resolved to make themselves independent as far as possible
within themselves, and that the States being an agricultural nation,
they could only export in quantities, *articles for food.* That this determination on the part of European nations has occasioned them great
embarrassments, arising, not from want of property, want of industry,
want of discretion on the part of merchants, traders, or bankers,
but simply from the circumstance that they as a nation, continued to
receive indiscriminately the manufactures of Britain, after she had
excluded their *bread stuffs.* That this has forced them to become a
manufacturing people, and this manufacturing will in time operate
to their relief. That cottons, woollens, and iron, have formed the
most prominent articles of import;—that they have the raw materials in their country, and were their manufacturing industry so aug-
mented as to supply only *half* these articles imported, it is easy to
see how beneficial the effects would be;—that the importation of
these cost them a loss from their specie capital in 1821 of near *two
million dollars.* That their embarrassments were seen in Britain and
exultingly commented upon by British writers, and some of them of
high rank; but the facility with which they have become manufacturers is a proof of their industry and energy, and the statesmen of
Britain will quickly find the people of the United States have it as
completely in their power to make themselves independent within
themselves for clothing, as the people of Britain are for food. That
the result will eventually be a blessing to both countries, that every
nation ought to be independent within herself for all her material
wants, and no nation can be great or respectable that is not. That
their agricultural ranks are full to overflowing. That their manufactures do not supply the demand by 30 *millions* of dollars annually;—that when that sum is added to their stock of *national industry,* British writers will have no cause to triumph over them. That
if they are true to themselves they will not only soon supply all
their own material wants, but will have a large portion to spare for

C

other countries, particularly the rising independent States of Mexico and South America. That the argument made use of by modern political economists, of buying where you can buy cheapest, is *unanswerable*, but applied to the social industry of a nation, it will generally be found that the *cheapest purchase* for a supply of all the material wants will be to *make the articles.* That their manufactures are on a respectable footing;—that the application of machinery has been extensively made;—that it is daily increasing, without increasing their *public burdens;* and though they have not reached the finer fabrics, there is a prospect, through the medium of machinery applied to manufactures, of their soon being relieved from every difficulty as a nation, if it be *judiciously combined* with agriculture and commerce." After, impressing the necessity for every nation to become independent within itself for all its material wants,—applying this maxim practically to the United States in plain yet forcible terms,—ascribing England's great wealth to her powerful machinery; and complimenting her inhabitants for their great industry, he thus concludes, " My decided opinion is, that in the augmentation of our manufacturing industry depends our independence and comfort and happiness as a nation; and that we must place the manufacturer by *the side of the agriculturalist.*"

Such are some of the sentiments contained in an address published in 1822 by their patriotic citizen, John Mellish. It may contain some errors, but every sentence teems with good and common sense, no bombast, no vagaries of the mind marching with modern philosophy beyond the sphere of human capability, every statement verified by the most authentic documents; no theories, but plain facts made clear by the plainest language, suited to the understanding of every plain and sensible mind ; and had every letter been cast in solid gold, and circulated gratis, 't would have been a cheap answer to the bales of theories published by humbugging modern political economists since that period. What a mass of misery might it have saved this country !

If such was their state of manufacturing in 1822, what is it now? They have their corn mills grinding with 17 pair of stones, their factories of 100 power looms; not thinly scattered over an extensive territory, but wherever power of water is, there ranks of factories are crowded. Even the grand Niagara is turned aside into a mill race, a second Manchester is rising there; and that mighty cataract is made subservient to human purposes, in working their native iron as well as cotton.

This address was published in 1822: the Americans, therefore, in 1822 well knew the effects of foreign trade,—that for every dollar that came into the treasury thereby, the value of four left their country,—knew the exact loss of it, the necessity of becoming manufacturers; and that the greater the power and the sooner applied, the sooner would they supply their deficiencies. They knew, England's superiority had been maintained by her superior machinery; and they have given employment to crowds of English artisans. They, knew also, price is not regulated by intrinsic value or labour

expended in production, but by demand, began to suspect that produce might be extended beyond the possibility of consumption, that
by producing an extra quantity of goods, *a greater quantity of labour
must be expended* (to use modern phraseology); and they might add
nothing to the *money value.* They knew that machinery applied to
manufactures as a branch of national industry, to be beneficial, must
be judiciously *combined with agriculture,* and they knew also it
could be applied without adding to their public burdens. They
knew its use and have applied it. They do now export cottons to
Mexico and South America. As in 1822 they knew it must be
judiciously combined with agriculture, and, that *then* it would not
increase any public burden, they will have penetration to discover
when it is detrimental to agriculture; and know how to curb its
application when the time arrives that its power produces any public burden. For the Americans well know also that industry to be
wealth, must be actively employed,—that the cheapest purchase for
a supply of all material wants will be to *make the articles,*—that the
best maintenance for a population arises from their own exertions,—
that idleness of itself is a loss to the community independent of the
deleterious effect it has on moral habits. KNOWING ALL THIS,
will they suffer themselves to be burdened to maintain a population
demoralized by idleness occasioned by the unrestrained use and
labour-saving power of machinery?

LETTER IV.

Although it is difficult to judge to what degree of misery competition
in machinery may reduce the inhabitants of Great Britain, yet some
notion of it may be formed when it is known, that machinery is extensively introduced into the East Indies, superintended by British
artisans, and that the rate of wages to the natives is about 2s. 6d.
per month, or 1d. per day. The power of machinery is the same
in every place, climate and seasons have little effect on it; goods
made thereby will wear the same appearance, and be appropriated
to the same purposes, whether made on the healthy shores of Britain, or in the fruitful but pestilential swamps of the East or West
Indies.

The love of money will lead men to brave every danger, and
unless restrained by wholesome regulations, to sacrifice every consideration—their friends, their countrymen, their country, to its
overwhelming influence. Political economists there are (and they
are more to be dreaded than foreign armies, or famine, or pestilence)
who are ready to sacrifice to the cry " Buy where you can buy
cheapest" the millions of the agricultural people of this country:
they are willing to sacrifice the millions of the manufacturing population to the population-starving (*therefore* cheap) power of machinery; who, as they have found out the impracticability of moving
these islands to some spot of everlasting summer, where the spon-

taneous fruits of the earth would abundantly supply the wants of the population, *surplus by machinery*, will move machinery to some rich torrid swamp, inimical to population, yet producing food in plenty. Such competition Britain cannot meet, must be supplied from thence with food and clothes (as long as she can pay in coin) at the cheap rate. All cultivation then would cease; all employment would be then unnecessary; the land become a wilderness, the people mere intellectual beings; their money spent, they would be aroused to prey upon each other, or be a prey to pestilence and famine; the wreck would till the earth, taught wisdom by so severe a lesson,— know better for the future! But to the point,

The British Isles do at this present moment furnish to every soul one acre of highly-cultivated arable land, one acre and a half of rich pasture, and more than one acre and a half of land at present in a state of nature—in all about four acres to each individual. Now as the United States have only 140 acres to each of their population, and that to the 1000th and 1000th generation, they are provided for, increasing as they do, not only by the laws of nature, but by a tide of people, flowing from all parts of the Old World, surely British fears are groundless for the present generation at any rate; if not, 'tis no argument to neglect Britain's little treasure; but, on the contrary, as she values her existence, to push her fertility by every device to her utmost capability. But will any one contend that four acres are insufficient to maintain one soul?

When Colquhoun wrote, about thirty-three in every hundred of the population of this country were actively employed; of these sixteen were engaged in agricultural pursuits, the rest in manufactures and in commerce. Since that time the relative numbers may have altered considerably, and the manufacturing population may have increased; the agricultural decreased. Many of the country labourers may have become weavers—from local circumstances being able to work cheaper than citizens, and have the preference; " cheap being the order of the day." The citizens, also from local circumstances, being unable to compete with the country people, have been and are unemployed. The application of machinery to agriculture rendering a less agricultural population necessary; and this competition must, under such circumstances, always thus effect the citizens, were *they* not rendered *surplus* by the application of machinery to *their* natural pursuits.

Population also ebbs and flows, and it may have flowed the last ten or fifteen years, but the increase ascribed to it is impossible. If history is to be depended upon—it is recorded, that in many places plagues have swept off as many as the present population; that in 1348 the plague carried off in this city 57,000, besides religious persons and beggars, and that one fifth part were left alive. Then Norwich was more populous than it has been since—it had *then sixty-seven churches* within the walls, *now there are but thirty-six*, the cathedral, and fourteen places of dissenting worship. The ancient evidences scattered everywhere over the country, the churches standing, the ruins of others, the barns, in which the forefathers of the present generation threshed out corn, the signs of cultivation on land in some parts of England known as downs and wolds, now untouched by the plough, are indisputable proofs of a numerous population. Britain was always populous, always will be, and as a nation, whatever change the state of any component part may undergo, will always bear a powerful sway.

Agriculture requires able-bodied men, manufactures do not; able-bodied men can more easily become inmates of a factory than inmates of factories become labourers in the field. Our agricultural forefathers never dreamt of applying machinery to render useless and burdensome members of society any part of their community: they were all employed on the land or in the barns, in *the very barns we see now standing* they did thresh out all the corn without machinery. Those *very barns* will at this moment find the same employment for all the labourers by the canting politicians of the present day called " surplus ;" and agriculture would, as in the days of our forefathers, occasionally require the assistance of some of the manufacturing population.

The British Isles have at this moment more than three acres of *profitable land* to every soul; and remember, *soul* means men, women, children, infants. Take half the population as agricultural, which I believe to be sufficiently correct, (though by some the manufacturing and commercial part are stated greatly to preponderate, and if they do it will leave a greater breadth of land,) there will be seven acres at the least to every agricultural soul. If Colquhoun's estimation of the numbers actively employed be correct, there will be sixteen only of that number employed, or about twenty-one acres to be cultivated by every person actively employed in agriculture; but by persons actively employed, women and big children are included; and as families average the number of $4\frac{1}{2}$ in each, there will be nearly thirty-two acres of profitable land to be cultivated by every agricultural family in this kingdom. Such are the facts as it regards these realms and their agricultural population. Will any one be bold enough to say the land does not require such a population? Whoever is at all conversant with the subject well knows the land of this kingdom, to push its productiveness to the utmost, would find ample employment for the millions of the manufacturing population, were they to change their employment; and so bountifully does the earth repay the labour spent upon it, that where it gives employment it is sure to give food. No ground for the agricultural-population-surplus alarm ! and *parliamentary returns give 66 acres to every agricultural family.* But crowds of able-bodied labourers are seen upon the roads wasting their time: but this is not all! wasting the country's wealth; and this is not all! the roads grow no corn, and the land may grow less wanting their labour; and that is not all! these men demoralized by idleness could not be disposed of like stock upon a farm ; fed, clothed, and housed they must be, as long as nature will bear them up under their privations. The price of produce not regulated by the intrinsic value, or the cost of its production, but subject to the experiments of intellect, compelled the farmer to dismiss from his employment the necessary labourers; horses and machines performing a great part of their accustomed occupation; they have been seen clustered in flocks upon the roads. Short-sighted and ruinous policy! affording but a temporary relief; —the burden soon returning with double weight; the labourers still in existence, every year becoming more wretched, requiring more relief; *food, raiment, shelter* still being requisite,—every year the land less cultivated must, in the end, grow less; and with that the means of relieving must be lessened.

In a case so clear as this, one would have imagined the machinery might easily have been dispensed with; but it could not, it had assisted mainly in reducing the capital employed in agriculture; had enabled the farmer to turn his crop into money as soon as harvest had ended, and, calculating on the growing crop, some farmers occupied farms larger than they could otherwise have done: others endeavouring to continue their farms, loth to lose their credit in business, continued to pay more than the *money produce* of the land would admit, wasted the capital necessary to carry their farms round; and, to meet their payments, had recourse to threshing machines. On the other hand, the landlord, seeing the crop upon the land, and knowing that the corn could be brought to market as soon as ripe, by the aid of these machines, would give the farmer more credit; that in very many cases no rent has been paid for land, but from the growing crop, and little capital is employed. The impossibility by the flail thus to meet their payments, would have deterred any men not mad from entering upon farms, without a sufficient capital to carry on a year, leaving the first crop untouched. But the poor and the occupier have not been the only sufferers; thousands of men who had invested their all in land, or had borrowed money on estates, were, with the decreasing value of produce, (not that the quantity was materially lessened or the intrinsic value of it, or land,) ruined, and the estates have fallen into the hands of money lenders; or if not, after having paid repairs, other unavoidable expences, and interest to these money lenders, have little left but name, of their estates. But their day is nearly past, and the capital they have mainly assisted in taking from the land must be returned; a whole year's rent must be forthcoming ftom some quarter; these money lenders, will they advance it? They are the persons who have reaped the greatest profit on this great loss.

Such has been the effects of these machines, and will not they be abolished? No theories, no intense intellect, none of the political economists, no Malthusians, none of the anti-population committees, no march of mind men, opposed their progress; but the good plain sense of common minds, of men, who, feeling their effect most keenly, seeing the barns in which their fathers earned an honest living, alive with these inanimate vermin, (their bellies rebelling against all law,) stopped not, knowing the cause, till in attempting to root it out, they have brought upon their heads the penalties of the law.

They could not understand with empty bellies the industry of machinery—they well knew if industry was wealth, they possessed that disposition—they well knew it must be active or it would avail them nothing—they knew little and cared less about any other wealth than that which fills the belly—they knew that without money they could get no food—they wished not to have that money without earning it, and they were not too blind to discover, that these threshing machines were the main cause of their not earning money, and rendering their wealth in industry of no avail. They have taken the laws into their own hands—they have violated the laws of the land, which protect all property—protect machines as well as lives; and for their error they await the punishment. They should have petitioned without ceasing till the grievance was removed. The law protects machines, and while that law remains, machinery will be protected, and revived as caprice may give occasion. Modern machinery must be *restrained* or *abolished by law*. No tax short of total prohibition can, in many instances, be of any benefit; any tax short of that would enable monopolists to continue some in use to the incalculable mischief to society.

What tax on thrashing machines could be equivalent to their detrimental effect on the community? See their effect in figures! And where is the man, or set of men, not to be startled, to find thrashing machines causing the agricultural population a direct loss, to the full amount of the agricultural poor rate,—that thrashing machines in thrashing wheat alone, on a moderate calculation, and not to be disputed, occasion the enormous loss of £3,339,886 8s. to the inhabitants of this country? Three Million Three Hundred and Thirty-nine Thousand Eight Hundred and Sixty-six Pounds, Eight Shillings!!! Every thrashing machine averaging sixty quarters of wheat per week, if taxed to the amount of direct loss to the community, must be taxed annually £868 8s.; and this pretty sum, Eight Hundred and Sixty-eight Pounds, Eight Shillings, is without calculating the mischief resulting from a lessened circulating medium, and the amount of capital withdrawn from the cultivation of the land through their agency. These machines cannot well be taxed. Who would propose an annual tax of £868 8s. when the gross earning of the same machine is but £234 in the year? but if taxed at all, such is the amount each ought to pay. And if the tax be levied as an equivalent to the mischief, this sum levied on every machine must be repaid the parties within the range of its pernicious operations.

A thrashing-machine, averaging sixty quarters of wheat per week, would earn in that time £4 10s. or 2¼d. per bushel, but would pay out of its earnings the wages of a man to superintend and direct it; FIVE men, FOUR women, and SIX horses would also be employed. The value of the *manual labour* will be equal to that of about EIGHT MEN. This quantity of corn would employ eight men TEN days; there then remain FOUR days to be provided for by the parish. The men, by the flail, would earn £9, if paid the usual rate of 4½d. per bushel; they earn only £4 10s.—Yet this machine costs the farmer more than flail labour! He loses the value consumed by the horses. And there is a loss to the community; for swine, sheep, bullocks, &c. would grow fat on horses' provender, and produce a greater plenty. The labourer loses half his earnings; and the parish bound to provide some maintenance in their lieu, loses the purchase of his pauperism.

In the following calculations I have given the superintendant 2s. per day, to the labourer 1s. 6d., to the women 9d.; but were wages increased to 2s. for men, to 1s. for women, and the rate of threshing by flail to 6d. per bushel, the loss would be the same, but, differently borne. Give greater power to the machine, the burden on the parish is greater; and prolonged the misery and deprivation of the labourer.

LOSS TO THE FARMER.

Cost of a thrashing-machine, thrashing 60 qrs. of wheat in 6 days } versus { Flail labour, thrashing and dressing at the rate of 6 bushels per day.

	£	s.	d.		£	s.	d.
Machine at 2¼d. per bushel less the labour of superintendent	3	18	0				
Six horses, each per week at 18s.	5	8	0	Flail labour on 60 quarters including dressing	9	0	0
Waste of fodder and deteriorated value of the straw	1	0	0				
MANUAL LABOUR.				Loss to the farmer by using a thrashing machine	5	16	0
Superintendent, 6 days		12	0				
Five labourers, ditto	2	5	0				
Four women, ditto		18	0				
Dressing 6 last at 2s. 6d.		15	0				
	£14	16	0		£14	16	0

LOSS TO THE PARISH.

Sixty quarters of wheat would employ the six men and four women with the flail, at six bushels per day each man, (or estimating the four women as two men,) would employ eight men ten days; they are employed only six, consequently there remain four days' work to be provided these eight men; they are sent to the overseer, and generally would not receive more than 12d. per day. This causes the parish to lose

£1 12s. 0d.

LOSS TO THE LABOURER.

	£	s.	d.		£	s.	d.
The 8 men with the flail would earn in the 10 days	9	0	0	The 8 men earn at the machine only	4	10	0
				They receive of the parish	1	12	0
				They receive less than they would earn — consequently they lose the difference	2	18	0
	£9	0	0		£9	0	0

LOSS TO THE COMMUNITY.

The six horses consume the value of 18s. each per week, which value, whether in hay, or oats, or grass, would be consumed by eatable animals, were there no machines. The straw when threshed by machine is wastefully consumed, and the chaff and colder, (always taken care of and consumed when produced in small quantities,) is by the machine completely lost as provender, adds but little to the muck heap; and the loss to the community is this and the value consumed by horses,

£6. 8s. 0d.

TOTAL LOSS BY THRASHING MACHINES PER ANNUM.

Paying old rate of wages to the labourer	Loss to the farmer.	Loss to the parish.	Loss to the labourer.	Loss to the community.	Weekly loss by a machine threshing in six days 60 quarters of wheat.	Supposed quantity of wheat annually threshed by machines.	Necessary number of machines each threshing 80 bush. a day.	Annual loss by each machine.	Total annual loss to the community by the use of threshing machines.
	L. s. d. 5 16 0	L. s. d. 1 12 0	L. s. d. 2 18 0	L. s. d. 6 8 0	L. s. d. 16 14 0	12 mill. qrs.	3846	L. s. d. 868 8 0	L. s. d. 3,339,866 8 0
Paying advanced wages.	3 17 0	3 4 0	3 5 0	6 8 0	16 14 0	12 mill. qrs.	3846	868 8 0	3,339,866 8 0

If any other reason were necessary, to induce the abolition of these machines, it is the encouragement they offer to monopoly and speculation, enabling the parties using them in a few days to bring to market their whole crop, and to avail themselves of the fluctuations corn (in spite of every regulation to the contrary) is subject to, as well as all things else. For who can regulate the seasons? as well might it be attempted to regulate the stature of the human race; the thing is impossible; though it is hard to say what intense intellect might attempt.

But thrashing machines are limited in their operation. They can but thrash the corn, and that once thrashed there is an end to their employment. But limited as is their sphere, their pernicious influence carries pauperism in the train and the apparent need for emigration, while there is land enough at home to employ the population, were they all engaged in agriculture. The philosophy of the present day encouraging the increase of machinery, not people, the country and the people must be sacrificed; but as the people have some voice, it will be as well to know the value of the sacrifice. About half the population are engaged in agriculture. The land—does it produce enough for their consumption? if it do, it is of that value to the agriculturalist. But does it not produce a vast deal more, a vast surplus compared to their consumption? it does no doubt; the value of that surplus then, must be the value of the land; and while there is a manufacturing population and that population consumes provision, that surplus must be valuable, and as long as there is coin, its price must be the *money rental* of the land; for while bellies inhabit the bodies of the manufacturers, food they must have; and were it necessary, would give their whole industry to procure it. But we have three acres of profitable land to every mouth, of which the forced produce will suffice the population's need for many generations! The manufacturing population, the other half, will be engaged (not in the culture of the land but in that which conduces to the comfort of society) in producing luxuries, things of secondary im-

D

portance compared to food, and unaided by machinery could minister to every want of their own community and their agricultural countrymen : the essential wants of all supplied, FOOD, RAIMENT, SHELTER, would find leisure plenty, to produce some " surplus produce," to procure " surplus produce" from other nations ; luxuries to us, but surplus produce whence they come; a source of wealth depending solely on the demand. Here are the elements of social happiness within ourselves, *food, raiment, shelter*, and if trading were the only source of wealth, of that too. Here then is no need for the excess of that machinery so much admired, experiments with which so fairly tried, have brought us to this pass of starving plenty! FOOD, RAIMENT, SHELTER,—these are the three essentials, to get which, in greater plenty, (without them what is gold) machinery has been used. What better argument need be adduced than that the experiment has completely failed ; and is this country to be sacrificed, and its inhabitants exposed to every ill social society can suffer, and starvation too, for sake of this machinery ? Machinery like the reptile race makes its deadly attack covertly, or if observed, the faculties of its devoted victims are so fascinated and bewitched, that they become its unresisting and most certain prey.

LETTER V.

That some cause, other than taxation, does exist for the great increase of crime and pauperism must be admitted by every one of common understanding, on examination of statistical and other documents; for on reference to them it will be seen that since 1815 taxes have been very much decreased and *are now decreasing*, but that crime and pauperism have been *increasing to the present moment.* That in 1815 the poor rate amounted to about FIVE MILLIONS AND THREE QUARTERS, that it is *now* nearly EIGHT MILLIONS.—That the commitments for crime in 1815 were only 7,818, that they have been in the last year nearly 20,000. Debt and taxes have had their share in this, no doubt: but cannot be the sole cause of this alarming increase. The money value of all commodities has been subject to the influence of intense intellect experiments, a greater quantity of produce has been required to pay a given sum, and the reduced taxation has pressed more heavily : *but it bears no proportion to the increase of crime.* In 1815 the amount of taxation was about SEVENTY MILLIONS, in 1822 it was only FIFTY-FOUR MILLIONS, yet so great was the reduction in the price of produce, that the *reduced taxation* in 1822 required *three millions and a half quarters of wheat* (had taxes been paid in wheat) *more* than would have been required in 1815 to pay the seventy millions. The unbounded importations of corn gave a temporary stimulus to commerce and manufactures, at the expence of agriculture. Agriculture first declined ; and the capital invested has gradually left the land to the amount of a clear year's rental. This never could have been, had not *thrashing machines* been used; had it not been for them, pauperism never could have made such progress among the agricultural labourers, the *flail* would have given them employment many months, other agricultural occupations would have left them but little time unemployed, consequently but little occasion to apply to the overseer for relief; capital might have been reduced but never to its present low ebb: BUT, THE LABOURER NEVER COULD HAVE BECOME THE ABJECT PAUPER.

The manufacturing and commercial community received a temporary excitement, but two such weighty interests in the same country cannot long exist in opposition, they must be *combined* for *mutual welfare.* In the pauperism of one half of the community the manufacturer lost his best customer, he may search the world for such another market and not find it. The manufacturer feeling a loss, improves machinery—forces trade—reduces prices—all to no purpose.—Competition does its utmost, it is met in every quarter by improved machinery.—Machinery acquires new powers—competition renders them unavailing—no matter how low in price commodities, there is no market—no matter how low wages, competition requires a reduction, till the very manufacturers cannot buy a rag to cover them.

But machinery was necessary to the country! Without machinery, some say, " taxes could not have been paid nor wars prosecuted," if wars were necessary! That the wealth of many individuals in this country may have arisen from machinery is not to be disputed, and while England commanded *all markets* in the world, all nations contributed to increase this wealth. But the vast extension of this machinery gave birth to that competition, the first act of which was to *reduce the wages of labour;* with increased machinery, came increased competition and still lower wages; that this wealth has been acquired at the expence of *Englishmen as well as Foreigners.* A vast sum of money has been taken from circulation and a vast sum of comfort from the people. But machinery paid no taxes. TAXES WERE LEVIED ON THE PEOPLE BY GOVERNMENT TO PAY THE INTEREST OF THE MONEY BORROWED OF THOSE WHO HAD ENRICHED THEMSELVES BY MACHINERY.

After the peace, foreigners became better acquainted with machinery, they were *shewn England's machinery,* and the competition, existing before between countrymen, became universal. When foreigners entered into this machinery-competition, the produce of this machinery, if sold, could realise but little profit; wages, before low, were further reduced by this foreign competition. *Foreigners live cheaper* on worse and coarser food than Britons, and Britons, to compete with foreigners, must live on the same fare as foreign nations live. By this foreign machinery-competition, foreigners became acquainted with the *intrinsic value* of manufactured goods; from the date of this foreign competition, the profit on manufactured goods has been gradually sinking, and had machinery created no surplus population—had all hands been fully employed, wages here must have sunk to the foreign scale of wages, or the goods could meet no sale in foreign markets; and this competition must in the end destroy all profit on goods subject to such competition, if it has not done so already.

Under any circumstances the country must be burdened with *part* of the maintenance of the *employed,* their wages by machinery-competition inevitably reduced too low to enable them to provide more than the meanest diet, nothing for old age,—nothing for sickness,—nothing for births, marriages, burials, clothing, fuel, rent, or any casuality. But machinery has created a *surplus population, they* are to be wholly maintained. Here are the causes of that burden known as POOR RATE which is levied on *visible property!* And, were the proprietors of machinery by any possibility to gain as much by its use as the country loses by poor rate, is it *fair* or *just* that any part *of the community* are to be burdened to such an enormous amount to enrich a *few individuals?* But the eight millions poor rate bear but little proportion to the mischief wrought by this machinery! The eight millions are expended to keep life and soul together! For what is the sacrifice, the misery, deprivation, and poverty, to be endured, before even that pittance can be obtained? It is almost incalculable. Where is the family not visited by the effect of this machinery?—Where is the house in which it has not put an end to domestic industry?—Where is the labouring man who does not feel its effect to the amount of half his earnings?—Where is the man in middle life not affected thereby?—Where is the profit on trade, if trade remain?—Where is the estate in city or country not depreciated in value by the weight of poor rate? Houses want tenants, people want food and employment, and goods want consumption. Is there a soul living, or any species of *visible property* not affected by the poverty and destitution brought upon the labouring class of the community?

Compared to this, what is the weight of debt, or taxation to pay the interest?—What taxes? These are relative evils, heavy or light in proportion to the currency, or to the quantity of labour they absorb. *But machinery absorbs the source of labour, and drives the currency from circulation into heaps.* Taxes take part of value when created: *machinery stops creation.* Levy all the taxes on machinery,—place to its account them and the poor rate, then will the people lose all the comforts and enjoyments of life, no less their due, though deprived of them by machinery. What is Rent compared to this? what Tithe? They are both, part only of created value; land must always (while it produces more than its cultivators consume) pay rent, houses always will, while dwellings are necessary, and tithe is part of rent, part of created value, obnoxious from the peculiar mode of its collection: the weight of all these are *mere bubbles compared to the evil workings of machinery.*

To attribute the misery and starvation everywhere surrounding to over-production of the fruits of the earth, to over-population, to competition or free trade, to high prices or low prices, to fire, sword, pestilence or famine, when there is *no famine,* would be worse than madness. Is not machinery the barrier between labour and labourers? Can Man, possessed of an immortal soul and of a mortal body compete with inanimate machinery? Does machinery *gratuitously clothe or feed* the mortal man? O! no; he *must buy clothes, buy food*. He must first get the money,—and from whence is it to come? Can he find it? Will it fall from the heavens? The labourers know well their labour and the poor rate are the only sources from whence they can get this money, and they know it is machinery, and *machinery alone*, that has superseded the necessity for their services; that machinery has robbed them of their only wealth, the value of their industry—rendering them burdensome to society, and their lives burdensome to themselves, having endured every pang but that of dissolution; so that to them death creates no terror.

To treat this subject fully in all its bearings would far exceed my leisure or my present intention. To reduce to any correct calculation the evil wrought to society by machinery is utterly impossible; but to elucidate this subject it is necessary to shew *in figures* the value of the direct deprivation suffered among the labouring population.

There are in this kingdom about THREE MILLION LABOURING FAMILIES, each averaging nearly five persons; let machinery have affected to the value of only *ten shillings each family per week*, what does it amount to in the year? SEVENTY-EIGHT MILLION POUNDS STERLING. *Seventy-eight millions annually* in value taken from consumption—from the comforts and conveniences of these labouring families! *Two shillings per week* from each individual! Is there a family of five persons whose experience will not respond to the truth of this? Is there a labouring family in this city not losing a great deal more? Where is the combing and spinning, cotton-weaving, silk-filling, cruel-filling, hemp-dressing, sack-weaving, paper-making, hand-sawing, hot-pressing and printing;—where the employment general till the last few years?—all absorbed by machinery. Where is the distaff and spindle,—where the employment in knitting, in the manufacture of hemp and flax,—where the employment for women and children, formerly carrying comfort and independence to the *home* of every cottager?—all absorbed by machinery, or sacrificed to the cry of 'cheap.' Rotten cotton has taken the place of hemp and woollen,—machinery has superseded manual labour; and the labourers remain to be maintained by the inhabitants, whose source of maintenance *depends principally* on the prosperity of the *labouring community*. *Seventy-eight millions* taken from annual consumption! *Seventy-eight millions* not to be hoarded, but would be immediately spent in the necessaries of life! Seventy-eight millions of *direct loss to this portion of the community!* Who can calculate the direct loss to the *other part*, the indirect loss, the loss to society brought about by such an unnatural state of things? What is foreign trade to this,—what can *the profit* be, when the total GROSS AMOUNT of it is not *one half* of this *direct loss of* PROFIT ? A loss of profit (to calculate after the *improved fashion* of modern times) equal to the employment of a capital of

TWO THOUSAND MILLIONS.

What is charity at best,—what is it compared to this,—what the utmost benevolence can do ? Innumerable charities there are, benevolence abounds; and can no society be found who will (at the expence of personal appearance) encourage *domestic manufactures,* and wear the *stronger, warmer,* in every respect *better,* productions of manual labour; who will encourage domestic industry, domestic virtue, domestic happiness? SURELY THIS IS WORTH CONSI-DERATION.

To those capitalists to whom their country is not dear, to whom home, friends, countrymen, offer no endearments, I can point out a kingdom now on sale, *equal in extent to England,* as a field in which to work their capital. It is south of the Arkansas river, and west of Illinois, lastely advertized in the States' Gazette, at one cent. per acre. To those who value England's happiness, her climate, soil, her people, *her domestic industry,* requiring the aid of a vast capital, a chance here offers for their mouldering wealth *locked up in coffers* to see day light, a capital equal to the direct production of seventy-eight millions yearly,—a capital equal to the increased trade such production must produce.

Need I answer that machinery is the cause of increased crime, the cause of increased pauperism, when it is proved the labouring population cannot annually lose less than the value of seventy-eight millions by its unrestrained use?

MACHINERY IS THE OTHER CAUSE, increasing every ill, with every ill increasing; and unless *restrained,* Misery, Destitution, Poverty, Want, Pauperism, and Crime will go on increasing till anarchy overturns all rule, or till the reign of UNIVERSAL PEACE ARRIVES ; when swords shall become ploughshares,—when the noise of war shall be heard no more,—when ALL NATIONS, ACKNOWLEDGING NO EARTHLY RULE, SHALL BECOME OF ONE FAMILY, of one language, of one interest, wanting no laws, but taking conscience for their guide, " do as they would be done by,"—when the fruits of the earth are equally enjoyed by all,—when the machinery of nature and of mankind so justly balanced that all are ministered to alike,—when millennium arrives then can machinery do no harm.

But is there no middle state; must society be thus cursed till that time arrives,—cannot the mind of man which has created this machinery devise some plan by which its services may render the human race the benefit its mighty power can accomplish? Is it not a libel on humanity to say the mind of man cannot do this? To say this is to set at nought that reason given to man, to subdue all things to his use, and to abuse the gift of the Deity. Man can do this, every man does do this. Societies of men can form communities of common stock, have all things in common, and use machinery; no one aggrieved, all equally receiving the benefit of its use,—all equally enjoying the leisure by it produced,—all will find time to cultivate the arts, the sciences, philanthropy, philosophy; to dive into deep mysteries, unravel the purposes of Providence; then may the mind march till it is lost in the expanse of the creation. Here then is happiness (if such an end produces happiness) within the reach of any such society! Compare the state of such a society to the co-operative schemes of petty dealings, so lately recommended with so much earnestness; defunct as soon as born,—of nature too ephemeral to survive their birthday!

And shall it longer be said of Britain that machinery is her curse; Shall it longer be said that England, bearing a proud sway among nations, is prostrate by machinery? This cannot long endure. *The time is fast approaching when England will shew the world, that she can so curb machinery, that its restricted power shall be so used* THAT HER INHABITANTS SHALL ENJOY EVERY HUMAN FE- LICITY HER SOIL, HER CLIMATE, AND HER CONSTITUTION ARE SO FULLY CALCULATED TO ENSURE HER SONS; AMBITION SHALL SUBMIT TO REASON, AND STARVATION (WHEN THERE IS NO FAMINE) BE NEVER HEARD OF MORE.

LETTER VI.

In conclusion, I beg most forcibly to impress that CHEAP is but a relative term, a term leading to the total destruction of every hu- man enjoyment, and of mankind. Where is the limit to man's invention,—where the limit to the power of machinery? By every new invention, by every improvement, by every increase of its power, it cheapens production, compared to manual labour; fresh bands of population are rendered surplus; fresh tracts of land ap- pear to be required. Hence the schemes of emigration and loca- tion! Where can this end? End there can be none; for could another world approach this earth and touch, and then conjoined, could they perform their revolutions,—then could not this new world, if ready peopled, and wanting clothes and every thing but food,— then could not this " new field," opened to the power of machinery, consume its produce. For who will say, the power of machinery could not *instantly be increased*, and increased its produce far be- yond the need of such new population, were they bound down by some overruling power eternally to spend their time in agriculture?

Unrestrained machinery must create surplus population. Human competition with machinery is unavailing, and humanity must sink in the unequal contest; the power of machinery must render popu- lation surplus; *and while coin is necessary to procure sustenance, and labour the means of procuring coin, so long must the surplus sink also, and cheap to them be mere mockery and delusion.*

The man who drinks *beer*, saves the expense, and can *work cheaper* than he who drinks *wine*,—the man who drinks *water* can *work cheaper* than he who drinks *beer*,—the man who lives on *vegetables, lives cheaper* than the one *indulged with animal food;* and *cheaper he* who denies himself half the plainest necessary sustenance. John Fransham (whose life is in our public library) a character well known here a few years since, by use of potatoes and salt (turnips and spring water he maintained were quite sufficient to support existence) reduced his daily meal in value to just one farthing. To this extremity must unrestrained machinery and *the cry of cheap* reduce mankind (if they can bear it); and even then their competition with machinery must be unavailing,—the poor's rate their only refuge.

Where the earth produces not spontaneously, but yields to the industry of man a fair return, that return is the *intrinsic value* of the labour; yet from the combination of circumstances labour cannot be so paid, for land wants *specie capital* as well as labour. The *intrinsic value* of the produce is equal to the value of the *capital and the labour.* If in such a country climate offers no inconveniences, and labour gets its due proportion, *there* life may be enjoyed to the full measure of happiness allotted to mankind;—that country must command the highest purchase;—THAT COUNTRY IS ENGLAND; and were machinery restrained such must be the lot of her inhabitants.

There are countries yielding *more* abundantly;—there the toil of labour is *less* and *less* the intrinsic value of the produce, although the intrinsic value of that country must be greater, yet a *worse climate* more than counterbalances these advantages.—There are countries yielding almost spontaneously sufficient food for their inhabitants.— There must land be of greatest intrinsic value: but the climate is inimical to human life, rendering its durance scarcely supportable. What can the intrinsic value of produce be in such a country? It is almost nothing, although purchased by the *sacrifice of every comfort known in temperate climes.* And shall the produce of this country be weighed in such a balance?—Shall this fine country, these fair fields, be pitted in such competition?—Is this climate no boon to us?—And are the people to be driven from their native land by this machinery, wandering emigrants in some foreign land, that they may consume the produce of this machinery, or sacrificed at home (their value measured by machinery) to the cry of cheap, the very cheapness purchased at their expence and unavailing to them?

But while unrestrained machinery exists in any country, individual self-defence opposes machinery to machinery, when the baneful effects appear as clear as " sun at noon." On that account alone can the project be countenanced of introducing to this city spinning machinery for wool. Look forward, a little, see the probable result! In Scotland, cabbages and barley form a principal article of diet: in the North of England, rye, oats, and vegetables: in Ireland, potatoes: to the same fare the people here are fast approaching. Scotch goods are cheap, Yorkshire goods are cheap, the secret is, the *cheapness is purchased at the expence of the inhabitants.* But to compete with Scotland and the North of England, the people here must make a greater sacrifice than just their mode of living The North possesses *natural advantages* not to be purchased here. Machinery, competition, and the cry of cheap, *must render unavailing* every attempt successfully to meet their goods at market in price or quality, unless some greater sacrifice be made. *The attempt must prove abortive, or the rate of wages must be reduced* to pay the difference. No preference will be given to native workmen, *those who will work the cheapest will be the men employed;* Rye, Oat, Barley, Cabbage, and Potatoe diet, will be substituted; these will be found too dear, and Turnip diet, without salt, the less than farthing daily diet, will then be tried. But is this the end of our existence?—For this end were these beauteous isles covered with plenty? God forbid!—But compared to the power of machinery, *may this farthing diet, these turnips be too dear, and " to the cry of cheap," too dear the very oil which keeps the monster moving.*

And now, my countrymen and fellow-citizens, I have endeavoured to discharge, what from the bottom of my heart, I conceived to be a paramount duty, in pointing out the *severest, pressing, all-pervading, never-ending cause,* of your calamities.—I have endeavoured to combat the prevailing cant of the day, *falsely called the* MARCH OF INTELLECT.—I have given you in the meteorological table, a correct and comparative view of your *libelled climate.* —I have shown you the *intrinsic value* of your land.—I have shown you the relative proportion of your country to the inhabitants.—I have shown that for many generations it can supply your wants.—I have shown sufficient of the evil working of machinery, to prove it to be the HYDRA OF THE PRESENT DAY; *and that its pernicious effects far exceed all other grievances.*

Having done this, can I point out a remedy? Most certainly I can. " *Man wants but little here below, nor wants that little long.*" Better had man MARCH LORD OF THE CREATION, in his pristine nudity, or clothed in skins, contented with the *dispensations* of ALL-WISE PROVIDENCE, than be cursed with machinery, deprived thereby of the blessings every where by Providence spread around; clothed in machinery's effeminating rags, scarcely sufficient to cover his emaciated form.

MACHINERY MUST BE RESTRAINED.

Unrestrained machinery demoralises society—substitutes idleness for industry—want for competence—immorality for virtue. It has pauperised the peasant,—pauperised the citizen. It has abstracted capital from agriculture; capital from manufactures.—It has abstracted money from circulation, and drawn it into heaps.—*It has created taxes.*—It has destroyed domestic trade,—domestic consumption,—domestic industry. It has concentrated the population, and collected the people into dense masses. Wherever it does give a scanty sustenance, it is in *crowded factories*, prejudicial to health; the nurseries of every evil; setting at defiance every endeavour to work moral improvement; where the very means used to that end,

E

are marshalled in formidable array, dangerous to social happiness. Where *children* are employed in the room of *men;* and the heads of families, instead of leading in the paths of virtue, are starving, turned adrift, to sigh for departed happiness; and to meditate on desperate plans to restore their *cherished, but long-lost independence.*

Such is machinery; and unless restrained, will, ere long, involve this country in every horror and calamity attending the bursting of all the bonds that hold society together.

Fellow citizens! a minister of the crown represents you in parliament; as your representative, HE has pledged himself to listen to your complaints. *Address yourselves to him,* and he will support the prayer of your petition. Fellow citizens and countrymen! should opportunity offer, (and it may be soon,) as you value your existence, return not one man to parliament who will not pledge himself to the restriction or abolition of modern machinery, in all that in him lays. And should such occasion not offer, FORM ANTI-MACHINERY SOCIETIES *to petition, nor let your petitions cease till you get them granted.*

Fellow-citizens! Fellow-countrymen! Fellow-sufferers! Thus have I thrown down the gauntlet in defiance of the *liberal opinions* of the day; and in the hope that men of leisure and acquirements will pursue this subject in all its bearings, I beg to subscribe myself,

Your devoted servant,

THE AUTHOR.

" LET THE POOR PETITION AGAINST MACHINERY, DE-PRIVED THEREBY OF DAILY BREAD. LET THE MIDDLE CLASS, FOR BY IT THEY ARE DAILY SINKING INTO POVERTY.—LET THE PHILANTHROPIST, THAT HE MAY RENDER THE HUMAN RACE MORE SERVICE.—LET THE RELIGIONIST, THAT HE MAY ASSIST IN PURGING THE COMMUNITY OF THE PROLIFIC CAUSE OF IMMORALITY; AND LET THE RICH THAT THEY MAY RETAIN THEIR POSSESSIONS."

1830. Norwich, Old England, 52° 47″ N.L. 0° 20″ E.L. from London. MONTHS.	Winds. Estrly, Days of	Winds. W'strly, Days of	Temperature. Highest.	Temperature. Lowest.	Temperature. Mean.	Atmosphere. Fine days.	Atmosphere. Fair days.	Atmosphere. Cloudy days.	Atmosphere. Rainy days.	Atmosphere. Foggy days.	Atmosphere. Snow or Hail.	Atmosphere. Frosty days.	Hottest Day.	Coldest Day.	Highest. Boston.	Highest. Philadelphia, or New York.	Highest. Norwich.	Lowest. Boston.	Lowest. Philadelphia, or New York.	Lowest. Norwich.	Mean. Boston.	Mean. Philadelphia, or New York.	Mean. Norwich.	Daily. Heat.	Daily. Cold.	Monthly. Mean excess of Heat or Cold.
January	15	16	38°	20°	32°	8	5	3	2	4	9	17	7	31	35°	48°	38°	5°	9°	20°	23°	28°	32°	36	13°	c 6°
February	12	16	59	18	34	18		4	1	1	8	19	25	2	50	42	59	1	Zero	18	29	34	34	-13	17	c 3
March	9	22	68	30	46	27		5			2	5	26	8	74	68	68	4	16	30	34	38	46	3	20	c 10
April	7	23	72	30	49	12	5	5	6			3	30	2	75	89	72	27	20	30	48	53	49	10	7	H 2
May	17	14	74	42	54	14	8	3	9				18	10	78	82	74	51	45	42	56	60	54	6	-6	H 4
June	8	22	74	46	57	12	5	1	8				27	9	98	95	74	50	56	46	67	76	57	22	-7	H 15
July	8	8	*89	52	65	21	7	6	3				30	9	87	96	89	57	70	52	67	78	65	5	-11	H 8
August	4	27	78	50	60	14	5	8	8				1	21	73	94	78	53	64	50	62	78	60	17	-8	H 10
September	10	20	68	45	55	15	3	2					22	30	75	76	68	43	44	45	58	71	55	-3	2	H 2
October	10	21	70	38	52	25	6	6	3		1		6	24	58	60	70	15	36	38	48	52	52	-3	4	c 7
November	4	26	60	34	46	21	1	8	3		1		7	24	54	60	60	8	22	34	39	40	46	-4	16	c 7
December	14	17	48	*8	35	13			5		5	13			42	45	48		27	8	27	33	35		-9	c 5
Total	118	247				200	35	51	48	5	26	58														
United States, Boston, 42° 22″ N.L. 5° 48″ E.L.	124	241	Mean 50° Heat of the year.			{ 235 { 224		84	35		22		*30th July.	*26th December.									The greatest excess of heat in any day 22°.	The greatest excess of cold in any day 20°.	
New England Philadelphia, 39 57″ N.L. 1 52″ E.L.			Ditto 47° ditto																				The greatest average mean heat en- during a whole month } 15°.		
New York 40° 43″ N.L. 3° 10″ E.L.	154	211	Ditto 53° ditto			216		85	55		9												The greatest average mean cold en- during a whole month } 10°.		

H means heat, c — cold, – before any figure means minus heat or cold:—for example, United States had in Febr. one day 17° colder, but none so warm as Norwich in England by 13°.

APPENDIX.

A work has just been published "*under the superintendence of a society for the diffusion of useful knowledge,*" called the "WORKING MAN'S COMPANION;" or, "Results of Machinery," addressed particularly to the working men of the United Kingdom.

Curiosity has led me to enquire of various booksellers "*if working men had been the purchasers?*" The reply has uniformly been "it is a book in great request, *but working men are not the purchasers.*" This one fact is additional evidence against "*cheap production.*" This is a proof that machinery giving so much increased employment has not in this part of the country diffused sufficient of its benefits, to enable the *working people* here to give *one shilling* for this very cheap work, this very great bargain, although it contains 216 pages, and about 50,000 words. I almost question if the *working people* would read it if given to them, unless loaves of bread were also distributed gratis, to feed on while wading through such an assemblage of words.

What a mistake does this society labour under! They seem to think people like work for work's sake! They think people dislike machinery, from ignorance of its effects. Let the people be well fed at the expence of machinery! Make that trial! and then hear their opinions about machinery!

On reading over the names of the central and local committees of this society, I felt some misgiving (the foregoing letters were prepared for the printer, they had also been advertised) in publishing my individual opinion in point blank opposition to the doctrines of this society as set forth in this work. I have read their publication attentively, and my firm conviction is, that there are the names of many persons attached to it, who will renounce any connection with a society advocating principles to which are ascribed nearly all the evils which at present afflict society.

With a society who have taken great pains to prove the vast power of machinery!—denied by no one.

With a society who have endeavoured to prove, *cheap production, increased employment, increased consumption,* and *increased enjoyment,* go hand in hand with *unrestrained machinery,* and this in the face of increased crime and increased pauperism! See page 189.

With a society who rather than put the least restraint upon machinery encourage emigration, in other words transportation, when *they* shew the United Kingdom contains 66 acres of land to every agricultural family! See pages 167, 182, 207, 208.

With a society whose doctrine is *buy, buy—sell, sell,* without in any way shewing how sales are to be made or whence is to come the money with which to buy! See pages 74, 77, 79, 117, 186, 187, 184.

With a society whose doctrine is also *change, change, change* *employment*, as if people could change employments between break-fast and dinner—as if a man could lay down at night a carpenter and as a book-binder earn his next day's bread ! See pages 162, 196, 197, 176.

With a society having proved that the competition between man-ual labour and machinery must be supported by the poor rate, im-mediately advocate the *propriety* of burdening the community with *eight millions poor rate*, to enable the proprietors of machinery *to make cheap goods* ! See page 181.

With a society who prove machinery has it so much in its power to reward the smallest improvement, that it is of importance in mak-ing needles to save even the wages of a child ! See pages 132, 165.

(Messrs. Taylors, St. George's-fields, London, have invented ma-chines to complete pins without manual labour; these when brought into full operation will displace ten thousand hands, these 10,000 persons will be thrown upon the poor rate, until they can find a change of employment !—to what can they change ?)

With a society who set ditchers to work with a mattock ! who tell farmers *as they are men of capital* to combine to advance the price of corn, and when they hire land cheap, they are of *necessity to farm carelessly !* See pages 28, 46, 170, 197.

With a society who have discovered England's unhappy climate ! See pages 48, 152.

With a society who encourage idleness ! See page 197.

With a society who deride old age ! See page 134.

With a society who endeavour to prove *strength of body* has been given man *for no purpose !* See pages 157, 158, 193.

With a society who would make mankind mere intellectual beings ! See pages 147, 149, 202.

With a society who insinuate that as our forefathers had little or no machinery, they enjoyed neither health, long life, nor the blessings of Providence ! See pages 141, 148, 149.

With a society comparing man, made in the image of his creator, to inanimate machinery ! See pages 29, 61, 135.

With a society endeavouring to persuade the Lords of the creation that they must submit to be starved by the work of their own hands ! See pages 5, 6, 180.

With a society holding up one Joseph Foster as a paragon of excellence, (surely this Foster is pensioned), because he confessed to the committee that as HE could not " *saw with his teeth, nor dig with his nails,*" HE could devise no antidote for the starvation of himself, family, and fellow-workmen, by machinery, against which competition is useless ! See pages 5, 6, 7, 45, 179, 180, 182.

With a society advocating cheap finery ! the certain ruin of the wearers. See page 101, 104.

With a society advocating factories as conducing to health and long life ! when it need not be asserted that they are the certain high road to the destruction of all health, morality, virtue, and domestic industry. See page 149.

With a society speaking of men as mere animals, of rearing them and sending them to market! See pages 23, 61.

With a society placing men in unnatural competition with animals, and, with that which is even worse, with machinery! See pages 20, 28, 61.

With a society after having proved beyond doubt that man must be reduced to the extremest misery by unavailing competition with machinery, (see pages 5, 61, 180, 181,) propose that the very men so beggared and very properly relieved as paupers, should become fundholders! should save money to invest in saving banks! to enable them, *not to combine for the advance of wages*, but to enable them to keep out of the *labour market*, "a march of intellect term," *that wages may rise!!!* See pages 197, 198.

And, finally, with a society whose watchword is " Knowledge is power!" (as if all men were wise, as if all men could be learned,) whose doctrines war with the very existence of mankind unless they can live upon iron, cotton, books, or air. God save us from such power of knowledge, and if this be the happiness of knowledge,

IGNORANCE MUST BE BLISS.

IT MUST BE FOLLY TO BE WISE.

Printed by Wilkin and Fletcher, East Anglian Office, Norwich.

THE SCOTSMAN'S

ADVICE

TO THE

LABOURING CLASSES,

ON THE

BEST MEANS OF RAISING THEIR WAGES,

AND

SECURING THEMSELVES AND THEIR FAMILIES AGAINST WANT.

[*Reprinted from the Scotsman of Nov.* 10. *and* 13. 1830.]

_____

EDINBURGH:

PRINTED FOR ADAM BLACK, **27.** NORTH BRIDGE.

_____

1830.

[*Price Twopence.*]

SCOTSMAN'S ADVICE

TO THE

LABOURING CLASSES.

FRIENDS AND COUNTRYMEN,

THOUGH the burnings and the nightly attacks on property in Kent may proceed partly from mistaken notions and bad passions, it is certain that labourers, who had a reasonable share of the comforts which belong to their station of life, would not be guilty of such atrocities. It may therefore be truly said that these disorders have their root in the misery of the working classes—of those classes to which you belong. Is this misery increasing? Or rather has it been increasing during the last forty years? My belief is that it has: but the problem is not easily resolved, and it is not my object at present to enter into it. I find from a document of unquestionable authority, that in 1824, there were numerous examples in various counties of England, of *unmarried labourers being paid sixpence per day by their employers, in parishes where no part of the wages of labour was paid out of the poor's rates* *!* Whether the situation of such persons was always as bad I do not know; but in facts like these we have a proof of wretchedness which it is fearful to contemplate, and which must be pregnant with evil. Insurrections of the belly, as Bacon observes, are the most dangerous of all: and in a country *full of wealth,* where thousands or millions are habitually on the verge of starvation, there can be no entire security either for life or property.

The more important question is,—what are the causes of the extreme poverty and misery of the working classes? Let us hear what Political Economy says upon the subject. Capital, it tells us, is the fund which puts labour in motion. When the capital of a country increases more rapidly than its population, competition operates in favour of the la-

---

* Abstract of Returns respecting Labourers' Wages, by a Committee of Parliament, No. 299, in 1825.—See Returns for Bampton in Oxfordshire, Arlesford, Fordingbridge, and Isle of Wight in Hampshire and many others.

bourer; capitalists outbid one another in their eagerness to get workmen, *and wages rise.* An opposite result ensues when population increases more rapidly than the capital which employs it; in this case labourers find it difficult to procure employment; they underbid one another, *and wages fall.* There are circumstances which qualify these conclusions; but in the main, their soundness is admitted by all enlightened men, and they comprise a truth of great importance to society. What some assert is quite true, that the United Kingdom could maintain twice as many inhabitants as it now holds; but we must remember that in this case its capital must be doubled.

It follows then, that the condition of the labouring classes may be deteriorated in two ways—By increasing their numbers too rapidly—and by diminishing the capital which provides them with employment. Now, capital is either diminished, or its natural growth is impeded, by the enormous sums paid to the government, by the tax on corn imposed for the benefit of the aristocracy, and by the many absurd restrictions on industry, which have arisen from the ignorance or misconceptions of our legislators. To repeal or reduce taxes, and relieve industry from the restrictions which fetter it, benefits the working classes, by enlarging the fund which creates a demand for their labour. The sufferings of these classes are therefore, in no small degree, imputable to the exactions and misconduct of the government; and in the present circumstances of the country, when ministers take a single shilling from the pockets of the people beyond what their necessities strictly require, they are guilty of an act of cruelty, and are adding to the misery which they ought to relieve.

Culpable and injurious. however, as the extravagance of the government has been, I am convinced that were all the public burdens annihilated, and all the obstacles to freedom of industry removed, the relief given would be but temporary. The misery of the working classes might be mitigated by such means, but it cannot be eradicated by legislation, nor by any human means except such as shall put some check on the increase of their numbers. Scientific thinkers regard this conclusion as established on the clearest evidence. How then is the principle of increase to be checked?—only in one way, by enlightening the minds of the working classes, by inspiring them with feelings of self-respect, by teaching them the immense importance of habits of prudence, forethought, and self-controul to their own happiness—by giving them true notions of their situation as moral agents, responsible for the consequences of their actions, and endowed with powers which, if rightly used, make them to a great extent masters of their own destiny.

It is a radical evil, that in the article of marriage men consider life as a *lottery*, and they rush into the most important of all ties, without making any provision for discharging the obligations it lays upon them. This applies to the middle ranks as well as the lower. Thousands and tens of thousands marry every year who are scarcely able with their utmost efforts to keep their heads above the water, or whose earnings hardly suffice for their own subsistence. Such persons shelter their thoughtlessness under the plea of " trusting to Providence," or " taking their " luck like their neighbours." If any one talks to them of the provision necessary for rearing a family, the reply is, that " Providence never sends a mouth without send- " ing meat for it." It is no exaggeration to say, that multitudes in this country throw their offspring on the world with as little rational consideration about its future well-being, as the crocodile shews when she drops her egg in the sand, and leaves it to the sun and the winds to hatch her young into life. How common is it to see two individuals, who have scarcely a mouthful of meat for themselves, marry and bring beings into the world, whose existence for the first fifteen or twenty years of their life must be a continual struggle with starvation and misery in their worst forms. Such a spectacle might make a humane man weep. It presents a picture of improvidence which can only result from the higher faculties of our nature being left in a state of brutish abeyance. Far be it from me to discourage any one from trusting in Providence. But is this to be an excuse for the most reckless defiance of the common rules of prudence? God has given us reason to regulate our conduct, and in most of the common concerns of life has enabled us to foresee the consequences of our actions. After making a right use of this faculty, our reliance on Providence is wise and rational; but to neglect its admonitions, and then trust to Providence to free us from the evils induced by our own thoughtlessness, is to call upon the Deity to work a miracle in our favour—not to promote our improvement, but to harden us in our folly.

It has often occurred to me that it would be extremely useful *to convert the burdens which marriage brings with it into money*, in order to show a man clearly the nature and amount of the obligations he contracts when he enters into it. Society is not in a sound state, till regular provision is made against these and all the other casualties of life which common prudence can foresee. Were this once done, nine-tenths of the misery—and of the crime—which exists would be extirpated. If philosophy and government had not been wide asunder as the poles in all countries, care would have been taken to instruct men in such subjects by the agency of the schoolmaster or the clergyman. But our legislators are themselves too unenlightened to think of any thing so rational and useful.

It is impossible to say beforehand what the condition of any individual will be as to health and sickness, the number of his family, the time he or they may live; but if we take 100 or 1000 individuals, we can answer these questions with regard to the collective body, with a certainty sufficient for the guidance of a reasonable man in the ordinary concerns of life. I am not ripe enough in the subjects of mortality tables and annuities to make the necessary calculations very correctly; but it can be done; and my statements will at all events illustrate the principle I wish to enforce. I would address a labourer who intended to marry thus—

You are about to marry. Are you aware of the burdens you bring upon yourself by this step? And have you a reasonable prospect of being able to meet them? If you have not, you are preparing a life of privation and misery for yourself, your partner, and your offspring; and you are injuring the community, first, by throwing upon it the burden of supporting those whom you ought to support, and next, by bringing labourers into a market that is already overstocked—to take food and employment from those who have not enough.

You have at present, I shall suppose, 10s. *per* week. Now a marriage produces on an average four children; sometimes more than four, sometimes fewer; but this is what a person of forethought ought to expect and provide for. In seven or eight years then you may calculate upon having five or six individuals to support from your wages. If you do not look forward to this, you are shutting your eyes to your true situation, and incurring heavy obligations blindfold. Will the same earnings which at present do little more than supply your own wants, be sufficient to furnish food and clothes for six persons, and education for four of these, for a course of years? Will a family under such circumstances not plunge you into extreme poverty? But supposing that you are able, by hard labour and pinching parsimony, to provide for your family while in health, what happens if you fall into a sickness of long duration, or if you die? Your wife, with three or four children to take care of, cannot even gain her own bread by her labour. She must live in misery; your children will die of disease from insufficient nourishment; or growing up without education, and amidst all the temptations of want, will contract depraved habits, and by their vices become a scourge to society, and a disgrace to their relations. Search the history of the criminals who crowd our Bridewells or come to the scaffold, and of the ruined outcast females on our streets, whose looks and demeanour betray the consummation of human wretchedness, and you will find, that most of them have become what they are, in consequence of neglect of education and moral training in their youth, or vicious habits to which want in their early years drove them, or dangers to which the poverty of their parents or their own misery exposed them.

But you will ask—Do I mean to deny to the poorer classes the pleasures springing from the exercise of the best social feelings of our nature? By no means. I only ask them to put their social feelings and their animal impulses under the controul of their reason, and not to wreck their own happiness and that of others, by disregarding the plainest dictates of prudence.

I shall sketch an ideal picture of the provision which I think a considerate labourer or tradesman ought to make against the accidents and misfortunes of life. I call it *ideal*, though I see nothing in it which may not be rendered practical in a well ordered society; and in the mean time it may serve as a standard to which the working classes may approach, in proportion as education is diffused, and they get clearer views of their condition. It will equally apply to the middle ranks.

Nineteen-twentieths of the poverty and misery which we see in the world arise from some species of improvidence, that is, from neglect of health, from want of diligence in improving the advantages we possess, or from want of due care in providing against those accidents which every one knows he is exposed to; and this improvidence again has its root, to no small extent, in our ignorance of the true conditions of our existence, and the laws of our nature. In illustrating this by an ideal sketch, I shall take the case of an industrious mechanic who begins to earn 16s. per week at the age of 18. I shall shew what he might accomplish by living economically, and deferring marriage till he was 28.

Let us suppose that he is able to live upon 12s. 6d. *per* week, and place 3s. 6d. in a Savings' Bank: his stock, including interest, would amount in ten years to about L.100. I have heard of journeymen mechanics who have accumulated a larger sum in the same number of years. I shall take it for granted that he expends L.30 of this money at his marriage in furnishing his house, and that L.70 remain to meet contingencies.

As others are now dependent on his health, his first care should be to make a provision against sickness; but in order to keep his stock entire, I shall take for granted that he effects this by a weekly contribution, which need not exceed fourpence for himself and his wife both.

The second casualty to which he should look forward is the infirmity of old age, which so often renders a man unfit for labour. The best mode of providing against this calamity is by an annuity sufficient to keep himself, and his wife, if she is living, above want. Such annuities are now embraced in the plan of benefit societies. According to a table calculated by Mr Finlaison for government, a sum of L.17 : 1 : 9 paid at once, (or an annual payment of 9s. 6d.) by a man at the age of 28, will obtain for him an annuity of L.20 *per annum* for whatever number of years he may live beyond the age of 68. By laying out L.17 therefore he can effectually secure himself against want in his old age; and I shall assume that he disposes of L.17 of his stock in this manner.

The third casualty he should provide against regards his wife. He may die and leave her a widow, unable to gain a shilling for herself, because encumbered with a family. The misery which ensues in such a condition is often great; and it is heartless in any man to expose the woman to it who has been the partner of his life, and whom he took from a situation where she was more independent and secure. Now, this and other calamities attendant on the uncertainty of life have been subjected to calculation, and data have been obtained for making provision against them. I find, from a table in the volume published by the Highland Society, that a man of 28, by paying down L.32, 12s. in one sum, may secure for his wife, (supposing her age to be the same,) an annuity of L.10 *per annum* for life, in the event of her being left a widow, at whatever period it may happen. It is now very common in the middle ranks for a man to insure a sum on his own life, to be paid at his death, to his widow or other relations; but, in my opinion, the plan of purchasing an annuity is better; because a smaller sum will answer the same purpose when it depends on the chance of survivorship, and because women often want the business-knowledge necessary for making a prudent use of a large sum received at once. The object aimed at in making such a provision is so plainly prescribed by the most common feelings of humanity, that nothing but the grossest ignorance and thoughtlessness could have induced men to regard it as a work of supererogation. When society is more enlightened, it appears to me that a provision against the chance of widowhood will be considered as indispensable at marriage as a suit of wedding clothes.

I mentioned that a marriage produces on an average four children. On this number an individual ought to reckon. Now let me suppose that the first is born within two years after marriage. This child depends on you for its support; and if you die before it is able to shift for itself, before it is 15 or 16 years of age, it must either starve, or be thrown upon casual charity, or the bounty of relations who have probably nothing to spare. The chances of your death happening within a few years may be small; but the expense of providing against them is small in proportion, and the misfortune, when it falls upon the child, is not the less heavy for being uncertain. What are your duties in such circumstances? To insure your child against the misery resulting from the loss of its natural guardian and supporter. This can be done most economically and conveniently by securing a small contingent annuity to it, of 3 s. *per* week for instance, up to its fifteenth year, only payable, of course, in the event of your death happening before it reaches that age. I have no tables which exhibit the cost of such an annuity, but supposing the purchase to be made at the end of the first year of the child's life, and when its father's age is 30, I infer from some rough calculations that the price would not much exceed L. 5 *. Five pounds, therefore, deposited in the first year of a child's life, would protect it from the severest calamity which impends over it—the misery and destitution arising from the death of a father. When so small a sum will accomplish so great a good, how powerful an inducement is presented to parents to make every possible sacrifice to give their child this advantage. Even though the child should never need it, the feeling of security and peace of mind which the parents procure for themselves, is an ample remuneration for the outlay. Reflect on the fact, that whether your child shall be in comfort or in beggary, whether it shall enjoy the blessings of education or be deprived of them, whether it shall be a useful member of society or an outcast, may depend on your making this provision to preserve it from destitution. Ought not a considerate man to place so necessary an act among the number of his indispensable duties?

A similar deposit of five pounds would be requisite at each addition made to the family; and as a marriage is assumed to produce on an average four children, the whole sum expended under this head would be L.20. I do not include those children which die within the first year, and the calculation applies only to ordinary cases. When the number of children amounts to six, eight, or ten, the additional burdens imposed on the parents, in such

---

* According to the Carlisle Tables about one-sixth of the fathers would die in the 15 years between the age of 30 and 45. One-sixth of the children would thus be orphans ; but in the same interval of 15 years, one-fourth of the children also die. The number, therefore, of the fathers diminished by one-fourth, and divided by six, will give nearly the proportion of the First Born, who are orphans at the end of 15 years. From these data, by the help of some tables, I obtained the result stated above, which is only offered as a loose approximation. Only about one-eighth of the children in whose behalf payments were made would ever come as pensioners upon the fund. Hence the smallness of the contribution necessary.

circumstances, must be met by additional economy or exertions.

The whole sum thus required to afford a working man a reasonable decree of security against the casualties of life for himself and his family would be—

Annuity for himself in old age,	- -	£. 17
Annuity for his widow,	- - - -	33
Provision for four children,	· - -	20
		£. 70

I have taken for granted that the young man saves the money necessary to bear this expenditure while he lives single, and it follows, that marriage shall be postponed till the sum is obtained. In some cases the female may have saved a little money; in others a small sum may have come to one of the parties by inheritance; and in others the deficiency might be supplied by strict economy in the first years of marriage, while the family is small. But the wisest course, in all cases, would be, to consider the possession of the sum by the parties jointly, as *indispensable*, before the bonds of matrimony are tied.

Marriage, however, often brings careful and frugal habits with it; and a couple who started with less than the full amount, and were inclined to make up their lee-way by subsequent economy, might proceed in this way. The provision for old age (L.20 *per annum* or 8s. *per* week,) might be divided into four portions of L.5 each. As soon as L.4, 6s. could be spared, one of these might be purchased, and 2s. *per* week thus secured. A year or two afterwards a second portion might be bought, and the allowance consequently enlarged to 4s. A third instalment would increase it to 6s., and a fourth to 8s., or L.20 *per annum*. If other demands were pressing, some might stop short at the second payment, and others at the third. Four shillings *per* week, though a small sum to subsist on, is a great deal when it stands between an old man and absolute want, or what is nearly as bad to an honourable mind—charity. The widows' annuity, and the provision for children, might be purchased by instalments in the same way; but it must always be remembered, that the longer the purchase is deferred, the greater the sum required. Of these various provisions, perhaps the widows' endowment ought to be held the most pressing, and be first secured. The provision for the children stands next; and the annuity for the husband in old age might be placed last; since in the event of its never being obtained, a family well brought up, and arrived at manhood, should be a protection to the parents against absolute want, at the latter end of life.

It might seem better suited to the humble circumstances of labourers and mechanics to purchase such provisions as have been described by weekly or monthly instalments; but this system seems to me to be appropriate only when the payments are so trifling as scarcely to be felt—the twopence or fourpence a week for instance, for insuring against sickness. When the payments are heavy, singly or collectively, the necessities of the day will cause them now and then to be suspended, and then the benefit is either lost, or a very troublesome species of accounting is required to ascertain its value. The objections are not so strong against annual instalments; but the best method in my opinion is, to put the weekly savings into a Savings' Bank, and let them accumulate till they reach an amount, with which some tangible benefit can be procured—either, for instance, the full provision desired for wife or child, or some determinate proportion of it. Thus, with L.2, an allowance of 1s. *per* week might be obtained for a child to its fifteenth year, in the event of its father dying in its infancy. With L.8, an endowment of L.2, 10s. might be secured for life to the widow *.

It will be said that in the present state of wages, the

---

* The system of annuities and endowments I have been describing, is quite as necessary for the middle classes as the lower; at least for all persons belonging to the latter who have no property or capital to rely on. But there is one additional provision required in their case—for unmarried daughters. There is not a more helpless and unfortunate being in the world, than a young woman genteelly educated, reared amidst all the refinements and luxuries of polished life, and not instructed in any method of gaining her subsistence when she loses the shelter of the paternal roof. Many unhappy marriages, and many degrading sacrifices are made by young ladies in this situation, from the mere dread of want. Nothing can prove more clearly how ignorant men are of their *duties*, than that we every day see examples of parents, who love their daughters, throwing them upon the mercies of the world in this way, without any adequate idea of the flagrant cruelty and wickedness of their conduct.

A correspondent suggests that all these allowances should be placed beyond the reach of legal attachment, and Parliament would of course be most willing to afford them this species of protection.

savings I have supposed a labourer to make are out of the question. I admit this to some extent, and have called my scheme *ideal*, without thinking that it is in any degree chimerical. Good is done when a sound principle is brought home to men's understandings, though some practical difficulties should stand in the way of its adoption. It will not be denied that there are many labourers and mechanics whose earnings exceed the sum I have assumed; let *these* act upon my suggestions, and the result will at least benefit themselves. But, in point of fact, when journeymen mechanics were earning a guinea a-week some years ago, they left their families as much exposed to the casualties of life as at present, from not knowing how their savings could be applied to such a purpose. Even in the case of those who are worst paid, if the husband with his wife and three or four children can subsist on his wages alone, the same individual, when living single, should surely be able to lay up a little. If a man cannot save L. 100 before marriage he may save L. 30; and L. 30 applied as I propose will go a certain length in warding off poverty and misery. Farther, if he cannot collect the requisite sum in seven years, he may do it in ten or fourteen; and it is surely better to make a prudent marriage at thirty or thirty-five, than a rash and perhaps ruinous one at twenty. The mere abstinence from marriage, as a means of saving a little money, would improve the condition of the labourers collectively, by diminishing their numbers, even though the immediate object should not be attained. But though desirous to recommend my particular plan, I am still more anxious to impress upon the minds of the labouring classes two truths of vast importance to their well-being, upon which it is based. The first is, that as no efforts of legislation can lift them out of their misery, *their happiness must always depend on their own habits of prudence, forethought, and self-controul.* The second is, *that no man has a right to bring human beings into the world, who is not able to provide for their support and education.* The law punishes severely the act of exposing a child; but the man who marries and becomes the father of children, without having any reasonable prospect of being able to keep them from beggary with all its attendant miseries, is guilty of the same crime in a lower degree.

But I shall be told that I have made no provision against the worst calamity which the labourer is exposed to—want of employment. My answer is, that I have made the only provision which the case admits of, and which will operate surely, though slowly, to remedy the evil. I call in the agency of what Malthus terms the *preventive check* to an excess of population, in the only form in which it can be rendered practical. To tell an individual that he should postpone his marriage for some years, because the world is too full of people, would be to offer an insult to his understanding. To talk to him of *prudence*, and ask him to wait till he has saved a little money, is tendering a good advice, in a shape too vague and general to be of any service. My aim is to convert the virtue of *prudence* in this particular, into pounds, shillings, and pence—to hold out a *definite object* to him, requiring a definite sum for its accomplishment. I neither counsel him to live single till he is 21 years of age, nor till he is 28; I simply advise him to abstain from marriage till he has saved a sum sufficient to secure his wife against the evils of widowhood, his children against the miseries of orphanage, and himself against the misfortunes of infirm old age. I ask him, not to consider whether the country is thickly or thinly peopled, but to take a rational view of his own situation. I consider society indeed entitled to demand guarantees from him against entailing burdens upon it, before he is permitted to bring a number of unbidden guests to the common table *. But still my counsel is merely this—let him consult *his own interest ;* let him fulfil the duties which common humanity enjoins to his wife and family, and which common prudence dictates, to himself; and in fulfilling these, he will completely satisfy the demands of society. In doing this I say he will contribute to meliorate the lot of his brethren ; for when the working classes generally act upon the system, of holding the accumulation of a specific sum indispensable as a preliminary to marriage, the most effectual check will be given to those premature unions, which deluge the

---

* In Bavaria the law allows no man to marry till he can show that he possesses a certain amount of property ; in other words, society demands security from the parties, that it shall not be loaded with pauper children in consequence of their union. The principle is sound, though it is probable that the law may sometimes be an engine of oppression.

country with a population of paupers. It is obvious, that when the general period of marriage is postponed for a few years, all who die in the interval leave no offspring behind them, and the unions which take place being contracted later in life, yield fewer children. This, in my opinion, is the only mode in which an efficient practical check to the increase of population can be applied. Were it in full operation, the country would soon cease to be crowded with miserable beings for whom there is neither food nor employment. Wages would rise, for the competition would then be *between capitalists*, to procure labourers; and we would no longer see multitudes of famished wretches underbidding one another for employment, and selling their labour for the veriest pittance which will keep soul and body together.

In all old countries where the land is entirely appropriated, there are but two methods of keeping down population to the level of subsistence. Either prudence must prevent men from bringing beings into the world till they are fully able to provide for them, or misery and disease will shorten their days and thin their numbers after they come. The schoolmaster, the priest, and the magistrate, who have taught the people many useful, and some silly and absurd things, have never taken any pains to impress this most momentous truth on their minds.

The system I recommend, then, would benefit the working classes in two ways. First, it would diminish their numbers relatively to capital, and as a consequence, *their wages would rise*. Secondly, it would rescue them and their families from extreme poverty, give them independence of character, secure to all of them the advantages of education, and thus break down the barrier which confines them to the sphere they are born in, and precludes them from obtaining any of the higher prizes in the lottery of life. To society the system would be equally beneficial. Poor's rates, with all the abuses they engender, would be done away; crimes would be rare when pauperism was eradicated; and by the universal diffusion of education, all the talent in society would be made available. And last, not least, when every grown-up man had either a small stock of savings in hand, or investments in a common fund, we should have the very best guarantee for the public tranquillity.

There is much truth in the Scottish proverb about the advantages of having a *nest egg*. Many who have both the means and the disposition to save money have not acquired the habit, simply because they never made a beginning; and a beginning probably was not made, because they had no specific object in view which they considered attainable with their limited means. By holding out to such persons *a tangible good*, we furnish them with a motive to begin the practice of economy; and the habit once implanted, will contribute to make them frugal, provident, and orderly through life.

I need scarcely say, that the improvements suggested can only be realised upon the system of *mutual insurance*, by Benefit Societies conducted by the working classes themselves. Government and the upper ranks may assist; but were they to appear as the managers, the scheme would never carry the full confidence of the working classes with it, and it would be impossible to keep it free of gross frauds and abuses. We cannot inculcate upon these classes too often, or in too many ways, that *the improvement of their condition must be their own work*.

Were the suggestions I have made adopted, were the whole working classes to operate upon them, I have no hesitation in saying, that nine-tenths of all the poverty, misery and crime, which we see around us, would disappear. We would in fact find ourselves in a new world, full of intelligence, peace and good order, in which life and property would be ten times more secure, happiness more equally distributed, and an admirable foundation laid for the further amelioration of the lot of mankind.

With best wishes for your welfare and happiness, I am, &c.

THE EDITOR OF THE SCOTSMAN.

Printed by James Walker,
Old Bank Close.

AN

Equitable Property Tax:

A FINANCIAL SPECULATION:

AND

A FAIR RATE OF WAGES

TO

THE LABOURING POOR.

BY A LOYAL BRITON.

The KING, by JUDGMENT, STABLISHETH the LAND.
PROV. xxix. 4.

LONDON:
PRINTED FOR
LONGMAN, REES, ORME, BROWN, AND GREEN,
PATERNOSTER-ROW;
AND RODWELL, NEW BOND STREET.
1831.

LONDON:
Printed by A. & R. Spottiswoode,
New-Street-Square.

EQUITABLE PROPERTY TAX:

A FINANCIAL SPECULATION:

AND

A FAIR RATE OF WAGES, &c.

INTRODUCTION.

As a poor, *worked-out* peasant, double with years and infirmity, was slowly creeping along the margin of his village brook, and warming his shrunken frame, in the full blaze of a July sun ; he observed a young athletic rustic, striving with persevering, but unavailing labour, to hoist the trunk of a pollard-ash, from the surface of the stream, to the summit of the bank, which rose above it, lofty, precipitous, and beetling. Many and hearty were his tugs : but the projecting ledge at the top, baffled every exertion. The log was caught by the over-hanging brow ; and, after a few moments of suspension, fell again into the water.

" Neighbour," said the kind-hearted Chrone, " can " *I* give thee any assistance ?"—Mortified, and, perchance, irritated, by his bootless toil, the lout muttered in reply,—" *Thee*, indeed ! What i' the world " canst *thee* do ? Why it goes hard with thy legs, " old one, to support thy body."—" True," returned the other, " I cannot aid thee by my *strength :* but, " mayhap, I may *point out a way* to thee, by which " thine own two hands will do the business. Neither " I, nor *thee*, as it seems, can lift out the trunk where " it *now* is : but, let it float two or three hundred " yards down the stream, where the shore is sloping ; " and then, half the strength thou art now putting out ; " and half the trouble thou art taking, will place it, " high and dry, upon the bank."—The potency of plain common sense, is, usually, irresistible. The rustic scratched his head; hesitated for a moment: took the hint; and, in a short time, was in possession of the log, and haling it to his cottage.

The *Apologue*, to a certain extent, may be applied to the author of the following pages, and their subject. The *log* shadows out our *financial system*, ignorantly, or wilfully mismanaged, for an indefinite series of years last past; and utterly unmanageable, in its present state, and under its existing form. The *speculator* finds his *antitype* in the *old peasant :* and the *advice* of the *latter*, has its similitude, in the *hints* offered in the following *speculation*.

To pass, however, from *Fable* to *Fact*.

An important *question* lies at the very threshold of my subject: the fair answer to which, must determine, whether any pursuit of it, be, or be not superfluous. The question is this. " Is the general con-
" dition of our country, financial, statistical, and po-
" litical, at this moment, so *prosperous* and *satisfac-*
" *tory*, as to make an enquiry into it, an ill-timed oc-
" cupation; and to render any suggestions for its
" amelioration, an impertinent interference ?"

To this interrogation, the members of the last administration (had they still remained in power) would have unhesitatingly answered in the *affirmative :* and repeated the language which they held in both houses of Parliament, during the ill-starred period of their ministerial domination. They would again have asserted; that the great political machine of the state, unimpaired by age, and unstained by the divers dirty hands through which it had passed, still boasted its original perfection—that it continued to work "well:" as powerful; as useful; and as bright as heretofore—and therefore, that any inspection into its machinery was superfluous; and every attempt at the alteration of its parts, as dangerous as unnecessary. They would again have insulted the understanding and the humanity of the country, with a repetition of their declaration; that its alleged "general distress," was quite imaginary: that the lamented pressure upon the middle and lower classes of its population, was merely "local:" that its finances were flourish-

ing: its resources inexhaustible: its prosperity un-
paralleled:—and therefore, that all, or any representations, opposed to this real state of national comfort
and splendour, could proceed only from party-spirit,
disloyalty, and disaffection: or, from a morbid imagination, creating those phantoms, with which it was
appalled.

Whether or not the retirement of these gentlemen
(by the *free* permission of our PATRIOT KING,) from
the dust of Downing Street, into the pure atmosphere
of their several rural residences, may have cleared
their mental vision, and enabled them to see " things
as they are;" or, " the REFORM BILL of our present
brave and honest ministers (dreaded as poison by the
outs, but hailed with rapture by 15,000,000 of the
people) may have acted with the effect of *Ithuriel's*
spear,

> —— " for no falsehood can endure
> " Touch of celestial temper :"

and made them feel and acknowledge, that their as-
sertions were untrue, and uttered merely to *root them
in their places*—I have no means of ascertaining—but,
of this I am confident; that, be the present opinions
and avowals of the late ministry what they may, there
is no man in the country, gifted with common sense
and common honesty, who will not answer the question that forms the groundwork of the ensuing sheets,
instantly and decidedly, in the *negative* — who will
not allow, that the existing state of the empire, is calamitous and appalling, to an unprecedented degree;
that unless speedy and efficient measures be adopted,
to check the evils which afflict it, neither health can
be restored, nor safety ensured to it: and therefore—
that even a SPECULATION, which has for its object the
cure or relief of the " sores of the land," may claim
attention, if not challenge applause :

> *O Navis* ——
> *Nudum remigio latus,*
> *Et Malus celeri saucius Africo,*
> *Antennæque gemant.*

Never, indeed, in the annals of our history, could a period be pointed out, when an administration entering upon office, burthened itself with such a " cumbrous charge," as our present ministers undertook, on their appointment to the direction of the public affairs. A huge mass of political corruption had been accumulating for more than fifty years, bred and matured, by a succession of cabinets, for the most part, unprincipled and selfish: or weak and inefficient: or reckless and headstrong: who had inflicted thirty years of WARFARE on the country, in the course of half a century: entailed upon it a PUBLIC DEBT of 800,000,000*l.* : begotten a TAXATION overwhelming in its bulk, and oppressive or vexatious in its collection: increased the POOR RATES of the kingdom, to the enormous annual sum of nearly 6,000,000*l.*: (or a seventeenth part of its yearly aggregate income ;) reduced the MIDDLE CLASSES of our population, to all but pauperism: and, finally, induced, *indirectly*, a want of employment, and a state of starvation, on an immense proportion of the LABOURING ORDER of society — while they had effectually banished every hope of an alleviation of the evils which they had created, by positively *denying*, from time to time, their actual existence ; and boldly avowing their *fixed resolve*, to oppose that PARLIAMENTARY REFORM, which alone could ascertain their reality, and originate their cure. It should form a subject of heartfelt and lasting gratitude, on the part of the people of this land, that, under circumstances so overwhelming, and amid omens so appalling, a MONARCH has been granted to them, who had the intelligence to perceive : the patriotism to lament; and the intrepidity to determine to redress, the all but universal suffering of his people—and that a MINISTRY could be found, able and willing to carry his just, generous, and enlightened views into execution, — men, who, unscared by those fearful forms of political corruption,—

" Gorgons, and Hydras, and Chimæras dire,"—

which, for an age past, had been at once the allies and the guardians, of successive administrations — men, who, competent to grapple with the complicated difficulties of the situation to which they were called, — disinterested in their own views, and clear, in the necessity and justice of their measures for the public good — while they would boldly and steadily pursue their patriotic *ends*, might fairly and successfully call upon the country, for its confidence and support, in the *means* which they should adopt, for their attainment of them.

It is highly satisfactory to observe, that, hitherto, the people of the United Kingdom appear to have been duly sensible of the blessings of such a KING, and such a MINISTRY—for, they have responded to the appeal of the former, with unqualified loyalty and joy; and afforded a testimony of their confidence in the latter, which cannot be denied or misunderstood : by actually returning to the British Senate (in every case in which they could exercise the rights of *unfettered constituents*) men pledged to support the great ministerial measure—REFORM in PARLIAMENTARY REPRESENTATION.

It cannot be doubted, that, by this happy union of the KING and his PEOPLE — this manifested accordance, between the generous wishes of the *one*, and the wants, and prayers, and determined purpose, of the *other* — an *engine* of incalculable power for the production of good, will be placed in the hands of the existing administration. "Give me a spot on which "I may stand," said the ancient mechanist, "and I "will move the earth." The REFORM BILL will, at once, form the *base*, the *fulcrum*, and the *lever* of a machine, capable of as mighty an operation on the political world : and we have every sound reason to believe, that, under the application and direction, of those to whom it is to be intrusted, it will work effects, as beneficial as they will be comprehensive : for, who can *fairly* call in question, either the sagacity; or integrity; or disinterestedness; or policy, of these accredited servants of the crown? If high intellect and long experience, be good securities for sensible, judicious, and discreet action — if unstained honour, ensure singleness of purpose; and the adoption of upright means for the attainment of beneficial ends — if a large stake in the property of the country; and a deep interest in the preservation of its existing institutions, and in the maintenance of its tranquillity and prosperity, be guarantees for the pursuit of prudent, cautious, and safe measures, in the "healing of its "sores," and the working of its cure — then, may we look forwards with confidence for the constitutional re-integration and political improvement of the state, to those eminent characters, to whom His Majesty has been pleased to commit the execution of this important task : fully satisfied, that, as they have the ability (if fairly supported) to effect it; so they will not be wanting, either in the honesty, or wisdom, necessary for its prudent and sure accomplishment. The critical situation of the country, indeed, and the loud tone in which the People have expressed their conviction of its embarrassments, and their discovery of the political corruption which has occasioned them; are in themselves sufficient indications, that the time is arrived, when the Ministers of the Crown, willingly or unwillingly, must "do their duty :" when Britain will no longer be trifled with : when official madmen may no more "cast about firebrands and death;" "war, pestilence, and famine," and cry, "Am I not "in sport?"—nor political peculators enrich themselves and connections, to the minutest ramifications of their families, at the national expense — "writing "down" thousands and tens of thousands of pounds to "the public service," which ought to be itemed "to private purposes."

Admirably adapted, however, as the Reform Bill may be, to originate the improvement, and induce the cure, of our national ills; and well qualified as our Ministers actually are, to try its present efficacy, and ensure its eventual success : yet, it must not, it cannot be expected, either, that the one should act with instantaneous completeness, like the wand of the magician; or the other, work its processes single-handed, and unaided by the co-operation of their countrymen.

It is among the ordinations of Providence, that every extensive and permanent good, should be of *gradual* growth. Prudence ever proceeds with deliberate steps : and, amid the complexity of ob ects, and multiplicity of obstructions, involved in a wide system of national reform, it is quite impossible (and it would be madness were it practicable) to spring to the desired goal by a sudden, single bound. The Ministers may do great things, but they cannot work miracles: they may administer alteratives; but cannot cure the disease with a touch. The course of the *political reformer*, indeed, is impeded by peculiar difficulties: for, while, on the one hand, he has to satisfy the just demands for redress, by those who have suffered the evils of mal-administration: he must, on the other, cautiously guard against any compliance, with the wild speculations of the political *enthusiast;* and the evil wishes and schemes of the political *anarchist:* and, at the same time, provide against, and encounter, the pertinacious opposition of those, whose deepest, dearest interests are identified with the unaltered state of " things as they are:" and whose vigilance is on the alert, to detect, expose, abuse, and take advantage of, every little error, into which *he* may fall, who endeavours to restore things to the *state in which they should be*. The country, therefore, will do both justly and wisely, to blend *patience* with *expectation:* and, in their earnest longing after relief, to repress disappointment, and withhold displeasure, should relief come more tardily than their sanguine wishes may desire; giving " fair play " and a clear stage" to the champions of Reform: waiting with due temper and equanimity, for the result of their struggle; and satisfying themselves, in the mean while, with a homely, but valuable truth, applicable to most of the concerns of human life — that, " nothing can be done *well*, which is done in a " *hurry*."

But, I have suggested, that the *co-operation* of *the country*, must go hand in hand with the wishes and endeavours of the KING and his MINISTERS, to reform the abuses, and revive the prosperity of the State. The expression, however, should be understood, in a limited, rather than a general, sense. A large proportion of the population of every country, consists of the poor, and the dependent. Exclusively occupied in obtaining the means of providing for their daily wants, *they* have neither the power, nor the opportunity, of promoting the general well-being; save, by the conscientious discharge of the duties of humble life; by the diligent exercise of their industry, in the useful and important offices of their servile station; and by a quiet enjoyment of those little comforts, which, in a *wholesome state of society*, animate their exertions, and reward their toil. Not so, with the more fortunate and favoured classes of the body politic: the ARISTOCRACY and GENTRY of the land: the co-partners of its riches; and the lords of its soil. To *them* we may fairly look, for a display of the loftier, and more public virtues — high and honourable feeling: a love of their country and its liberties: disinterestedness; munificence; and a cheerful sacrifice of a part of their advantages, on the altar of the general weal. From *them* may be expected, not to say demanded (more especially in times, and under circumstances, similar to those in which our united kingdoms are at present placed), a LOYALTY which shall echo the wishes, and aid the exertions, of our philanthropic Monarch, for the universal benefit of the country — a PATRIOTISM, that will support those MINISTERS, to whose especial agency, he has been pleased to commit the execution of the great and good work — and a LIBERALITY, that rejoices more in the participation of its abundance, than in the exclusive selfish enjoyment of it.

Two opportunities are, at this moment, presented to the more prosperous classes of our countrymen; the great, the affluent, and influential; of evincing the high-minded conduct of which we now speak — namely: First: their ready acquiescence in such an EQUITABLE PROPERTY TAX, as (in the language of the truly excellent and benevolent Bishop of Bath and Wells *) " *shall throw the burthen*" (of taxation) " *on the rich, and them alone ; and that in exact proportion to their wealth and means of discharging it;*" — and secondly; such a management of their *landed property*, and modification of their *rents*, as shall increase the *demand* for agricultural *human* labour; and make

* " Remarks on the Present Distresses of the Poor." Rodwell, New Bond Street, 1830. P. 22.

provision for its larger and more equitable *remuneration*.

The mode in which (as it is conceived) the PROPERTY TAX, above alluded to, might be adjusted, will appear in the subsequent pages. With respect to the other topic, a few observations will, with propriety, be offered in our INTRODUCTION to them.

The present distressed condition of the labouring poor, owing to the *supply* of labour being much greater than the *demand* for it, is so notorious, as to obviate the necessity of formal proof. A large proportion of this class, throughout all England, more especially in its southern moiety, are without *regular* employ, for the greater part of their time; and the wages which those receive, who are fortunate enough to procure work, (in consequence of the present great *competition* for labour,) are both insufficient, as a means of support; and inadequate, as a remuneration for their toil. I speak advisedly when I assert, that, in the twenty parishes around the one in which I reside, (and the observation applies to many hundred other parochial districts,) the present average of wages (except during hay harvest) cannot be estimated at more than 16*d.* a day, or 8*s.* per week; while crowds of labourers, who only pick up accidental, or *caddle* work (as it is called): or, are employed on the roads; would actually starve upon the gains of their toil, if the deficiency were not supplied, by a dole from the parish pay-table.* To those who have not

---

* The atrocious acts of incendiarism, which, last winter, so naturally alarmed and horrified the country, had the effect of raising the rate of agricultural wages. It is deeply to be regretted, however, that this rise, endured (in most cases,) only for a time. The alarm passed away; and wages sank again to their customary level: a sum far inadequate to the claims of justice, reason, and humanity. " The labourer is worthy of his hire." He has a *right* to live; and to live comfortably, on the profits of his honest industry: and, for my own part, I am free to acknowledge, that I should blush for the act and deed of my right hand, could it offer to him who was doing that work for me which I could not do for myself, LESS THAN TWO SHILLINGS for his twelve hours' laborious occupation in it. The example of raising agricultural wages to an *equitable rate*, has been given in an instance which may be influential. The humane and patriotic Bishop of Bath and Wells (G. H. Law) has announced to his numerous

the opportunity, or, having the opportunity, lack the inclination, of entering the hovels of the labouring poor; inspecting the condition of their families; witnessing their destitution; the struggles which they make, and the privations they endure—a representation of the actual state of their domestic life, habits, and resources, would wear the appearance of an exaggerated picture, or an idle tale: for the general information, therefore, of such persons, on this interesting point; and their conviction of the existence of this social evil, and of the necessity of meliorating it; I would beg a moment of their attention, to the following few *facts;* derived from much personal inspection, and diligent and extensive enquiry.

The *wages* of a labourer, in the southern moiety of England, may be estimated, (at a *high average*, throughout the year, and supposing him to be *constantly* employed) at 8s. *per* week; or, 20l. 16s. *per annum.*

The *number* of persons depending upon every labourer, for maintenance and support, may be averaged, throughout England, at *three* (that is to say, a wife and two children); making, together with himself, *four* persons to be supplied with all the means of living, clothing, &c. from the profits of his toil.

Potatoes constitute the almost sole food of the labouring poor, because they are the cheapest article of life. What then will be the *consumption* of this article by a family of four; and the *cost* of the quantity required?

No man capable of performing a good day's work, can be supported in health and strength, under ten pounds' weight of potatoes, (or, half a peck,) during the twenty-four hours. His wife and two children will (at a low estimate) require two thirds of the same quantity.

Potatoes cannot be *averaged* lower than 6s. *per sack,* or 6d. the *peck.* The cost of the labourer's food, therefore, (presuming that this *cheapest of all*

labourers, that he will henceforth give 12s. per week to every sober and industrious labourer, who is able and willing to do a good day's work.

aliments constitutes his entire support) for the whole year, will amount to 4*l.* 16*s.*; the charge of sixteen sacks. The wife and children will consume two thirds of the same quantity; amounting to 3*l.* 4*s.*; making, together with the first-mentioned sum, 8*l. per annum.*

The cottage or lodgings, occupied by every labourer's family, may be fairly *averaged* at 3*l.* 3*s. per annum.*

Every labourer must expend, at the least, 12*s.* annually in shoes; for a new pair, 9*s.*; for repairing the old ones, 3*s.* The expense of this article, for his wife and children, will be under-estimated at 8*s.*: making the total 1*l.*

The various articles of clothing, independently of shoes, required by a labourer, will cost, annually, at the lowest estimate (including mending), 2*l.* 5*s.*; those for his wife and children, 1*l.* 10*s.*: making a total of 3*l.* 15*s.*

The fuel of a labourer's family, will (upon an *average*), cost 1*l. per annum.*

The above totals, added together, will amount to the sum of 16*l.* 18*s.*; leaving a surplus, out of the labourer's annual earnings, of 3*l.* 18*s.* to furnish tools, candles, soap, and the numerous other little articles, which are necessary for the support of a family, under the most humble circumstances, in a civilised country.

It is to be recollected, that the above statement confines the diet of the labourer and his family, exclusively, to *potatoes* and *water*, instead of allowing him the *more expensive luxury of bread :* and supposes him to be regularly employed during the *whole year ;* when the fact is, that this is not the happy lot, of more than half the class !

    " Ah ! little think the gay licentious proud,
    " Whom pleasure, power, and affluence surround ;
    " They, who their thoughtless hours in giddy mirth,
    " And wanton, often cruel, riot waste !
    " Ah ! little think they, while they dance along,
    " How many —— —— —— drink the cup
    " Of baleful grief, or eat the bitter bread
    " Of misery ! "

The simple fact is, (and the truth ought to be told,) that we have *done a wrong to the labouring classes :* a wrong which it is high time for us to redress. We have taken from them several advantages ; without giving them any boon in return. We have enclosed those commons, forests, and wastes; (a wise and beneficial measure, in a *general* point of view,) which, formerly, furnished the working man with pasture for his cow : or mast for his pig; or grass for his geese ; or turf for his hearth. We have swept away those humble tenements, in our cities and towns, for the sake of improvement, or of lessening the burthen of the parish rate, which heretofore gave shelter to him and his family, at an easy rent ; and, in our villages, we have demolished, as far as it could be effected, the same description of lowly dwellings, for the same reasons ; rendering an habitation for a labourer an object of competition, and, of course, of increased expense. And what have we placed to the *credit* side of his account ? — diminished wages, and scant employ : the wretched alternative, of an insufficient parish relief ; or, emigration from his native land !

The ignorantly-incredulous may deny, and the heartless may disregard, the truth of the foregoing statement ; but, every wise, good, and humane man, whilst he admits and laments its accuracy, will anxiously enquire, what measures must be pursued, to cure the evil, and avert the fatal consequence of its prolonged continuance. It is clear, that we cannot, with propriety or justice, look to His Majesty's ministers, for its remedy ; as the adjustment of wages, cannot be the subject of legal enactment : nor a provision for the constant employment of labourers wanting work, be made by any exertion of Government. From the great body of farmers, in their *present condition ;* with, (for the most part,) lessened or exhausted capitals ; at high rents ; and on short leases ; and crushed with a heavy weight of poor-rates — nothing can be expected. *Necessity* (for it would be utter want of charity to say inclination) compels them, to reduce the wages of the peasant to the lowest Minimum : to lessen, as much as possible, the number of their workmen ; and to substitute *artificial helps,* wherever they can be made applicable, in the room of *human labour*. To look to *them*, therefore, for an equitable rise, and future reasonable standard of wages, would be equally absurd and disappointing. We must direct our attention and hopes to a higher quarter.—The bane and the antidote rest, exclusively, with the NOBILITY and GENTRY of the country: with the LANDLORDS: the OWNERS of the soil: the POSSESSORS of LARGE ESTATES: and to their sense of justice; feelings of humanity; and patriotic spirit, must the appeal be made—to raise the labouring poor from their present distressed and degraded condition; to give them some share in the blessings of social life: and to award to them an equitable remuneration, for that toil which provides for the use, of what are called the genteel and independent classes, all those necessaries, conveniencies, comforts, and luxuries, which it pleases God to permit them to enjoy.

The means by which they may effect this beneficial change in the present condition of the labouring poor, are sufficiently obvious:—

1. By dividing all their large farms, into two or more smaller ones *: none exceeding the annual rent of 300*l.* a year; and *not* letting more than one farm to the same individual: a practice, which, if universally adopted, would increase the demand for human labour to an indefinite amount.

2. By granting long leases, on a moderate rent;—a measure which would be equally beneficial to tenant and landlord; affording to the one, encouragement to improve; and ensuring to the other, a bettered condition of his estate, when the lease shall have expired.

3. By binding the farmer, in a clause of the lease,

* " The proprietors of large estates have it in their power, to " facilitate the maintenance, and thereby to encourage the esta- " blishment of families, (which is one of the noblest purposes to " which the rich and great can convert their endeavours) by " BUILDING COTTAGES: SPLITTING FARMS: erecting manufac- " tures: CULTIVATING WASTES: embanking the sea: DRAINING " MARSHES; and other expedients, which the situation of each " estate points out. If the profits of these undertakings do not " repay the expense, let the authors of them place the difference " to the account of CHARITY. It is true, of almost all such pro- " jects, that the public is a gainer by them, whatever the owner " be." *Paley's Mor. Phil.* v. i. p. 260.

(in consideration of his easy rent and long term) to employ a certain number of labourers; and to pay to each individual of that description, a certain equitable rate of wages: such number and payment to be settled between the landlord and tenant.

4. By allotting to the peasantry on their estates; or, by obliging the tenants of their farms to allot to them (on certain just rents and judicious conditions), portions of land, averaging a quarter of an acre to each family, for their own exclusive use; and unfettered cultivation: — which would at once, afford them food; furnish occupation; generate, or maintain, industrious habits; improve their morals: and give to them, more of home society, and family intercourse, than they at present enjoy.

5. By building on their farms, and their own domains, small, but comfortable cottages; and letting them at low rents to the labouring poor: an outlay which would be returned in a two-fold manner, — by a fair interest for the money expended: and by securing to themselves the respect and attachment, of a benefited, grateful, and decent peasantry.

6. By manifesting the same solicitude, for the preservation, subsistence, and comfort of the working classes, as for the *preservation of game;* and thus crowning themselves with the favour of Heaven; and the blessings of those who are now ready to perish; and averting from their country, the evil alluded to by the Poet: —

> " Ill fares the land, to hast'ning ills a prey,
> " Where wealth accumulates, and men decay.
> " Princes and lords may flourish, or may fade;
> " A breath can make them, as a breath has made:
> " But, a *bold peasantry*, a country's pride,
> " When once destroy'd, can never be supplied." *

* " It is a mistake to suppose, that the rich man maintains his " servants, tradesmen, tenants, and labourers; the truth is, they " maintain him. It is their industry which supplies his table: " furnishes his wardrobe: builds his houses: adorns his equi- " pages: provides his amusements. It is not the estate; but the " *labour* employed upon it, that pays his rent. All that he does " is to distribute what others produce, which is the least part of " the business." *Paley's Mor. Philos.* vol. i. p. 240.

AN EQUITABLE PROPERTY TAX:

A Financial Speculation.

1. That the present system of taxation presses, (either directly, or indirectly,) with a disproportionate weight, on the middle and lower orders of the community, is a fact generally acknowledged. It would seem to be desirable, therefore, to render its imposition impartial: and, in the room of some of its objectionable items, to substitute others, (or another,) which, without occasioning any defalcation in the amount of the revenue, would diffuse the burthen of providing for it, more *equally* and *equitably*, (than is the case at present,) over all classes of the population.

2. The taxes which are supposed to be of this partial, and therefore oppressive, description, are the following : —

Windows, producing annually,	£1,185,283	and a fraction.
Inhabited Houses, Do. -	1,361,625	Do.
Horses for riding, Do. - -	362,675	Do.
Other Horses and Mules, Do. -	62,450	Do.
Hides, tanned and untanned, Do. -	43,402	Do.
Soap, Do. - - -	1,249,684	Do.
Candles, Do. - - -	482,413	Do.
Malt, Do. - - - -	3,436,272	Do.
Making a total to be provided for by some other means of	£8,183,804	

3. The national debt amounts, it is said, to nearly eight hundred millions. The annual income of England, Wales, Scotland, and Ireland * : derived from rents; tythes; dividends; annuities; canals; docks; rail-roads, &c., has been stated, in round numbers, at one hundred millions. The revenue of the coun-

* The rents of Ireland, including glebe lands, are said to amount to fourteen millions. Of this sum, six millions are supposed to belong to absentees. A reasonable system of taxation; a judicious body of poor laws; and the residence of the Irish gentry upon their estates, can alone cure the ills, of that unhappy country. Four millions are calculated to be annually expended by British subjects, residing on the Continent: to the immense loss of their own native land. A heavy absentee tax should repair the injury.

try, furnished by the customs: excise: stamp-duties: land and assessed taxes: post-office; and miscellaneous imposts, amounts to a clear net sum, (after all deductions and drawbacks,) of 50,523,429*l.*, and a fraction. The sum of 8,183,804*l.* would be deducted from this total, were those taxes liquidated, which are proposed to be taken off: a deficiency which it is intended to supply, by a general EQUITABLE TAX on PROPERTY.

4. PROPERTY is a SACRED THING * : so sacred, that LOCKE asserts : "Government has no other end, than " the PRESERVATION of PROPERTY :" and if he included the RIGHTS: and LIBERTIES: and WELL-BEING, of the GOVERNED, in his idea; the proposition is incontestably true. But, if PROPERTY be (and it must necessarily be) protected by GOVERNMENT, in order that its legal use may be preserved to its possessor, it is but *just,* that it should PAY for this protection : and that, too, in an EQUITABLE PROPORTION to its AMOUNT — a proposition, which the next paragraph will more clearly explain.

5. " We are accustomed to an opinion," (it is

---

* Among the many objections which have been urged against the REFORM BILL by its opponents, there appears to me, to be only ONE which deserves an answer; viz. that in the disfranchisement of CLOSE, (and therefore CORRUPT) BOROUGHS, government would violate the sacredness of PRIVATE PROPERTY, by arbitrarily taking away from its owner, a possession, which he had either acquired by purchase, or obtained by inheritance. The argument is specious, but unsound. A BOROUGH (or, in other words, an ESTATE which carries with it the right of returning one or more representatives to parliament) may, unquestionably, be bought, sold, or inherited, like any other freehold property : and, as such, ought to be sacredly guaranteed, by the government, to its possessor. But, the RIGHT of COMMANDING or DIRECTING, or INFLUENCING, by threats, promises, or rewards; the VOTES of the BURGESSES, can neither be bought, sold, nor inherited. It is a species of property, legally and constitutionally faulty; politically and morally injurious ; and therefore ought, in justice and propriety, *to be taken* from its possessor. The PROPERTY (correctly speaking), and its LEGAL USE, still remain with the owner : he is deprived, merely, of the power of ABUSING it. Can a single instance be pointed out, for a century last past, in which the possessor of such a BOROUGH, as those alluded to, has NOT been in the habit of exercising an ILLEGAL INFLUENCE over the VOTES of its BURGESSES? Or, was it ever known, that a man purchased such a borough, without an INTENTION to exercise it, on every befitting opportunity; thus involving himself in a BREACH of the STATUTE, and driving the voters into the CRIME of PERJURY? — The questions do not merit a reply.

the reasoning of Paley,) "that a TAX, to be JUST,
" ought to be accurately proportioned to the CIRCUM-
" STANCES" (or, more correctly perhaps, to the AMOUNT
" of the PROPERTY) of the persons who pay it. But,
" upon what, it might be asked, is this opinion
" founded : unless it could be shown, that SUCH a
" PROPORTION, interferes the least with the general
" CONVENIENCY of SUBSISTENCE ? Whereas, I should
" rather believe, that a tax constructed with a VIEW
" to THAT CONVENIENCY, ought to rise upon the
" DIFFERENT CLASSES of the community, in a much
" HIGHER RATIO, than the SIMPLE PROPORTION of their
" INCOMES. The point to be regarded, is, NOT what
" men HAVE, but, WHAT they can SPARE : and it is
" evident, that a man who possesses a THOUSAND
" POUNDS a year, can MORE EASILY give up a HUN-
" DRED, than a man with a HUNDRED POUNDS a year
" can part with TEN : that is, those HABITS of LIFE
" which are reasonable and innocent, and upon the
" ABILITY to CONTINUE which, the formation of fami-
" lies depends, will be much LESS AFFECTED by the
" one deduction, than by the other. It is still more
" evident, that a man of a HUNDRED POUNDS a YEAR,
" would not be so MUCH DISTRESSED in his SUBSIST-
" ENCE, by a demand from him of TEN POUNDS, as a
" man of TEN POUNDS a year, would be by the loss of
" ONE : to which we must add, that, the POPULATION
" of the country being replenished by the marriages
" of the LOWEST RANKS of the society, *their accommo-
" dation and relief become of more importance to the
" state, than the conveniency of any higher, but less
" numerous, order of its citizens.*" Upon the undeniable truths propounded in the above extract, the
SCHEDULE at the conclusion of these observations is
constructed : which proposes, to affix CERTAIN RATES
of TAXATION, upon certain AMOUNTS of PROPERTY, proportioned to " the general CONVENIENCY of SUBSIST-
" ENCE," of those by whom such payments are to be
made — or (to place the nature of the impost in a
clearer point of view) to make a man pay taxes to the
state, in PROPORTION to his INTEREST in the GENERAL
FUND of PROPERTY.

6. A PROPERTY TAX, in order to be EQUITABLE,

must NOT be levied upon the profits of PERSONAL INDUSTRY, like the INCOME TAX, under which the country struggled, for some years, during the last bankrupting war—but, on actual REALISED PROPERTY; whether in land: houses: mortgages: funded stock : or money, hoarded, or however employed.

7. By the adoption of a PROPERTY TAX, constructed on the principle laid down in paragraph 5., in lieu of those taxes proposed to be repealed, in paragraph 2., several IMPORTANT OBJECTS would be attained—the RELIEF of the MIDDLE and LOWER classes of the community: a just STANDARD for the AUGMENTATION of TAXATION, in times of great national emergency, without compromising PUBLIC FAITH, by a REDUCTION of INTEREST upon FUNDED PROPERTY: greater simplicity, and LESS EXPENSE in the COLLECTION of this SINGLE, than in the collection of VARIOUS OTHERS to the same amount: and more CERTAINTY in its PRODUCT, and greater STEADINESS in its PAYMENT, than is the case, with respect to the financial impositions just alluded to.

8. The PERSONS LIABLE to an ASSESSMENT on the PROPERTY TAX in question: and those EXEMPTED from the same, would be as follows—LIABLE: the PROPRIETORS of all freehold: leasehold (for life, or terms of years): copyhold: funded; or hoarded property, producing, or capable of producing, an annual income of ONE HUNDRED POUNDS, and upwards: annuitants for life; and OFFICERS on PERMANENT HALF PAY — EXEMPTED: all persons whose actual property does NOT amount to 100*l. per annum :* OFFICERS in the NAVY and ARMY on service, as far as respects their PAY: persons in OFFICIAL situations, who are REMOVABLE AT PLEASURE: and CURATES. Such persons, whatever their income might be, as derived from their OFFICIAL SITUATIONS, would be EXEMPT as to SUCH INCOME: but liable to the tax, upon their ACTUAL PROPERTY, provided that it amounted to 100*l. per annum,* or upwards.

9. The CALCULATION of every individual's property, and the ADJUSTMENT of the sum to be paid upon it, (according to the RATES established by the following SCHEDULE) ought to be left, exclusively, to such in-

dividual. But, in order to secure to GOVERNMENT a just, true, and correct RETURN of every individual's property: and to prevent FRAUD, CONCEALMENT, or COLLUSION, on the part of the TAX-PAYER; a DECLARATION, signed by such person, should be transmitted by him to the collector, at the time of his payment of such tax, drawn up in terms similar to the following form: —

" I A— B— of, &c., do hereby solemnly declare,
" in the presence of ' Almighty God, unto whom all
" ' hearts be open, all desires known, and from whom
" ' no secrets are hidden,' that the just and true
" amount of my PROPERTY TAX, for the last whole
" (or half) year, according to the SPIRIT and MEAN-
" ING of the act of Parliament imposing the said tax,
" is the sum of
" So help me God! A. B." *

10. The AMOUNT of all PROPERTY should be calculated by its POSSESSOR, with a DEDUCTION of all legal LIENS upon it: such as mortgage interest: dowers: annuities, &c., without reference to PERSONAL DEBTS, not charged on ACTUAL PROPERTY.

11. The METHOD by which every individual might determine the ACTUAL AMOUNT of his property, so as to enable him (*in case of doubt*) to make a correct estimate of, and a just and conscientious return, upon it; would be — to throw the whole of it into NOMINAL CAPITAL (after deducting the charges alluded to in the last paragraph) — to estimate the total at *four per cent.*—and make his RETURN, according to the INCOME resulting from such a calculation. Two EXAMPLES may be given, as illustrations of this suggestion. 1st, The ANNUITANT for LIFE, might estimate the *market price* of his annuity, according to the annual amount of the same, and his own age, (calculating from the *tables* drawn up, and published, on that subject): make a NOMINAL CAPITAL of the

* As government would accept of a *declaration* instead of an *oath*, it must feel fully satisfied of the *honesty* and *accuracy* of the *return*: which can be provided for, only by awarding heavy penalties upon a CONVICTION of a FRAUDULENT one."

total : and charge this IMAGINARY AGGREGATE with four per cent. per annum, to be reckoned as part of his yearly income. 2d, The HOLDER of any dignity or office in the CHURCH, and the RECTOR or VICAR of any LIVING, might readily come to the same satisfactory result, by following the same easy process. The INCUMBENT holding his own PERPETUAL ADVOWSON, would be included in the class of those, who were assessed for REAL PROPERTY; and be chargeable, according to the CLEAR PROCEEDS of the preferment, after deducting the stipend of the curate, if he retained such an assistant.

12. The ACT establishing the proposed EQUITABLE PROPERTY TAX, should contain clauses of EXEMPTION or MODIFICATION, with respect to the NUMBER of CHILDREN; or such other peculiar circumstances in families, as might reasonably claim the attention and favour of the legislature, in their particular cases.

THE SCHEDULE:

Particularising the AMOUNTS of INCOME, and RATES of
PAYMENT thereon.

	Per Cent.
100*l*. annual income (inclusive) up to 250*l*. per ann. (exclusive) to pay - - - -	1
250*l*. annual income (inclusive) up to 500*l*. Do. (exclusive) - - - -	1½
500*l*. annual income (inclusive) up to 750*l*. Do. (exclusive) - - . -	2
750*l*. annual income (inclusive) up to 1000*l*. Do. (exclusive) - - - -	4
1000*l*. annual income (inclusive) up to 2000*l*. Do. (exclusive) - - - -	6
2000*l*. annual income (inclusive) up to 5000*l*. Do. (exclusive) - - - -	9
5000*l*. annual income (inclusive) up to 10,000*l*. Do. (exclusive) - - - -	13
10,000*l*. annual income (inclusive) up to 20,000*l*. Do. (exclusive) - - - -	18
20,000*l*. annual income (inclusive) up to 40,000*l*. Do. (exclusive) - - - -	24
40,000*l*. annual income (inclusive) up to 80,000*l*. Do. (exclusive) - - - -	31
80,000*l*. annual income (inclusive) up to 150,000*l*. Do. (exclusive) - - - -	39
150,000*l*. annual income (inclusive) up to 200,000*l*. Do. and upwards - - -	48

Should the amount of the EQUITABLE PROPERTY
TAX, constructed according to the above SCHEDULE,
be found (after minute and accurate calculations) to
be redundant or deficient, with respect to the sum
required to supply the diminution of taxation, recognised in paragraph 2.; the rate of the said PROPERTY
TAX, must be made either HIGHER or LOWER, to meet
the case; preserving, in its fearless adjustment, the
same EQUITABLE RATIO observed in the same SCHE-
DULE.

THE LORDS AND THE REFORM BILL.

It has been asked: "How will the Lords act with respect "to the REFORM BILL?"

The high character of that august assembly, authorizes us to answer; "They will act as they ever have done—LOYALLY —CONSTITUTIONALLY—POLITICALLY."

LOYALLY—by aiding the accomplishment of the patriotic wish of our most GRACIOUS KING, to establish, as a Statute of the Realm, a political measure, obviously adapted to confirm the STABILITY of the THRONE; to ensure the PEACE of the COUNTRY; and to pave the way, for the relief of the DISTRESS, and the promotion of the WELL-BEING, of the MIDDLE and LOWER classes of the PEOPLE!

CONSTITUTIONALLY—by affording their sanction to a BILL, which, purifying our present system of PARLIAMENTARY RE-PRESENTATION from the corruptions that pollute it; will restore to health, soundness, and vigour, our GLORIOUS CONSTITU-TION—the PALLADIUM of the liberty; prosperity; and respectability, of the BRITISH EMPIRE.

POLITICALLY—by sympathizing in the feelings and aspirations of an immense MAJORITY of their FELLOW COUNTRYMEN —of the inmates of almost every dwelling through the United Kingdom, from the PALACE to the HOVEL—and thus securing the continuance of the ATTACHMENT and RESPECT of the PEOPLE, towards that integral and important branch of our form of Government—the HOUSE of LORDS!!!

THE END.

LONDON:
Printed by A. & R. Spottiswoode,
New-Street-Square.

ADDRESS

TO

THE FARMERS

OF

THE UNITED KINGDOM,

ON THE

LOW RATES OF PROFIT

IN AGRICULTURE AND IN TRADE.

By R. TORRENS, Esq. M.P.

Second Edition.

LONDON:

LONGMAN & Co., PATERNOSTER ROW.

1831.

Price Threepence.

LONDON:

PRINTED BY T. BRETTELL, RUPERT STREET, HAYMARKET.

FARMERS

THE UNITED KINGDOM.

GENTLEMEN,

IT is my intention, should no other Member of more influence and experience undertake the task, to propose, in the approaching session of Parliament, a revision of the Corn Laws, upon the principle of gradually abolishing all restriction, and all duties, upon the importation of the products of foreign agriculture. In the mean time, permit me to solicit your attention while I state, in as few words as possible, the grounds upon which I confidently anticipate, that, in endeavouring to carry through a measure, upon which the prosperity of all the industrious classes of the community essentially depends, I shall receive, from the enlightened agriculturists of the United Kingdom, not opposition, but support.

It is the interest of the farmer, no less than of the manufacturer, that the rate of profit should be high. The cultivator of the soil, like every other producer, is prosperous when his returns considerably exceed his expenses, and is depressed and embarrassed as the return he obtains bears a diminishing proportion to the capital he lays out. Now I undertake to show, by proof amounting to demonstration, that a free importation of the products of foreign agriculture, without restriction and without duty, would render the rate of profit, in all the branches of British industry, agriculture included, permanently high. Should I succeed in this undertaking, may I not expect to receive from the farmer, as well as from the manufacturer and trader, cordial support and co-operation, while endeavouring to obtain the sanction of the Legislature for a gradual introduction of a perfectly free and untaxed trade in all the first necessaries of life?

It was proved before a committee of the House of Commons, and it is a fact which must be familiar to every practical farmer, that the soils under cultivation in this country vary very widely from each other in fertility ; some lands, as stated in evidence before the Select Committee of the Commons, yielding no more than from eight to nine, and others producing as much as from thirty-six to forty bushels of wheat per acre. The expense of cultivating bad land is greater than that of cultivating good land. I will, however, concede this point ; I will admit that cold reluctant soils are tilled at no greater cost than alluvial mould ; and I will assume, for the sake of illustration, that on every quality of land the farmer's annual outlay, in cultivating his farm, consists of ten bushels, or the value of ten bushels of wheat per acre.

These things being premised, we will assume that, in consequence of the free importation of foreign corn, the demand for farms is so limited that the farmer can obtain, for a very small, or merely nominal rent, land yielding an annual crop equivalent to 20 bushels of wheat per acre. Under these circumstances, the farmer will pay rent for those lands only which yield *more* than 20 bushels per acre ; and for these lands all the produce above 20 bushels per acre will go to rent. The farmer, therefore, for all the lands which he cultivates, will obtain, after the deduction for rent, a produce of 20 bushels per acre ; and as his expenditure is only 10 bushels per acre, his profit will be 10 bushels, or cent per cent. upon his capital.

Let us now suppose that an increasing population requires an increased supply of corn ; that a protecting duty limits importation ; and that, in consequence, the demand for farms becomes such, that that quality of land, which the farmer can obtain at a nominal rent, yields only 15 bushels of wheat per acre, and that, on other lands, the excess of produce above fifteen bushels per acre is paid as rent. His profits are reduced from one hundred to 50 per cent. Laying out 10 bushels per acre in cultivation, he obtains a return of 15 bushels.

Should increasing supplies of food continue to be required, and high protecting duties upon importation continue to be imposed, then no lands may be obtainable at a nominal rent, except those which, cultivated at an expense of 10 bushels of wheat per acre, yield respectively no more than 11 or even 10 bushels per acre. It is self evident that, on the lands yielding 11 bushels per acre, the farmer's profit would be reduced to one bushel per acre, and that on those yielding only 10 bushels per acre, the profit would altogether disappear.

Upon the supposition that the expenses of cultivation can be accurately represented by a given quantity of the produce obtained, it can be established by proof, simple and obvious, and amounting to strict demonstration, that restrictions imposed on the importation of foreign corn lower the rate of profit upon the capital employed in domestic agriculture. I am fully aware, however, that the intelligent practical agriculturist may object, that this supposition is not sufficiently conformable to fact and experience to render the inductions from it completely satisfactory. Hence the question, whether the rate of profit upon the capital employed in domestic agriculture, is raised or lowered by restrictions on the importation of foreign corn, becomes one of considerable complexity, involving, as it does, considerations respecting the value of farm produce and of manufactured articles, in relation to each other and to currency. I entreat the patient attention of the intelligent farmer, while I endeavour to disentangle this complicated question, and to present it to him reduced to its simple elements.

For this purpose, I assume that the expense of cultivating an acre of land consists of the labour of one man, to whom seed and food, equivalent to five bushels of wheat, and implements and clothing, equivalent to five yards of cloth, are advanced; while the cost of procuring 60s. in money also consists of the labour of one man, to whom the same identical advance is made. By this supposition, the produce of an acre of land, paying only a nominal rent, will sell for 60s., whatever the quantity of such produce may be. The reason why the varying quantity of produce thus obtained from an acre of land will always sell for the same price is this. The principle of competition constantly tends to bring the rates of profit, obtained in different trades, to an equality; and profits cannot be equal, unless products obtained at equal cost are, on the average of years, of equal value.

While the produce of an acre of land, paying a nominal rent, sells for 60s., I suppose further, that the cost of producing 15 yards of cloth consists of the labour of one man, to whom raw material and food, equivalent to five bushels of wheat, and tools and clothing, equivalent to five yards of cloth, have been advanced. On the principle, that goods produced at equal cost are of equal value, 15 yards of cloth will be equivalent to the produce of an acre of land, and will always sell for 60s., or at 4s. per yard.

On these data, the question—in what manner restrictions upon the importation of foreign corn affect the profits of the farmer—becomes one of simple arithmetic. And let me here distinctly state, that I have assumed these data, not because they are in any peculiar way favourable to the conclusion which I wish to establish, but merely because *some* data must be taken, in order to state the complicated questions we have to consider with clearness and precision.

CASE I.

The farmer occupies, at a nominal rent, a tract of land yielding an annual crop equivalent to 30 bushels of wheat per acre. Upon the data assumed, wheat must, in this case, be 2s a bushel, because the same cost which raises 30 bushels procures 60s. *Question,* What is the rate of the farmer's profit?

EXPENDITURE, PER ACRE:

	s.	*s.*
Farm produce, seed and food, five bushels of wheat, at 2*s.* per bushel	10	
Wrought goods, implements, and clothing, equal to 5 yards of cloth	20	
		30

RETURN:

Produce, per acre, 30 bushels at 2*s.*	60	
		60
Profit		30

CASE II.

The farmer's profit being cent. per cent., when he cultivates, at a nominal rent, land yielding 30 bushels per acre, we have now to ascertain what the rate of his profit will become, should restriction on the importation of foreign corn create such a demand for farms, that the land which can now be obtained at a nominal rent, yields only 20 bushels of wheat per acre, and that on the superior lands all the produce above 20 bushels per acre is paid as rent. In this case, as 20 bushels per acre constitute the farmer's nett return, 20 bushels will be worth 60*s.*; in other words, the price of wheat will rise from 2*s.* to 3*s.* the bushel. *Question*, What will be the farmer's profit?

EXPENDITURE, PER ACRE:

	s.	*s.*
Farm produce, as before, 5 bushels of wheat, at 3*s.*	15	
Wrought goods, as before	20	
		35

RETURN:

Twenty bushels, at 3*s.*		60
Profit		25

CASE III.

Increasing population, and continued obstructions to the importation of foreign corn, create such a demand for farms that the capitalist who wishes to engage in cultivation can obtain, at a nominal rent, land yielding only 15 bushels per acre, and is obliged to pay, as rent, all the surplus above 15 bushels per acre yielded by lands of a superior quality. As 15 bushels per acre will in this case be the farmer's nett return, after the deduction of rent, 15 bushels will be worth 60s., and wheat will be 4s. per bushel. *Question*, What is now the farmer's profit?

EXPENDITURE, PER ACRE:

	s.	s.
Farm produce, as before, 5 bushels of wheat, at 4s. per bushel	20	
Wrought goods, as before	20	
		40

RETURN:

Produce, 15 bushels, at 4s. per bushel..............................	60
Profit	20

Thus we see that restrictions on the importation of foreign agricultural produce, and the consequent increase in the cost price of wheat, from 2s. to 4s. per bushel, have reduced the rate of profit upon the capital applied to domestic agriculture, from cent. per cent. to 50 per cent. Let the population continue to increase and the restrictive system to be enforced, until the land, which can be obtained at a nominal rent, yields only seven and a half bushels of wheat per acre, and until, on all superior lands, the excess above seven and a half bushels is paid as rent. In this case, seven and a half bushels, being the nett return upon the farmer's capital after the deduction of rent, will be worth 60*s*., and the price of wheat will have risen to 8*s*. per bushel. *Question*, What now will be the farmer's profit upon the capital he invests in cultivation?

CASE IV.

EXPENDITURE:

		s.	*s.*
Farm produce, as before, 5 bushels of wheat, per acre, at 8*s*. per bushel		40	
Wrought articles, as before......		20	
			60

RETURN:

	s.
Produce, seven and a half bushels, at 8*s*. per bushel	60

Farmer's Profit .... *nil.*

Thus it appears, with all the certainty of demonstration, that those restrictions on the importation of the products of foreign agriculture, which, in ignorance or in fraud, are represented as beneficial to the class investing their capital in domestic agriculture, have a direct and necessary tendency to lower the rate of the farmer's profit. But the full extent of the injury, which such restrictions inflict upon the industry of the country, cannot be seen until we have traced the manner in which they affect the profits of the artisan and the manufacturer.

It will be remembered that, in order to state the question under consideration with distinctness and precision, I have assumed as data, that the same identical expenditure that serves to cultivate an acre of land, may likewise serve either to procure 60*s*. in money, or to prepare fifteen yards of cloth, which are taken as equivalent to that quantity of wrought goods which is expended in cultivating three acres of land. It must also be borne in mind that, on this supposition, it follows, from that principle of competition which tends to equalize the rate of profit, that the varying quantity of produce raised from one acre, the constant quantity of goods employed in the cultivation of three acres, and 60*s.* will all be of equal value. Now, if the results obtained by the employment of equal capitals are of equal value, then, in the first of the preceding cases, when land paying a nominal rent yields 30 bushels of wheat, selling at 2*s.* per bushel, the profit of the manufacturer, as well as of the farmer, will be cent per cent. For the account of the manufacturer employing a capital equal to that with which the farmer cultivates an acre of land will stand thus :—

EXPENDITURE :

	s.	*s.*
Food and raw material, equal to five bushels of wheat, at 2*s.* per bushel	10	
Clothing and implements, equal to 5 yards of cloth	20	
		30

RETURN :

Fifteen yards of cloth	60
Profit.........	30

In Case III., in which restrictions on the importation of foreign food and material have created such a demand for farms, that a nominal rent is obtained for land yielding only 15 bushels of wheat per acre, and when, therefore, corn is at 4*s.* per bushel, the manufacturer's profit will have sunk from cent. per cent. to 50 per cent. His amount will now stand thus :—

EXPENDITURE :

	s.	*s.*
Food and raw material, 5 bushels of wheat, at 4*s.* per bushel ...	20	
Wrought goods	20	
		40

RETURN :

	s.
Fifteen yards of cloth............	60
Profit.........	20

In Case IV., when increasing population, and restrictions on the importation of food, have caused a nominal rent to be paid for land yielding only seven and a half bushels, then the profits of the manufacturer, as well as those of the farmer, altogether disappear. The account of the master manufacturer, employing a capital equal to that employed in cultivating one acre, will stand thus :—

EXPENDITURE :

	s.	s.
Food and raw material, 5 bushels of wheat, at 8s. per bushel...	40	
Wrought goods	20	
		60

RETURN :

Fifteen yards of cloth............	60
Profit.........	*nil.*

It is this necessary fall in manufacturing profits which prevents the farmer from obtaining more than a temporary benefit from a permanent rise in the value of corn; and which, by the principle of competition, converts into rent all the produce of the land which exceeds what is necessary in order to give the cultivator the same rate of profit obtained by other capitalists.

But the gradual reduction, and ultimate extinction of profit, in all the branches of industry, form the smallest portion of the evil inflicted on the country by that iniquitous system which deprives the people of cheap supplies of foreign food. As the profits of the capitalist diminish, interest urges, necessity drives him to resort to expedients for producing the same quantity of goods at a less expense. But, if he be a farmer, he cannot, without still greater loss, reduce the quantity or quality of his seed, or dispense with his plough and his team; and if the capitalist be a manufacturer, he cannot " make bricks without straw;" he cannot fabricate the same quantity of wrought goods with a less quantity of material, and with inferior machinery. The cost of production can be diminished only by reducing wages. On the labourer, therefore, the calamity falls with grinding pressure. He is trodden to the earth, without the possibility of recovering his lost position. When things have arrived at that state at which the capitalist, in order to realize a living profit upon the capital he employs, is driven to the necessity of reducing wages, every effort of self-preservation on the part of the working people, serves but to aggravate their misery. This is a point of vital—of fearful interest. Let us consider it more in detail.

In the preceding Cases, when the farmer, in cultivating an acre of land, advanced seed and food equivalent to five bushels of wheat, and implements, and clothing worth 20s., it is assumed that the food and clothing, received by the working man, were just sufficient for his comfortable support. Now, when the farmer cultivates land, which will not yield a produce sufficient to replace the expenditure, with a living profit, it is plain that he must either reduce wages, or abandon tillage. If the working people submit to a reduction of wages their condition is degraded; if they struggle to escape this degradation, and resist the reduction of wages, the land cannot continue to be cultivated, and the demand for their labour ceases altogether. By our restrictions on the importation of food, and by our tithes, and other taxes on production, the portion of the produce of industry, left to the producers, is so small, that it is insufficient to afford, at one and the same time, a living profit to the capitalist, and adequate wages to the labourer. Collision is the consequence. The capitalist and labourer are brought together, like two shipwrecked mariners upon a plank incapable of supporting both. Self-preservation urges them to a deadly contest against each other. Every where the struggle of despair is carried on. In the towns we have seen the manufacturer become a Truck Master, forcing the labourers to receive arbitrary payments in kind, while the labourers have formed themselves into Trades Unions, in order to escape from what mistaken suffering fancies to be the injurious influence of capital. In the rural districts, the farmers have reduced their labourers to the state of parish paupers, and the labourers have become incendiaries, in order to terrify the farmer into the payment of adequate wages. Where is this to end? Is it too much to say, that, if a speedy remedy be not found for these deep-seated evils, a servile war—the dissolution of society, is at hand?

Were a total stranger to the institutions of this country cast upon our shore,—were he made to understand the practical operation of our corn laws, tithes, and other taxes upon industry, and desired to estimate the character of the legislature by the tendency of its enactments, to what conclusion would a strict induction from the facts conduct him? Certainly it never could occur to him, that those who had brought us to the verge of social dissolution, should oppose themselves to change, upon the grounds that " the system had worked well." This stranger to the state of society in England could not be persuaded to believe, that the oligarchy which had employed the legislative power for the purpose of raising the rent of land, by depressing the profits of capital almost to nothing, should have ventured to put forth, to those who employed their capital in the business of cultivation, the gross delusion, that their interest would be sacrificed by extending to the industrious class a control over the laws by which industry is regulated. Nor could it " enter into the heart of our stranger to conceive," that any portion of the working people should be so debased by ignorance, as to view with indifference an extensive measure of reform, taking power from the faction which had deprived the people of cheap bread, and placing it in the hands of ten-pound householders, who, whether they live upon the profits of their capital, or on the wages of their labour, have a direct, and a common interest, in causing the necessaries of life to be procured at the least possible expense.

When a wrong course has been pursued, difficulty and embarrassment are experienced in getting right. A fall in the price of corn, *after* the farmer has invested his capital in cultivation, would, in the first instance, reduce his profits. Should the farmer, under a restrictive system, have cultivated, at a nominal rent, land yielding 15 bushels of wheat per acre, and have paid a rent of five bushels per acre for land yielding 20 bushels; then, as in Case III., wheat would be 4*s.* per bushel, the rate of agricultural profit would be 50 per cent. But a sudden opening of the ports, and admission of foreign corn, duty free, reducing the price of wheat to 2*s.* per bushel, instead of raising the profit of the farmer to cent. per cent., as in Case No. I., when wheat was also at 2*s.* per bushel, would immediately involve him in absolute loss ; for his account would now stand thus, for the land yielding 15 bushels, and held at a nominal rent :—

EXPENDITURE PER ACRE :

		s.	*s.*
Seed and food—5 bushels of wheat, at 2*s.* per bushel	......	10	
Implements and clothing	......	20	
			30

RETURN:

Fifteen bushels of wheat, at 2s.
per bushel   30

Profit ....   *nil.*

With respect to the land yielding 20 bushels per
acre, and held at a rent equivalent to five bushels
per acre, when wheat was 4s. per bushel, the farmer's
account, upon the fall of prices from 4s. to 2s. per
bushel, would be still more calamitous. It would
stand thus :—

EXPENDITURE PER ACRE:

	s.	s.
Seed and food—5 bushels at 2s.	10	
Implements and clothing	20	
Rent—5 bushels, at 4s. per bushel	20	
		50

RETURN:

Twenty bushels at 2s. per
bushel   40

Farmer's loss   10

Upon the data assumed, it is not until all lands yielding less than thirty bushels per acre have been abandoned, and the rents of the lands yielding only thirty
bushels per acre have been reduced to a merely nominal consideration, that the opening of the ports, and
the reduction in the price of wheat from four to two
shillings per bushel can have the effect of raising the
rate of profit from fifty to a hundred per cent.
Nay, unless the process of withdrawing capital from
the inferior land, and of bringing down the rent
upon the superior, should be extremely gradual;
great loss would, in the first instance, be incurred,
and great temporary suffering experienced. To
prevent this loss, and to avert this suffering, the

return to a free trade in foreign agricultural produce should be made step by step, and should be preceded by the repeal of all taxes upon industry, particularly by the abolition of that most injurious of all taxes—the iniquitous tax of tithe. I have already given notice of a motion for the repeal of all such taxes, and for substituting in their stead a regulated property tax; and I trust I shall be able to follow up this motion, by presenting, for the favourable consideration of the Farmers of the United Kingdom, a measure for a return to a perfectly free trade in all the products of foreign agriculture, so cautious and so gradual, as ultimately to increase the profits of capital, and the wages of labour, throughout all the branches of national industry, without occasioning any immediate loss to the farmers, who have now invested their stock in tillage, or any throwing out of the labour actually employed upon this soil. I entertain, indeed, a full conviction, that a judicious return to a free trade in corn would so increase the general opulence and prosperity of the country, as to tend to raise, rather than to lower the rent of the landed proprietor. The grounds of this conviction I have already presented to the public*, and it is not necessary that I should here repeat them. My present purpose will be fully effected, if I shall be found to have succeeded in demonstrating to the intelligent farmer, that the necessary tendency of restrictions on the importation of foreign agricultural produce is, to reduce the rate of profit upon the capital, which seeks employment in domestic agriculture.

I have the honour to be,

Your obedient, humble servant,

R. TORRENS.

Chatham, Nov. 28, 1831.

---

* *Essay on the Corn Trade,* p. 156.

FINIS.

Printed by T. Brettell, Rupert Street, Haymarket, London.

THE

STATE OF THE NATION,

AT THE

CLOSE OF 1830.

Two Shillings.

STATE OF THE NATION,

AT THE

CLOSE OF 1830.

BY

T. POTTER MACQUEEN, Esq.

LONDON:

JAMES RIDGWAY, 169, PICCADILLY.

———

M.DCCC.XXXI.

TILLING, PRINTER CHELSEA.

STATE OF THE NATION,

&c.

MORE than six months have now elapsed, since my former remarks upon the Condition of the Country were laid before the Public. Although I can have no reason to complain of the manner in which those observations were generally received, yet there were not wanting individuals who were inclined to censure me as an *Alarmist*,—as one who had adopted a partial and distorted view of the state of the labouring classes. These self-complacent persons were entirely convinced that the " *System worked well;*" and, admitting the existence of some little temporary distress, were prepared to administer the matronly comfort of patience, under the assurance that affairs would soon amend, and permanent prosperity be created. His Majesty's Ministers seemed perfectly of this opinion.—They received repeated warnings from those who could have no interest in deceiving them. The wretchedness (and consequent discontent) of the peasantry was fully detailed ; still it pleased them to

B

cause their Sovereign to declare from his Throne, that merely *partial* distress existed; and in strict accordance with that declaration, they scouted Parliamentary Petitions, ridiculed the sources from whence those petitions emanated, and neglected every effort made in either House to enter upon enquiries calculated to elucidate the subject.— Six months have gone by; have their predictions been verified? has the cloud passed away? has the condition of the labourer (I beg pardon, I ought to say of the pauper,) been ameliorated? has the independence of the cottager been increased? has his dependence on the parish been diminished? have his morals, his happiness, his comforts, and his general welfare, been advanced? The answer is short, but decisive.—Look to the rates:—look to the expression of public feeling wherever it has found utterance— above all, look to the present wretched insecure state of public and private property, and the manifestation, day by day, more unequivocally expressed, of a determination to escape by violence from impending starvation.— That the late numerous conflagrations in so many parts of England are deeply alarming, I will readily admit; still I regard them as comparatively insignificant, when I look to the expression of public sentiment so openly declared on these lamentable occasions. In former disasters of this description, we have always found the peasantry anxiously disposed to defend the property of their employers, to assist their neighbours, to brave the danger whilst it lasted, to respect the goods of the sufferers, and to afford every aid and consolation in their power.—Now regard the contrast;—it is notorious, that at recent conflagrations, the people could scarcely be induced to work the engines, much less to act with promptness and energy in resisting the danger. In some places they have been engaged in plundering the premises, and have even beheld the work of destruction with an almost fiendish feeling of exultation, that so many more were reduced to their own level of pauperism and abject destitution.—At meetings in various parts of the country, when efforts have been made to enrol special constables, such efforts have been defeated, by the avowed and discontented refusal of those who ought to have formed such force. In a word, the old honest spirit of the peasantry is completely broken down;—no longer " *their country's pride;*"—no longer possessing the comforts which Goldsmith has described, as belonging to the inhabitants of his Arcadian Auburn:—

" The whitewash'd wall, the nicely sanded floor,
The varnish'd clock, that click'd behind the door;
The chest, contriv'd a double debt to pay,
A bed by night, a chest of drawers by day;
The pictures, plac'd for ornament and use,
The twelve good rules, the royal game of goose."

All this is now gone by; and were those, who have sneered at the ideas of the labourers trials, to visit, as I have done, their abodes in the agricultural coun ties, a fearful and horrid lesson might be conveyed. From the utter inadequacy of these hovels to the wants and numbers of their occupiers, and from the consequent packing together of sex and kindred, old and young, married and single, scenes have occurred, and are daily taking place, revolting to humanity, and too disgusting to place on record. The unfortunate creatures, callous to good feeling, and indifferent even to the appearance of propriety, sink into brutal degeneracy, and become the willing and desperate agents of the first evil spirit who may be sent to excite them to acts of insubordination and violence; and for all this what remedies have been devised? 'Not to institute, on the part of Government, a deliberate inquiry into the causes of this universal depression;—not to bear in mind, that, in the common course of human nature, man will not starve in silence;—but to take off the duty on beer, has been the sole and solitary measure of relief. Certainly, if this proceeding were intended to conciliate the labouring classes, never was dissatisfaction or ingratitude more strongly exhibited, than by the conduct of those classes to the Ministers, within a very few days of the operation of this act of grace. The measure itself I consider one of the worst that could have been suggested. A number of persons will be plunged into inevitable ruin, by entering on speculations for which they are wholly unfitted; spurious, perhaps deleterious, liquors will be produced, to an incalculable extent; but as no private individual can eventually compete with the large wholesale brewer, the trade will soon revert to its original proprietors. In the country districts, however, the publican, especially he who brews for himself, has no chance with the retail vender; the latter is removed from the power and authority of the magistrates; he may entertain gamblers, poachers, and vagrants, at his own pleasure, and at his own hours, and with common caution may defy summary conviction. Had the malt duty been taken off, a real and permanent benefit had arisen to all classes, and to no one more than the cottager. The master would have readily granted the use of his brewing utensils to his own labourers, and the peasant be enabled to obtain a genuine article, for the support of himself and his family, at a reasonable price, whilst the abuse of drugs and dangerous ingredients would be abandoned, from the comparative cheapness of the material.

But the poorest ranks in society are not the only sufferers; the yeomen, the respectable farmer, the shopkeeper, the tradesmen; in a word, the middle class of society, are now loud and clamorous in their complaints; and whilst the vengeance of the labourer is directed against machinery, the outcry of the other class is raised against taxation : under this impression, every abuse of patronage, every symptom of influence, every manifestation of favouritism, finds its way before the Public ; and in an age in which knowledge and information have made advances in a degree wholly inconceivable in former days, instances of this description are greedily listened to, and freely discussed. On these subjects, however, as is generally the case in popular ferments, much falsehood and much delusion have been exercised. In viewing the powers of machinery, as beneficial or adverse to the welfare of the labourer, there are many and conflicting facts to be regarded and considered. In the course of 1829, I made very minute enquiries as to the extent of the *automaton* power caused by machinery in England and Scotland, and after setting aside all powers connected with navigation, collieries, and mines, (shafts,) and draining, I believe I am warranted in concluding the following statement to be not very remote from the fact.

First, That to the close of 1828, the steam and mechanical engines of England and Scotland represent the power of 1,920,000 men.

Secondly, That these engines are put into operation by the power of 36,000 human beings, of whom a considerable proportion are women and children.

Thirdly, That they consequently give an addition to the population equal to 1,834,000 labourers.

Now let us ask how this calculation will affect taxation ?

The mode in which taxation has ever been computed has been in reference to *population.* Taking, then, the National Debt of this Country at £800,000,000., and the amount of Annual Revenue at £70,000,000., with a population of 22,700,000 souls, the proportion considered as a Poll Tax would be £3. 1s. 8d. for each individual; but as England is taxed in reference to Ireland in the proportion of five to three, the fair estimate will be about £4. for each inhabitant of England and Scotland. Apply, then, this calculation to the numbers I have given, and allow each man to represent so little as three in family, and the return will be 5,502,000 superseded human beings, with a deficiency in revenue of £22,008,000. It is evident, however, that this calculation, though *numerically* right, is *practically* wrong. No man will be rash enough to assert, were every engine to be destroyed to-morrow, that the personal labour of 1,834,000 men would be immediately substituted. The comparatively low price of the commodity has been caused by the quantity produced—a quantity, however, so infinitely exceeding the demand, as to glut every market in the known world to which English manufactures can be conveyed. In refer-

ence, then, to this part of the subject, it may be
fairly urged, that machinery of this description ought
to be subjected to a moderate scale of taxation, so
as to render an equitable return to the revenue for
the number of persons who may *really* be dispos-
sessed of employment.

Let it not, however, be supposed, that I entertain any apprehensions of this automaton power, *as·
far as it has yet extended itself;* or any desire to
destroy its present operation. My firm belief is,
that under a Government really disposed to look
to the means and resources of the country, ample
employment might be developed, and new provisions enacted for relief, which would speedily
rescue the labourers from their present dangerous
and unnatural state—would open new channels for
industry and capital, and render mechanical power
a most useful auxiliary, instead of being regarded,
as it now is, as usurping the remunerative occupation of the poor.

Amongst the various suggestions which have been
clamourously put forward, no greater delusion has
been urged than the panacea of a great reduction of
the rent of land. In this error there is, however,
much specious argument, requiring more close enquiry than what is usually bestowed. The tenant
who now pays £400. per annum for his farm, would
doubtless infinitely prefer paying £200. per annum,
but the real political question is, how far the substi-

tution of £200. for £400. would benefit the community. If it be said that the farmer by this diminution would be enabled to employ so many additional labourers, and at a higher rate of wages, the answer is obvious—unless the farmer can *beneficially* and *profitably* set to work the now unrequired labourer, the entire system is not merely wrong, but is in direct and hasty progress to destruction. If the population be so redundant in 1830 as to call for the sacrifice of half the landlord's rental to support such redundancy, in labour which will not pay itself, it follows, as a matter of course, that in 1840 he will be called upon to pro ceed farther in this agrarian experiment; and in 1850, he may himself cultivate his remaining acres. But let us look to the *facts* establishing the proportion of rent to produce, and deliberately enquire into the consequences of a large reduction.

I will assume two principles for the following calculation :—

First. That 25*s*. per acre be the average value of wheat land ; if it be less, the balance is in my favour.

Secondly. That such land yield an average produce of twenty-eight bushels per acre ; if it be more, then the advantage is on my side.

Thus then,

$$25s. = 300 \text{ pence,}$$

and 28 bushels = 112 pecks = 224 half-pecks ;

therefore $\frac{300}{224} = 1\frac{1}{4}\frac{1}{3}d.$ = the landlord's profit on each half-peck.

But the weight of the bushel of wheat, according to the Northampton Tables, averages 60 lbs., and when ground into meal, equals 58 lbs.

To compensate fully for this difference, say $1\frac{1}{2}d.$, or three half-pence, are the actual portion of *rent* out of every half-peck loaf.

But the average price of the half-peck loaf for the last three years is 1*s.* 4*d.*

Again, eight bushels of wheat form the average annual consumption of an able-bodied man.

Now 8 bushels of wheat = 64 half-peck loaves, $\therefore$ 64 + 6 farthings = $\frac{384}{4}$ = $\frac{96}{12}$ = 8*s.*

So that eight shillings is the portion of rent paid to the land owner. But the consumer pays 64 + 16 pence = $\frac{1024}{12}$ = £4. 5*s.* 2*d.*, of which eight shillings is the amount of rent.

Again,

The price of the quartern loaf = price of the quartern of flour plus the profits, past the farmer. Now there are 80 quarterns in a sack of flour.

$\therefore$ Price of quartern loaf = $\frac{1}{80}$ price of a sack of flour plus contingent profits.

A sack of flour is uniformly $\frac{4}{5}$ the value of 8 bushels of wheat.

$\therefore$ Quartern loaf = $\frac{4}{5} \cdot \frac{1}{80} = \frac{4}{400} = \frac{1}{100}$ price of 8 bushels of wheat plus contingent profits.

Hence the variation in price of the quartern loaf

$= \frac{1}{100}$th part the variation of the price of 8 bushels, or one quarter of wheat; or if wheat fall 100 pence, it will only make a difference of one penny in the quartern loaf, or one fourth in the daily consumption of an individual. With these calculations before us, allow that the object so called for of reducing rents 50 per cent. were accomplished, then the half-peck loaf would sell for 1s. $3\frac{1}{4}d$. instead of 1s. 4d.; a reduction of three farthings, the half of three half pence, being effected. The consumer, at the end of his twelve months, would expend £4. 1s. 2d. instead of £4. 5s. 2d., thus saving the 4s. in the year to be gained from the land owner.

But the average rental is estimated at £40,000,000. By this measure £20,000,000. would be at once struck off. Admitting, then, that one half of the present rental is expended in the necessaries of life, and the other half in the superfluities, which last is now removed; how will this affect the home market? the importer of foreign produce? the manufacturer? the artist? and the many dealers in articles of comparative luxury, who depend wholly on the excess of income beyond the supply of the necessaries of life? The landowner heretofore of £4,000. a-year is reduced to £2,000. The man will live on; he will reduce his establishment, and send many of his servants to the parish; he will be less hospitable, and limit as closely as possible his consumption in exciseable goods. His wife and daughters must

wear less of the manufactures of Spitalfields and
Glasgow, of Nottingham and Worcester; and
this, even should he possess *sufficient patriotism* to
remain at home, instead of letting his paternal man-
sion for any trifle it may produce, and carrying his
£2,000. of diminished income to a foreign residence, where it will still produce him the full enjoyment of his former and habitual comforts. The
holder of £1,000. is now brought down to £500.;
he too must make his sacrifices; he must give up
the use of wine; must, with his family, perform
every possible duty hitherto employing others;
must adopt a coarser and cheaper clothing, more
rarely renewed, &c. Say all this is done.—Is this
the mode to enrich a country, mainly dependent on
its commerce and manufactures, or to enable it to
bear up under a National Debt of £800,000,000?
If, then, we ask what becomes of the large difference in value between the proprietor of the soil,
and the consumer of the produce, it will be found
to be divided between two branches—*taxation*, and
the parties who obtain an intermediate interest and
profit. The farmer is satisfied with a return of 10
per cent. on his capital—the miller ought to be content with a much less rate of advantage,—but unfortunately of late years, other traders have arisen
whose share of actual profit, depending much on
the success and extent of their speculations, it is
impossible to define. In former days there existed

great jealousy in our common law towards acts
of engrossing, forestalling, and regrating; and
although it was held, that two of these acts must
mainly apply to goods purchased in open market, or on their way to such market, still the
market being then the only place where sales
were negociated, the principle of preventing high
prices to the community, by discouraging too
large stores in the possession of any individual,
was clearly established. There is a remarkable
case of this nature recorded in Easts Reports, I.
143, 145, the King versus Waddington, wherein
the court ruled that the following were offences
at common law, and not removed by the repeal
of the 5th and 6th of Edward VI., viz.

" Ingrossing large quantities of hops, by
buying, with intent to sell the same again at an
unreasonable profit, and thereby to enhance the
price."

Also, speaking of defendant,
" getting into his hands large quantities, by
contracting with various persons for the purchase, with intent to prevent the same being
brought to market, and to re-sell, at an unreasonable profit."

If this system be unlawful, in regard to hops,
surely it is a far greater injury in respect to
corn ; and the original intention of the law is
distinctly visible. I will not now discuss the

propriety of enforcing such regulation at the
present day, and under what are called the
principles of free trade; but in viewing the
causes which actually give a high price to the
consumer, it is only just to observe the *real* profits which occur to the farmer, and, through
him, to the owner of the soil. But then it is
said that the necessaries of life are infinitely
cheaper, and have fallen to the favourite and
assumed standard of 1790. In examining
strictly this assertion, however, which I readily
admit, if incontrovertible, were deserving of
much weight, I find that the line of distinction
may be thus drawn; and so far corroborates
most fully every former argument; that where
the effects of machinery are felt, prices are lowered; thus, muslins, calicoes, cotton goods,
silks, stockings, are certainly much cheaper,
whilst those depending on manual labour are
nearly the same as twenty years since. The tailor,
the shoemaker, the sadler, the coachmaker,
make no comparative diminution of charges.
The wages of household servants, especially of
male servants, preserve the same rate as twenty
years since, or during war prices. As to the
wages of tradesmen, &c. in 1790, the period to
which landowners are to be thrown back upon,
their amount, according to Parliamentary returns, were as follows:—carpenters, 2*s.* 6*d.* ;

bricklayers, 2*s*. 4*d*.; masons, 2*s*. 10*d*.; plumbers, 2*s*. 3*d*. Have these proportions been maintained in 1830?

Perhaps this is the first instance in the history of any civilized country, that a remedy for its oppressive distress has been proposed, by causing it to *retrograde* forty years. To admit that all the advances of learning, all the improvements of science, all the extension of knowledge, all the efforts of skill and industry, all the investments of enlarged capital; in a word, that the entire experience of forty years, must be regarded as a dead letter, and England be called upon to start anew from so remote a barrier. But even to this ingenious problem there is one small difficulty, which may probably solve the mystery of the difference of prices, and which may show the folly and injustice of asking any one class of the community to consent to the self-spoliation by which such a transfer can *only* be accomplished. I mean this incontrovertible fact, that in 1790, the National Debt was £200,000,000., that in 1830, it is £800,000,000. If, then, it be understood that the National Debt is to be thrown back to the scale of 1790, I suspect the landed interest will be perfectly content to make a similar reduction; but until such arrangement be completed, nothing can be more atrocious, than to call for the ruin of one class, for the immediate aggrandizement of another, but the eventual destruction of both.

Another favourite remedy, which has amongst its advocates many amiable and well meaning men, is the cultivation of waste lands at home. It has been suggested, that lands now useless might be cultivated, and thus furnish employ- ment within the country for the destitute poor. Since the reign of Queen Anne, above 4,000 enclosures have passed through Parliament, comprising above 6,000,000 of acres : of these, however, only 244 Acts, comprehending about 340,000 acres, were in operation previous to the accession of George III. It is evident, then, that the high prices of corn during the war, in- duced the enclosure of a *quality* of land which could only repay cultivation during the exist- ence of high prices, and which, on a perma- nent depreciation in the value of corn, must return to their former value ; and though they could not be restored to their unenclosed state, inasmuch as the common rights, tithes, &c. had probably been commuted, still the population, which a few years of prosperity and high prices had collected, would now become, for the most part, unoccupied, and burthensome. Any land, by outlay of capital, may be made to produce corn ; but it is obvious, that when the produce can realize less than the outlay, the cultivator must stop short, or be ruined. It is true, these frequent enclosures, by abolishing cottage rights, pasture for cattle, poultry walks, and other advantages once possessed by the peasantry, have largely swollen the rates. Still, it is remarkable that the unenclosed parishes within my own observation, present as grievous complaints of inadequate wages, and destitute pauperism, as those which are, and have long been, enclosed. The plain fact I believe to be this, that the system of the poor laws is so radically bad, at least in its present application, or rather perversion, that all emulation is destroyed. The labourer is taught from his birth to make no reserve, to act with neither energy nor enterprise, to abandon all confidence in his own resources, and to place his single and entire dependence on the overseer, to whom he resorts under every circumstance that may arise; granted that he has a cottage right of pasture for a cow and three sheep, he has not the capital for purchasing such stock. Time was, when every labourer had his pig and small stock of poultry; this is no longer to be found, except occasionally in retired and isolated situations. If, then, Epping Chase, or Dartmoor, or any other of the many places pointed out, were selected for home colonization, whence is the capital to arise? Let it be remembered, that this part of the subject has been carefully investigated before the Committee on Emigration. The expense of so settling a man, his wife, and three children, has been proved to be £75., before a blow could be struck in the way of cultivation. And as to establishing a sort of petty republic in such places, I would ask any rational man, what are the chances of its success in a country constituted of all grades, and depending on the relative workings of such various classes for its general prosperity. Look to Lanark, and the ingenious visions of Mr. Owen. Nothing could look more pretty on paper; rows of cottages, hospitals, literary institutions, chapels, wherein free trade in religion was some how or other to be arranged. The theory was delightful, and amply gratified many of the philosophers of the day. Need I ask, where are the *practical* results?

As to the proposed method of giving a rood, or half an acre of land to each cottage, the first question is, will the peasant commute his right to parish relief for such grants? If he do, it then becomes a kind of agrarian system; if not, you take nothing by your motion.

Having thus far performed the comparatively easy task of proving the existence of individual misery, public insecurity, general disaffection, and universal dismay, carried to an extent probably unknown since the wars of the Roses; we must, after such humiliating admissions, turn to the more doubtful subject of remedies. Under this consideration, a question of paramount importance presents itself, which I approach with diffidence; but which, at the same time, I feel I cannot, dare not, avoid—I mean the subject of Currency. In this discussion, the acts of 1819, known by the name of Peel's Bill, forms the primary object. The substitution of bullion for property, and this too at a period when the national debt was little short of £900,000,000.; a sum, which though recognisable so long as general property could be rendered liable to valuation, was almost inconceivable as a matter of *cash*. And yet a change of this unlooked-for, this unjust character, is the entire feature of that fatal measure. I think I am justified in using the term *fatal*, although I cannot be misunderstood in attributing, in the slightest degree, any improper motives to the zeal which dictated it; but what, I would ask, were the advantages then held out to the country by the adoption of that measure? We were told, it was essentially necessary, that we return to a natural standard of money; and that could this object be effected by a sacrifice of three or four per cent., the benefit to be obtained of permanent and integral security, were cheaply acquired. Now how have these desirable results been realized, and how far have the anticipations of the most strenuous advocates of the measure proved correct?

Only two years since, Mr. Bankes, one of the Committee from which the Bill of 1819 emanated, in speaking in the House of Commons of the *consequences* of that Act, stated, "that since 1819, events had proved, that a tremendous mistake had taken place, and that the depreciation in the value of money could not be considered less than 25, probably 40 or 50 per cent. Sir R. Peel himself has admitted, that the alteration was far greater than the Committee had supposed, but gave no positive opinion as to the extent. The person on whose authority that measure mainly rested, and who stated before the Committee his belief, that the utmost variation would be three or four per cent., was the late Mr. Ricardo. I have long had reason to believe, that, previous to the demise of that gentleman, he had seen his error, and deeply regretted the dire mischief which resulted from his calculation. This belief, however, has lately been placed beyond all doubt, by the assertion of Sir Francis Burdett in the House of Commons, that he himself had heard from Mr. Ricardo's own lips, that he was at length convinced of the fatal error which had been committed, and the ruinous consequences entailed upon the country.

Under these facts, the only two points of consideration are these:—first, Can we be *honestly* expected to discharge a present debt in *pounds*, formerly contracted in *crowns*? Can we be fairly called upon to make good engagements, commenced in depreciated paper, and now demanding in payment actual bullion? And, secondly, If the objection be in the fullest degree admitted, *can* we, in the present day, discharge such obligations with rentals reduced 30 per cent.; industry taxed until the *next straw* will be fatal, and our working population reduced to crime and despair? The limits of this work preclude me from further enquiries at this time; but it will be a point well worthy of the serious consideration of Ministers, if, under the mistakes and errors now no longer a matter of doubt, some fair and just principle of modification be not within their reach; which, though perhaps not satisfactory to *many*, may yet avert the ruin of *all*.

Under the present circumstances of the country, I can only conceive three measures calculated to produce permanent relief.

First, To alter the Corn Laws, so as to raise

the prices sufficiently, to enable the farmer to cultivate inferior soils, in a mode which would ensure returns for encreased labour; and if this be not done, every effort to cultivate *waste lands* will be in vain.

Secondly, To alter the present regulations respecting banking, and give greater facility to dealing in money.

And, thirdly, To provide new employment, and open fresh sources of labour, to the present *dangerously* superabundant population.

The first proposition I will at once dismiss, by declaring my belief that no Administration *dare* adopt it. The second may be divided into two parts; a partial repeal of the Act of 1819, and an improved system of public banking. The one of these is, in some measure, dependent on the other. If the *grinding* monopoly of the Bank of England were at an end, there can be no doubt of the policy of encouraging Banks upon the Scotch principle. In that case, the perfect security which that system would create, might warrant a return to some smaller paper than the £5. note. I do not ask for a renewal of £1. notes; but were even 50s. paper, to a certain extent, permitted, even on *special security*, the benefit would be most important, as it would tend to that diffusion of property, and facility of representing such property, which now constitutes so great a feature in the public distress.

The superior practical effects of the Scotch banking system are now generally appreciated. I will shortly state, that, at the period of the Union, the delegates for that country proved their shrewdness and good sense, by the introduction of a clause, providing, that the financial arrangements of each kingdom should be kept separate. Thus, the monopoly of the Bank of England, prohibiting more than six partners in any banking house, could not affect Scotland; consequently, her national banks consist of a great many partners, contributing various sums. And whilst in England, between 1798 and 1818, no less than 230 commissions of bankruptcy were issued against English establishments, inflicting ruin on individuals, and the severest shock to trade; the experience of a century records one only failure, (the Ayr Bank,) as resulting from the Scotch system. Of late years, I believe, *two* have taken place; one, a very small concern, occasioned by the defalcation of a confidential servant; the other, by the ignorance of the parties of the first lines of their business; but in neither case was any material loss occasioned to the public.

The third suggestion, as it refers to the most alarming evil, ought to obtain the most deliberate examination. I consider that the working classes of the country, in return for their loyal and peaceable conduct, have a right to expect from their rulers such regulations as may always ensure to the honest and industrious a return calculated to secure something beyond the supply actually required for the *necessaries* of life; and where this is not the case, it is evident that something wrong must exist, which is worthy of immediate attention and amendment. The extraordinary difference in the numbers of rate-payers and rate-receivers, may be inferred from the opposite Table, which was obtained by the Right Honourable Wilmot Horton, and is published in his work upon the Causes of Pauperism; but as it relates to the Hundred in which I reside, and is capable of illustrating my views, as well as Mr. Horton's proposed measures, I do not hesitate to avail myself of its authority.

This, then, clearly proves, that in this Hundred there is a redundant population of 681 able-bodied men; that taking their families in so low an average as four each, a total of 2,724 human beings will be given from a population of 13,512; or, in other words, one-fifth of the entire number are actually consuming *unprofitably* that extent of capital which ought to be divided amongst the remainder; and which, if so divided, by raising their wages at once 20

A Synopsis of the Results of certain Queries proposed to the Overseers of the Poor of the several Parishes within the Hundred of Redbornstoke, in the County of Bedford.

QUESTIONS.	Ampthill.	Cranfield.	Elstow.	Flitwick.	Houghton Conquest.	Kempston.	Lidlington.	Maulden.	Millbrook.	Marston-Moretaine.	Ridgmount	Slepping-ley.	Wilsham-stead.	Wootton.	The Hundred at large.
1. What is the number of acres within the parish of ———?	1928	3500	1522	1700	3380	5160	2520	2574	1450	4500	2248	1060	3027	3468	38,037
2. What is the amount of its population?	1719	1272	644	537	769	1625	811	1268	425	1166	956	370	789	1161	13,512
3. What is the number of rate-payers?	198	100	40	40	42	86	50	108	42	62	92	33	39	50	982
4. What is the number of able-bodied labourers, accounting two boys for one man?	136	129	103	88	155	370	152	130	85	260	123	63	158	225	2,177
5. What proportion of those able-bodied labourers receive assistance from the parochial funds?	32	64	24	40	51	90	48	46	23	70	31	20	25	82	616
6. What is the number of persons composing their families, and with them dependent, either wholly or partially, on the parochial funds for support?	290	331	151	160	170	550	263	108	140	700	300	51	130	442	3,786
7. What is the rate of relief granted to able-bodied pauper labourers?	*s. d.*	*s. d.*	*s. d.*	*s. d.*	*s. d.*	*s. d.*	*s. d.*	*s. d.*	*s. d.*	*s. d.*	*s. d.*	*s. d.*	*s. d.*	*s. d.*	*s. d.* *s. d.*
———— single men?	4 6	3 6	3 6	3 6	3 6	3 6	3 6	4 0	3 6	3 6	3 6	3 6	4 0	3 6	From 3 6 to 4 6
———— man and wife without children?	5 0	5 0	5 0	4 0	5 6	5 0	3 6	4 0	3 6	4 0	5 0	4 0	4 6	5 0	,, 3 6 ,, 5 6
———— ditto, with one child?	6 0	6 0	6 6	5 6	6 0	6 0	6 0	5 6	6 0	6 0	6 0	....	6 0	6 0	,, 5 6 ,, 6 6
———— ditto, with two children?	8 0	7 0	7 6	7 6	7 6	7 0	8 0	7 0	7 0	7 6	7 6	....	7 6	7 0	,, 7 0 ,, 8 0
———— ditto with three children?	10 0	8 6	....	9 0	8 6	8 6	9 0	8 0	9 0	8 6	9 0	....	9 0	8 6	,, 8 6 ,, 10 0
———— ditto, with four children?	12 0	9 0	....	11 0	9 6	10 0	10 6	9 0	....	10 0	10 6	9 0	10 0	10 0	,, 9 0 ,, 12 0
———— ditto, with five children?	14 0	....	....	13 0	11 0	11 0	12 6	....	....	....	....	....	11 0	11 0	,, 2 0 ,, 14 0
8. What system is adopted with respect to the employment of able-bodied labourers	In almost every instance in digging materials for and repairing the parish roads.														
9. What sum has been expended in the maintenance of the poor during the last three years?	£. 3947	£. 4050	£. 2123	£. 2357	£. 3497	£. 7630	£. 3895	£. 2350	£. 1546	£. 6472	£. 3189	£. 892	£. 2781	£. 6012	£. 50,761
10. What proportion of that expenditure has been incurred for the support of *able-bodied labourers?*	465	870	1248	1023	1350	1509	768	300	690	3000	381	....	720	1350	13,674
11. What proportion of that expenditure has been incurred for the support of *their families?* (N.B. This return includes all the allowances made to the paupers of the whole parish)	210	840	138	1167	312	1500	462	....	135	900	378	....	450	2937	9,429
12. Is there a poor-house in the parish?	Yes.	Yes.	Yes.	Yes.	Yes.	Yes.	Yes.	Yes.	Yes.	Cottage.	No.	No.	Yes.	Yes.	In 12 out of 14 Parishes No.
13. What proportion of the labourers now belonging to the parish would be sufficient to perform all the labour necessary to be habitually performed, including repair of roads, &c.?	118	104	78	72	125	166	117	110	58	174	82	53	118	121	1,496
14. What number can be spared?	18	25	25	16	30	204	35	20	27	86	41	10	40	104	681
Annual increase of male population, most of whom are labourers	12	7½	6	3	7½	13	4½	15½	3½	10½	9	3	2½	13½	111
Number of acres to each able-bodied labourer	..	27	14	20½	22	14	16½	20	20½	17⅓	18	17	19	15½	18¾
Average annual amount of poor's-rates for ten years, up to Lady-Day, 1827	1381	1338	625	376	1150	2347	1178	742	546	2064	940	279	800	1948	15,714
Annual amount of poor's-rates per acre	..	*s. d.* 7 7	*s. d.* 8 2	*s. d.* 7 2	*s. d.* 7 8	*s. d.* 9 1	*s. d.* 9 3	*s. d.* 5 9	*s. d.* 7 6	*s. d.* 9 2	*s. d.* 8 4	*s. d.* 5 3	*s. d.* 5 3	*s. d.* 11 2	*s. d.* 7 10

per cent., would relieve them from their present too powerful temptations to criminal courses. But apply this principle, in the first place, to the entire County of Bedford, and subsequently to five other leading agricultural Counties:—

Counties.	Population.	Surplus.	
Bedford ········	85,000 ····	one-fifth ····	17,000
Bucks ··········	136,800 ···	———— ····	28,160
Herts ··········	132,400 ····	———— ····	26,400
Kent············	434,600 ····	———— ····	86,920
Norfolk ·········	351,300 ····	————· ····	70,260
Sussex ····· ····	237,700 ····	———— ····	47,540

266,340

£8. per head being the average expense of main-   8
   tenance of paupers throughout England.   ———————

£2,130,720

Thus, then, it appears, that, in these six Counties, the superabundant population may, on the lowest calculation, be estimated at 266,340 human beings, with an aggregate annual taxation of £2,130,720. upon the industry of the country. If, then, the measure which I have so long but so fruitlessly advocated, were effected, whereby each of these now wretched and destitute persons would be placed in a condition where he might exchange his honest industry for a rate of wages sufficient to enable him to consume to the extent of £4. per annum of British manufactures; the result would be an actual saving to the country of £12. for each person so provided, or an annual addition to the wealth of the mother country of £3,196,080., and this merely in reference to the six counties already enumerated. Take the total superabundant population of the Empire, and allow sufficient time for the necessary machinery to expand itself and get into play, and a system of gradual remunerative employment might be created, to an extent which can scarcely be contemplated.*

In speaking of emigration, or rather of colonization, as a measure so calculated to relieve the superabundant population of this country, as to deserve (especially under present circumstances) the most serious attention of Government, I would, first, wish to protest against the mistake so continually made of confounding colonization with transportation; whereas no two points can be more distinctly contrary; the one being necessarily a wilful and voluntary act, the other forced and compulsory. If then the voluntary going forth to a distant land is to be so misrepresented, our Cadets and Writers in our Indian possessions are to be regarded as transports. I can hardly conceive a more nar-

---

* Vide Appendix, A. and B.

row-minded prejudice, than to tell the people
of England that they may not avail themselves
of territories which have been obtained and
possessed by means of taxation levied on themselves, and constitutionally held for their benefit.
What I have ever complained of, is the *practical*
effect of our laws of settlement, that they hold
together our people in unmanagable masses, as
if within the limits of an enchanter's circle;
beyond which, if they presume to extend themselves, they are liable to be seized, if overtaken
by distress, and dragged back almost as criminals to their original place of confinement, their
own registered parish; whereas, give them fair
scope for their industry, their talents, and their
perseverance; allow them to ascertain the real
value of the change; assure them of the enjoyment of the rights of British subjects; convince
them of a certainty of constant and largely productive labour; establish a system by which
these advantages would be made known; and
the only difficulty will be in the selection and
limitation. The measures proposed for encouraging the colonization of public claimants,
would secure a supply of a superior and educated rank. I had very lately an application
from a distinguished Officer of a large and favourite regiment, for the purpose of ascertaining
the probability of my recommendation being

carried into effect; as in that case there existed
a disposition in many of the officers on half pay
of the —— regiment to form themselves into a
community or district, in which they had no
doubt of being joined by many, perhaps most,
of the pensioners of lower ranks. The advantages of such a system were too evident to require demonstration.

The system of transportation ought to be
entirely changed. It is obvious that it cannot,
at least as at present administered, form an
efficient secondary punishment. It is a most
injudicious mode of disposing of what are commonly called gentlemen convicts, who are value-
less as labourers, and are the proper inmates for
home penitentiaries. In a word, it now daily
becomes more evident that Australia should
emerge from the situation of a penal colony;
that she possesses means infinitely too important to become a mere refuge for crime, or to
be marked as an asylum for the outcasts of society; and that if it be held necessary to per-
severe in the punishment of transportation,
some less distant and less populous place should
be selected. In fact, by the method now recommended, transportation would be infinitely
diminished. *Forced* emigration I wholly dis-
claim; but I am convinced, that were the
means of voluntary colonization freely afforded

to the destitute before such destitution had driven them to courses which produce transportation, much of the forced necessity for banish-
ment would be avoided. The moral advantages
are equally obvious: instead of separating a
man from his wife and children, plunging both
parties into habits of vice and depravity, and
enormously encreasing the home rates to maintain those who are now deprived of their proper
head and protector; the entire family might be
transferred from poverty and discontent to independence and comfort ; and this without any
real additional outlay, if the various expenses
arising from the different parties now responsible were consolidated and rendered effective.
Take for example, the cases of the unfortunate
persons who are now (or probably soon will be)
under sentence of transportation as concerned
in the late disturbances, and whose misconduct
may be wholly attributed to their want and
misery. These persons will cost the country
about £34. a head to send out, and £26. per
head of subsequent annual expense, their average cost to their own parishes as paupers being
heretofore £8.; but their wives and children
being now thrown on the parish, will each average £8.; and this too, whilst the annual expenses drawn for New South Wales from the
British Treasury amount to little less than

£500,000. sterling. From these respective sources a fund might be created, which, added to the bounty or voluntary encouragement offered by the Australian Settler, who only asks for manual labour to ensure his own prosperity, would shortly enable the starving labourer to exchange his present state of squalid and hopeless misery, for one of remunerative employment and satisfied content.

To those who may yet entertain any doubt of the propriety, nay, I would say, of the absolute necessity of colonization, I would recommend an attentive perusal of the Report of the Committee on Emigration, April, 1827. There they may find an elaborate enquiry into the distresses of the various working classes, and the probable chances of amelioration or encreasing wants; they will find there the opinions of a body of men, whose names and characters are sufficient to relieve them from every suspicion of improper motive; and who, after giving the subject every possible consideration, arrive at this deliberate resolution, 1st, That there is little hope that any revival of trade can bring back the employment of the distressed manufacturers; 2dly, that satisfied of the efficiency and permanency of the benefits to be afforded by emigration, they recommend a grant of public money to be devoted to such desirable object. This Com-

mittee, be it recollected, made special enquiries into the condition of the suffering hand-loom
weavers ; but every proof of misery then produced, and every argument urged in favour of
colonization, is tenfold applicable to the starving
agricultural labourer of the present day.

The result, then, of these enquiries may be
thus briefly stated. In England, with every
constitutional and legal manifestation of humanity, dire and deep distress exists; not a
week passes, but some poor wretch dies by his
own hands, or by actual want, in the streets of
London. With all our boasted charity, our hospitals and asylums, such things occur. And
why? From privation, worked up to insanity;
from the unhappy patient outstripping hope,
and finding no resource beyond him but the
grave.— Grant what I ask, and you disarm despair; you offer to the redundant population a
resource, which otherwise they never could
have contemplated; and you subtract from the
ranks of misery to add to the class of happy,
independent, and grateful occupiers of another
Britain.

APPENDIX.

(A.)

Here, then, is a country prepared to our very hands, for all the purposes of civilized life. While England is groaning beneath a population for which she cannot provide bread, here is an unmeasured extent of rich soil that has lain fallow for ages, and to which the starving thousands of the north are beckoned to repair. *The great want of England is* EMPLOYMENT; *the great want of New South Wales is* LABOUR. England has more mouths than food; New South Wales has more food than mouths. England would be the gainer by lopping off one of her superfluous millions; New South Wales would be the gainer by their being planted upon her ample plains. In England the lower orders are perishing for lack of bread; in New South Wales they are, like Jeshurun, "waxing fat and kicking" amid superabundance. In England the master is distracted to find work for his men; in New South Wales he is distracted to find men for his work. In England the capitalist is glad to make his three per cent.; in New South Wales he looks for twenty. In England capital is a mere drug—the lender can scarcely find a borrower, the borrower can scarcely repay the lender; in New South Wales capital is the one thing needful—it would bring a goodly interest to the lender, and would make the fortune of the borrower.

Then let the capitalist wend his way hither, and his one talent will soon gain ten, and his ten twenty. Let the labouring poor come hither, and if he can do nothing in the world but dig, he shall be welcome to his three and twenty shillings a-week, and shall feast on fat beef and mutton at a penny or two-pence per pound. Let the workhouses and gaols disgorge their squalid inmates upon our shores, and the heart-broken pauper and the abandoned profligate shall be converted into honest, industrious, and jolly-faced yeomen.

Average Retail Prices of Articles in New South Wales, May 22, 1830.

MEAT.		s.	d.		s.	d.
Beef	per pound	0	1	to	0	2
Mutton	——	0	1½	—	0	3
Pork	——	0	5	—	0	6
Veal	——	0	4	—	0	6
Ham, { English	——	2	0	—	2	6
{ Colonial	——	1	0	—	1	3
Fish	——	0	2	—	0	4

BREAD.

		s.	d.		s.	d.
Finest Wheaten, per loaf of } two pounds }	——	0	4	—	0	5
Seconds (none made but for prisoners).						
Rice	——	0	2½	—	0	3

VEGETABLES.

		s.	d.		s.	d.
Potatoes	per cwt.	6	0	—	8	0
Yams (Island)	——	5	0			
Pumpkins	per pound	0	1			
Cucumbers	per dozen	1	0	—	1	6
Radishes	per bunch	0	2	—	0	3
Cabbages	per head	0	2	—	0	3

D

		s.	d.		s.	d.
Turnips	per bunch	0	2	—	0	3
Beans	per peck	1	6	—	2	0
Peas	——	2	0	—	3	0

FRUIT.

		s.	d.		s.	d.
Oranges	per dozen	1	0	—	1	6
Apples	——	1	6	—	3	0
Pears	——	0	6	-	3	0
Peaches (sometimes 1s. per bushel)	——	0	0½	—	3	0
Loquets	per quart	1	0	—	1	6
Grapes	per pound	1	0	—	1	6
Nectarines	per dozen	0	6	—	2	6
Apricots	——	0	6	—	2	6
Raspberries	per quart	1	6	—	2	0
Green Figs	per dozen	0	6	—	1	6
Melons	each	0	2	—	2	0

POULTRY.
(Dear in consequence of drought.)

		s.	d.		s.	d.
Fowls	per cple.	2	6	—	3	0
Ducks	——	4	0	—	5	0
Geese	——	10	0	—	12	0
Turkies	——	11	0	—	14	0
Eggs (dear in consequence of drought)	per dozen	2	0	—	3	0
Butter (Fresh)	per pound	0	9	—	1	0
Cheese (Colonial, as good as English	——	0	5	—	0	9

DRINK.

			s.	d.		s.	d.
Wine,	Madeira	per dozen	25	0	—	36	0
	Port	——	40	0	—	50	0
Rum (best Jamaica)		per gall.	8	4	—	10	6
Gin,	best Schedam	——	13	6			
	Colonial	——	10	0			

		s.	d.		s.	d.
London Ale	per dozen	13	6	—	16	0
London Porter	——	14	0	—	15	0
Colonial Beer	per gall.	1	8	—	2	6
Colonial Ale (very superior)	per dozen	8	4			
TEA, (by the chest 1s. 6d. per pound	} per pound	2	0	—	2	4
COFFEE	——	1	0	—	1	9

SUGAR.

		s.	d.		s.	d.
Mauritius	per pound	0	3¾			
West India	——	0	4	—	0	5
Loaf	——	0	9	—	0	10

SOAP.

		s.	d.		s.	d.
English (seldom used)	——	0	5	—	0	6
Colonial (equal to English)	—— —-	0	3	—	0	5

CANDLES.

		s.	d.		s.	d.
English moulds	per pound	0	6	—	1	0
Colonial (very good)	——	0	5	—	0	6

SPICES—much cheaper than in England.

SALT.

		s.	d.		s.	d.
Best Liverpool	per basket	1	6	—	2	0
Colonial	per pound	0	1½			

VINEGAR.

		s.	d.
English (best)	per gallon	3	0
Colonial (good)	——	1	6

TOBACCO.

		s.	d.		s.	d.
Best Brazil	per pound	2	0	—	3	0
Colonial (nearly as good)	—— -	1	3	—	1	6
Horses (not including first rate bloods)	} per head.	£10		—	£35	
Horned Cattle (sometimes sold at 9s. per head)	} ——	£1		—	£2	

		s.	d.		s.	d.
Sheep	—–—	3	6	—	7	6

Clothing and Haberdashery—about £25. per cent. above
fair English prices: by purchasing a piece of cloth, a
suit of good clothes may be had at about £5. or £6.

Furniture—cheaper than in England.

WAGES.

		s.	d.		s.	d.
Carpenters .... per day		7	0	—	9	0
Bricklayers and Masons	—–—	7	0	—	9	0
Day Labourers	—–—	3	6	—	4	0

*** The above has been compiled with the utmost care,
and has received the corrections of the most respectable
merchants and retail dealers.

Sydney Gazette,
May 22, 1830.

(B.)

Extract from the Sydney Gazette. Aug. 12, 1830.

Wanted in Sydney the following Tradesmen and Mechanics.

Bread and Biscuit Bakers.
Butchers.
*Boat Builders.
Bellows Makers.
*Blacksmiths.
Bell Hangers.
Brass Founders.
Brewers.
Boatmen.
*Brick Makers.
*Bricklayers.
*Collar Makers.
Confectioners.
Chair Makers.
*Curriers.
*Carpenters.
*Caulkers.
*Coopers.
Cart and Coach Makers.
Compositors.
Candle Makers.
Cabinet Makers.
Cheese Makers.
Coach Spring Makers.
Cooks.
Colliers.
*Coppersmiths.
Cutlers.

Dyers.
Dairywomen.
Distillers.
*Engineers.
Farriers.
Flax Dressers.
Fencers.
Fellmongers.
Gardeners.
Glaziers.
Glassblowers.
Glue Makers.
Gilders.
Gunsmiths.
Hair Dressers.
Hat Makers.
*Harness Makers.
Horse Breakers.
Hoop Benders.
*Joiners.
Japanners.
Ironmongers.
Iron Founders.
Leather Dressers.
Lime Burners.
Locksmiths.
Millers.
Mealmen.

*Millwrights.
Milliners.
Malsters.
Mustard Makers.
Nurserymen.
Nailers.
Painters.
Parchment Makers.
Ploughmen, and Makers.
Pump Makers.
Paper Makers.
*Plaisterers.
Provision Curers.
Plumbers.
Printers.
Quarrymen.
Rope Makers.
Sadlers.
Shoe Makers.
*Sawyers.
Shipwrights.
*Stone Masons, and Cutters, and Setters.

Sail Makers.
*Slaters.
Shepherds.
Sheep Shearers.
Soap Makers.
Sign Painters.
Sailors.
Sail Cloth Makers.
Starch Makers.
Straw Plat & Hat Makers.
Tanners.
*Tinners.
Tailors.
Tin Plate Workers.
Tobacco Growers.
Tobacco Pipe Makers.
Tallow Melters.
Vine Dressers.
Upholsterers.
Wheelwrights.
Wool Sorters.
Weavers.
Wire Drawers.

Those marked * are particularly wanted, and earn 10s. a day, and upwards, all the year round. Engineers and Millwrights earn 20s. a day. All articles of provisions particularly cheap. Beef and Mutton, 2d. per pound by the joint, and 1d. by the quarter; Tea, 1s. 6d. per pound; Sugar, 3d.; Indian Corn, 1s. 6d. per bushel.

PROPOSAL

FOR

THE ESTABLISHMENT

OF

VILLAGE SCHOOLS OF INDUSTRY,

SUBMITTED TO THE CONSIDERATION

OF

LAND-OWNERS AND CLERGYMEN.

LONDON:

EDWARD BULL, 26, HOLLES-STREET,

CAVENDISH-SQUARE.

1831.

LONDON:
PRINTED BY THOMAS DAVISON, WHITEFRIARS.

VILLAGE SCHOOL OF INDUSTRY.

"Teach a child what it will be useful for him to know when he is a man."

LOCKE.

I. The object of such a school is to make industry the leading feature : to make it subservient to the formation of character, and the acquisition of as much knowledge as may be deemed necessary : to render it beneficial to the neighbourhood, and to make it pay its own expenses.

II. A piece of ground should be provided of a sufficient size, according to the number of children to be taken. It should be the property of the owner of the school; or if on lease, the landlord should pay for all improvements at the expiration of the lease. A piece of waste land would not be objectionable (provided the soil were easy to cultivate), because it would be cheaper, and the result, if successful, would be more decided.

III. A man should be hired to cultivate the ground, part with the plough or spade, part as a garden. He must be intelligent generally, and understand his business thoroughly; he should be of a kind disposition, and should comprehend and approve the objects of the school; he should undertake to communicate to the children all the knowledge he possessed, and consider their instruction as of still more importance than his manual labour—not, however, neglecting the latter; he should direct their labour in the most useful manner, both for the garden and themselves.

IV. A schoolmaster should be obtained for the direct teaching of the children. He must understand that the chief sphere of his teaching would be in the garden and work-shops—making himself acquainted with the processes going on, and with the principles of gardening and farming as well as the practice. By means of the interest which the child would feel in the objects before him—their nature and uses—much more would be learnt than through any system of book instruction not illustrated by visible and tangible facts. The qualities and produce of the soil, and the habits of the animals fed upon it, would naturally become subjects of inquiry, and afford opportunities of useful information. The schoolmaster must work with the children. When the gardener points out the work required for the garden, the master must distribute the work, and superintend it. The children must work in groups, under monitors, as far as is possible. Each child must be employed, down to the very youngest, who must have some work allotted, as picking stones, sticks, counting cabbages, &c.

V. The labour must be adapted to the age; and regularly at stated hours, the children must adjourn to the school, or take lessons in the open air, according to the weather or convenience. There they would learn reading, &c.; great part of the lessons, exclusive of scriptural instruction, would consist of explanations respecting the objects, animate and inanimate, in the garden, taken from books adapted to this purpose. Besides gardening, the children should be taught such trades as local and other circumstances might render desirable: masonry, shoemaking, tailor's, carpenter's, blacksmith's work—netting, knitting, &c.: some of these might form also direct subjects of instruction.

VI. The girls, under the direction of a competent female superintendent, should be taught household-work, washing, cooking, baking, &c. They should not be exempt from out door-labour—its healthiness is a recommendation for all.

VII. A cottage must be found for the gardener and schoolmaster, but all the other buildings should be erected by the labour of those persons and the children. The convenience and comforts of the inmates should grow gradually, and in proportion to their own exertions. If instructed in classes, they might use any small room that could be obtained for their temporary accommodation. The first thing to be erected in addition would be a large shed. If this were begun on a proper plan, it would be enlarged by degrees till it answered every purpose. The children would soon pave the floor with stones, if directed. The building would serve for a school, for work-shops, and for a place of exercise in bad weather.

VIII. A great object would be to collect manure ; cattle must be kept for this purpose, and every other means resorted to. The children might be usefully employed sometimes in collecting and fetching it from a distance. The parents might be encouraged to keep pigs, and be supplied sometimes with food for them, giving the manure in return.

IX. Besides the regular work of the garden, &c., the children should have gardens of their own, of which the whole produce should be their own, to carry home to the parents. The children should be allowed to bring linen from home to wash, and to make articles of furniture for presents to the parents, or to mend any articles about the house.

X. The objects of the school should be fully and patiently explained to the parents, who should be invited to second them. The privilege of purchasing the garden produce, as well as the manufactures of the school, at a lower price from the school shop, should be offered to the parents ; and the rewards of the children should be composed of such articles as would be valuable to their families. Give the parents, in short, as great an interest as possible in the school, as experience pointed out the best mode of doing it. Let them feel the school to be, as it were, their own. Let them see that they reaped all the advantage, except in the gradual improvement of the property ; but let this improvement benefit them in a *palpable* manner. Here they might bring their assistance, viz.—labour to the school, as a common fund ; a DEPOSIT of labour, to be returned in produce, or in education to the children.

Whatever trade a parent exercised, let him at his leisure time give his labour or instruction to the school. The complaint is that the parent cannot get employment—then he would have more time to give to the school. Invite a stocking-maker, or weaver, &c., from an over-peopled manufactory, to settle near the school, teach the children his trade, work for the neighbourhood, and vary his labour, or work at leisure hours in the garden. His health, comfort, and character would improve. It would be easy to keep a labour-account of hours' work against every one who gave his labour to the garden; this would be valued and repaid in produce*.

XI. As the children would improve daily, and their labour become more valuable the longer they staid, it would be right to enter into a contract with the parents, to continue the children at the school a certain number of years. This would not only repay the school more completely, but would promote the general objects of the establishment;—the formation of good habits, and the acquisition of practical knowledge. If the children were detained at school when they could earn something, and the parents might wish to remove them on that account, this would be precisely the test of the experiment. By keeping them out of the labour market, the price of labour would rise, and the parents would be benefited; if the children's labour were worth sixpence a-day in the market, it would be worth sixpence to the school. At this period the proprietor might decline receiving the payment due, or give a meal a day, or make some arrangement mutually satisfactory. Besides, in making the contract at first, the parent, instead of giving the child no education at all, secured an education during the years when the child's labour would have been worthless; followed by a period of profitable labour at school. And again, at the end of this term, the boy's labour would be worth much more than it would have been without such training.

XII. Of course, tools of all kinds must be provided by the proprietor; the mode in which he would look for remuneration would be, the payment of the children, their labour in garden produce, and the permanent improvement in land and buildings. He would also form a collection of books for the school, containing the requisite information on the subjects of their labours.

XIII. The Bible should not be made a class-book, but read at stated times as a book of divine instruction, and proper passages

* This is no more than what is done at the Brighton work-house. Every vegetable used in the house is valued, credited to the garden, and debited to the house. All master-workmen charge for the time of their men to a quarter of a day; and the mode of making a bill is to calculate time, materials, and profit.

learned out of it. Doctrinal religion should not be taught in the school: but what is taught should be entirely practical, and made to go hand in hand with the work. Mutual regard and kindness should be hourly insisted upon as the sum of practical religion; and our destiny in a future life should be represented as depending on this, according to the text:—" I was hungry, and ye gave me meat, &c." Then the principles of independence and prudence should be inculcated; and the nature and consequences of improvident marriages should be pointed out to the children, when they were old enough to understand such considerations.

There should be a plan of the garden and premises. This plan should be studied in the school, and would exemplify the elementary principles of land-measuring, &c. Each boy, as he grew old enough, should make one for himself on a reduced scale. The children should learn the distances, in feet, of all parts of the garden, and the number of square feet in the whole, and in each part; the plants growing in each bed, their number, value, &c. The children should be allowed to propagate plants for themselves, for pleasure or for sale; and in the course of time might have the means of erecting a green-house.

Exact registers should be kept of all the occupations and expenses of the school: these should form the study of the children, and from them the arithmetical sums should be chiefly taken.

XIV. A Saving's Bank should be established in the school for the children.

——————

The fundamental principle of the above plan is, that every labourer should be taught all the knowledge which bears immediately upon his situation. This should form the school exercises.

Labour must be made more honorable, as it was in the early times. It is to be valued, not only because it is " the source of wealth," but because it is the only means of forming virtuous and religious habits. It subdues the passions and appetites. It causes natural hunger for simple diet, and weariness for natural rest. Idle habits and stimulating food are the certain fore-runners of moral ruin. Judicious labour, spare diet, and good example and instruction, will not only form good habits, but cure bad ones. There is, therefore, a double error, or vice, or crime on our part, in allowing bad habits to be formed at all.

It is the aim of these remarks to investigate, if there be ground to believe, that a gentleman, disposed to prevent pauperism, and misery, and vice, has the power to do so without a great outlay of capital, which he may not possess. And even if the capital could be found, we want to be assured that the same evils would not recur, in a certain period, when the capital has been expended. Emigration is a remedy liable to this objection. If it answered at first, the same causes which produced the present apparent surplus of popu-lation would produce it again. Emigration was formerly prohibited, now it is encouraged. This, like every other thing, should be left perfectly free. A man with a certain capital finds a new mode of increasing his surplus produce, either by emigration or foreign trade ; the government immediately take a useful producer, make him an unproductive consumer, in order to prevent the trader from increasing his surplus produce. Thus the country loses the labour of the work-man, turned constable or preventive man, and the surplus produce of the trader ; and creates one enemy, and one sinecurist, whose trade is to rob the public.

Classes of mere gentlemen, of men of science and literature, are useful and necessary ; but men of science and literature, and would-be literature, are increased far beyond what is desirable. While a por-tion of our literature is good, a portion of it is most pernicious to the public. Besides these classes, there is a large one of idle, abandoned consumers, whose sole object in life is to corrupt and plunder society : they have no other idea of existence. All ranks are so poisoned with the desire of show, idleness, and luxuries, that the sole object is to consume without producing : and to set a few stout hands to work, while all the rest stand still, look on, and quarrel for the produce.

Our notion is, that by the establishment of village schools of in-dustry, the vagabond children of cities, as well as the children of the industrious poor, might be educated to habits of productive labour, simple diet, virtue, and religion.

If it be asked, what is to become of the children when they leave school ? we reply, if they could not then find work elsewhere, let them remain, and be paid for their work in food, on the premises. When a child was grown up in good habits and useful works, he *would* get a good place. But why should any one employ him?—solely, because his labour would be worth more than his wages. If so, why give that valuable labour away? Why not keep a man who produces more than he consumes? If every labourer produces more than he consumes, the more labour the more surplus produce. Why then does one man reject a labourer, and another hire him? Merely because one has capital, and the other not; or one man employs the labourer for show and vanity, and not profit. But if a man had not the vanity to have idle people about him, every man he employed would produce more than he consumed; and then the more labour the more surplus produce.

But a man wants capital for this. But where is the surplus produce or capital produced by the lad during his education? In the school, which has grown from a simple shed to a large establishment, from a waste to a fertile garden*. Then every lad properly educated, creates enough capital during youth to work upon afterwards. Say that during the last year of his education he has dug and sown the ground: then he leaves the school, and leaves his produce for another. But, had he remained, he might have lived on that crop, have had a surplus, and dug and sowed for another year. Then why dismiss him?—You have kept him while his labour was least valuable —you dismiss him when it is most valuable.

As a proof that each labourer can, out of his own labour, earn enough capital to work on for ever, we have only to ask, who made the capital of the world? The labourers have created enough capital, not only for themselves, but for all the world besides.

Therefore, it should seem that there is no occasion to dismiss the lads at the end of their education, for want of capital, since they have already produced it.

This argument presumes that the owner consumes no part of the produce unproductively; that it is not applied to any thing not

* For the proof of the practicability of such a school, we must go to Fellenberg. He has been at work forty years with perfect success. After forming his chief agricultural school, he sent ten boys, with a master, into a wood. He supplied them with food, tools, &c.; they cleared the ground, cultivated it, and built a house. In seven years they maintained themselves, and the value of the improvements greatly exceeded the capital laid out. He considers that the world has never yet seen the importance of labour in forming character. He thinks two hours a day given to direct instruction quite enough: the children consider this as a recreation. But the master works with the children, and instructs them by conversation, giving a moral tone to their intercourse with each other.

essential to the maintenance of the establishment; but that all who consume, re-produce by labour, the food and clothes, &c. they consume : and that a judicious division of labour is employed.

We reckon the superintendence of the head of the establishment as labour. His management and direction render the labour of others more productive. We would introduce the division of labour, and all improvements, as far as possible. We would not turn the schoolmaster into a labourer; let him teach as much as is useful, and labour or direct as much as is useful.

The really useful and practical knowledge, which has been accumulated by the studies of men of science, might be transferred to these schools. By judiciously hiring land, as the children grew up, they could, as has been shown, support themselves*: or they could hire themselves in the labour market, when it would remunerate them; or they might emigrate, as valuable servants, to those capitalists who have purchased estates in new countries. This would be natural emigration. But to emigrate by act of parliament, supposes an evil arising out of fixed causes; which evil will assuredly return again, unless the causes are known and altered. In speaking of the possibility of conducting a School of Industry, or any establishment for enabling the poor to support themselves without charity, we should not forget the assistance to be continually derived from investing the surplus of their labour in machinery, which should work *for* them, instead of *against* them. All the contrivances for saving labour which have been invented, should gradually, as capital permitted, be brought to the assistance of the labourer. Machinery has improved the condition of the labourer by supplying him with cheaper clothes, and by preparing his food cheaper; but in some respects it has rendered his labour unnecessary. This labour, unnecessary in some departments, should have been bestowed upon fresh land : and it remains now to turn it upon fresh land, assisted by machinery, for his own benefit.

Thus, if a set of labourers were to build a mill at their leisure

---

* In the Brighton work-house, children from ten to fourteen weave sacking, calico, toweling, shirting, &c.; and the younger ones spin and wind thread. A machine for weaving costs only a few pounds, may be made by a common carpenter, and lasts for ever. Boys as well as girls will learn, in a few months, to mend their clothes; making them is more difficult. Both may be employed in plaiting straw for their hats and bonnets. Thus the children might be made to supply most of their own wants.

hours, they could then grind their corn cheaper; if they had stocking-frames, they could make stockings at leisure hours; so they could make their own hats, &c. If it be said, this would ruin the miller, hatter, &c., we reply, let them adopt the same principle—go upon fresh land, give their leisure to the cultivation of it, and raise their own food. Should it still be alleged that they would not be qualified for any work but what they had been used to, it is obvious that these schools for teaching various trades would provide the remedy.

Thus agriculture should be made the staple employment of the great body of workmen, who should be so educated as to be able to employ their leisure time in some manufacture.

It must be considered that the employment of agriculture is not constant. It varies much at different times of the year, and sometimes nothing can be done. During one part of the year men are employed in thrashing. If this were done by machinery, the men might be making ploughs, harrows, repairing buildings, digging pits, preparing house-frames, &c., road-making, &c.

That division of labour which confines one man to one trade, which only occupies half his time, must be worse than that which teaches him two trades, and employs his whole time.

A gentleman, whose sole object was the comfort and good character of his tenants, might adopt a system of this kind, employ all his labour productively, and grow rich in proportion to the number of his workmen: and upon the principle that each workman produces more than he consumes, and that children, by the age of twenty-one, repay all the expenses of their education, his population could not increase too fast.

He would employ his rent productively instead of unproductively, and re-invest a portion of it upon his own estate, in permanent improvements.

Thus, any one who can command labour, may grow rich in proportion to the number of labourers he has. The more productive labour the more wealth.

By the same rule, a School of Industry employed on land will maintain itself; fifteen children, of ten and twelve years old, will cultivate an acre, which may be reckoned at 300 bushels of potatoes, which will maintain a family.

Should this plan be approved of, and gentlemen or noblemen be desirous of submitting it to the test of experiment on their estates, or in their parishes, there will naturally at first be a difficulty in obtaining proper teachers : the difficulty, however, will be one rather of form than of substance. The mechanism by which large schools are now conducted by one master will by no means be abandoned, but it will not be so constantly, nor exclusively at work : on certain days, or for a certain time each day, or in bad weather, the whole school might work together; but at other times there will be a division of school work :—part of the children may be at school, while part may be at industry. The master having a smaller class, may deviate from the strait mechanical method, and communicate much useful instruction upon the plan of the Edinburgh Sessional School.

No gentleman will establish such a school except he be himself enlightened. He will then make the art of instruction an object of attention ; for which purpose he will consult, with advantage, Mr. Wood's account of the Sessional School, "Hints to Parents, on the Plan of Pestalozzi," (Harvey and Darton,) and other similar works, and he will find that both he and the master have enough of the substance of instruction, and only want to vary the form of it.

Thus by degrees the master will learn to see his art and office in a new light, and become more and more competent to its discharge. This system will raise the character and importance of the profession of masters even higher than it is at present ; and it will be right to select from the children those whose dispositions are suitable, and to train them more especially for masters. The monitorial system at present pursued will afford the means of doing this. The duties of the monitors will take a new direction. In the sessional school monitors are found fully competent to instruct, question, and examine a class, upon the new principle of teaching ; and, indeed, the principle is so much more improving to the teacher than the mechanical one, that his progress in acquiring it is extremely rapid.

The difficulty, therefore, of obtaining competent teachers though great at first, would diminish daily, and perhaps in two or three years cease altogether.

It will become a question, in the event of such schools being established and found to answer, whether some of the children should not live entirely in the school. Those children who are now found in work-houses ought undoubtedly to do so. All orphans, or those whose parents are bad characters, ought to do so. In the case of large families, instead of allowing parish relief, a certain number of children should be taken off their hands. The rule for this, as well as for every other question, would be decided by local circumstances. The vagabond children of towns might be sent to such schools, and thus relieve society and maintain themselves.

Care must be taken not to supersede the family ties, only to aid and regulate them : they are the most sacred of all earthly ones. We want to make parents and children blessings to each other, not to sever them as an unnatural union. Where the circumstances of home are vicious or dangerous, children might be entirely at school. Where the distance is great, it might be the same : nor would this, with periodical meetings, injure family ties, any more than it does in the upper classes, where children are absent for four, six, or even twelve months at a time.

It may be useful to consider what influence these schools, in which judicious labour shall be the leading principle, are likely to have upon the future rate of increase of population. It is much apprehended that whatever remedies we may discover at the present moment, to counteract the effects of a surplus population, the same will again occur in a certain number of years, and render all care useless.

On this we may observe, first, that we are not called upon to provide for the future contingencies of the world, but we leave future generations to regulate for themselves. It is sufficient for each to act for its own circumstances. When a remedy for a present evil is discovered, the argument against it must not be a possible, but a probable, or certain evil. The evil apprehended in this case is only possible and contingent. Secondly, in the present notions of the abundant powers of population, there is much indefinite exaggeration. It is forgotten that population must have laws by which its rate of increase is determined ; we must form our conclusions by these laws, not by a fearful imagination.

Without going into the depth of this subject, we may say, that the two great causes of over-population are vice and improvident marriages, and the latter is by far the more powerful of the two. Supposing schools of labour to be established in every parish, or in certain districts, in which the children should be apprenticed till the age of twenty or twenty-one. They would strike at the root of both these evils, first by preventive regulations ; secondly, by the inculcation of opposite habits and principles. Besides what is called religious instruction, the greatest possible care should be taken to prevent immoral and improper actions of all kinds, by a constant or close inspection; without this the plan would be useless. This would only require a certain number of inspectors or masters; and surely it would be a most useful change to convert some of the present surplus population, who are maintained, idle or criminal, at the public expense, into intelligent and useful inspectors.

The question of improvident marriages up to the age of twenty-one, would be disposed of by the apprenticeship.

The only question which remains is the future probability of imprudent marriage. Is it more likely for a man to be improvident who has been all his youth brought up to habits of labour, moderate diet, knowledge of his trade, and moral and religious intelligence, or for one who has during that time lived in idleness and mischief, unaccustomed to restraint, ignorant of any useful employment, a beggar by profession, or an intailed pauper?

Though we seem to see many good effects following from Village Schools of Industry, yet we think one of the most important would be the engrafting provident habits on the lower orders. These habits would bear upon marriage principally, and upon every transaction of life in proportion to its importance. When a workman had been accustomed to act upon a principle of prudence and self-respect, he would think twice before he put his comforts, character, and happiness in doubt. At present he either does not think at all, or thinks only how he may extort money from the parish.

These schools would also afford opportunities for promoting the more intelligent and better conducted children to be upper servants, headmen, or bailiffs to gentlemen of property. This would tend to diminish relative numbers of the lowest class, which is the most troublesome, because the most inprovident one, and to reduce the surplus population.

In proposing this method of education, we have the same object in view as the gentry and clergy of country villages. They wish to have their peasants virtuous, religious, and good workmen, instead of vicious, unprincipled, degraded paupers. We recommend, then, forming their habits from the cradle, instead of allowing them to be formed in the streets, in the robber's den, in the garrets of thieves and prostitutes. As our faith in Revelation leads us to expect a curse upon a system of idleness, discord, profligacy, and pauperism, so we look for a blessing upon a system of early industry, habits of sobriety, frugality, and neighbourly kindness; of Christian condescension and practical charity in the upper classes—and intelligent independence in the working classes.

THE END.

LONDON:
PRINTED BY THOMAS DAVISON, WHITEFRIARS.

iety,
and
nce

A PLAN

FOR IMMEDIATELY AMELIORATING THE PRESENT
DISTRESSED CONDITION OF THE

Agricultural Poor,

AND

PERMANENTLY IMPROVING THEIR MORAL CHARACTER:

CONTAINED IN

A LETTER

ADDRESSED TO THE

RIGHT HON. VISCOUNT MELBOURNE,

SECRETARY OF STATE FOR THE HOME DEPARTMENT.

BY

WILLIAM MILNER FARISH, M. A.

LATE OF CORPUS CHRISTI COLLEGE, CAMBRIDGE; CURATE OF
WIMESWOULD, LEICESTERSHIRE.

" ...... the labourer is worthy of his hire."—LUKE x. 7.
" ...... this we commanded you, that if any would not work, neither should he eat."
2 THESS. iii. 10.

LONDON:

C. AND J. RIVINGTON, ST. PAUL'S CHURCH-YARD, AND
WATERLOO PLACE, PALL MALL;

PARKER, OXFORD; DEIGHTONS, CAMBRIDGE; BENNETT, NOTTINGHAM;
BEMROSE, DERBY; CARTWRIGHT, LOUGHBOROUGH; AND
COMBE AND SON, LEICESTER.

A PLAN,

&c. &c.

Vicarage, Wimeswould, near Loughborough,
December 13, 1830.

My Lord,

In times like the present, " *England expects every man to do his duty.*"

The firm conviction which rests on my mind that, at a crisis in the national affairs like that which we now witness, every man *ought* to do what he *can* towards the restoration of public tranquillity by every method in his power, consistent with moral rectitude, and sound policy—this firm conviction, my Lord, is the only apology which I have to offer for obtruding myself and my plan on your Lordship's attention.

Much is in the power of private individuals—much more, I apprehend, than they are apt at first sight to imagine : but perhaps no class of the community have it more in their power to do good, at the present juncture of affairs, by vigorous and well-directed efforts, and by a judicious use of that influence which they derive from their official situation, than *the Resident Country Clergy.*

Were the Clergy with zeal and diligence to adopt rational means (each in his own parish) for bettering the condition of the Labouring Population, and at the same time relieving the land-occupier from the intolerable pressure of the Poor Rates:—were they (by explaining to their parishioners the advantages which would result *to all classes of the community* from elevating the condition of the Labourer,) to induce them to return to that rational and wholesome method of administering the Poor Laws, which (and which *alone)* was contemplated by the Legislature in *those charitable enactments,* they might, by the blessing of God on their endeavours, become (as instruments) THE SAVIOURS OF THE COUNTRY. And were they thus to exert themselves, the fruit of their labours would return into their own bosoms:—they would raise themselves in the opinion of all ranks of people;—the farmer and the labourer would alike look upon them as their friends:—they would gain a moral influence over the minds of their parishioners which would predispose them (so far as any outward circumstances can) to listen to those lessons of piety, which in the discharge of their pastoral office, they are called upon, both in public and in private, both "in season and out of season," to inculcate on the flock committed to their charge:—but above all, my Lord, they would bring down on their heads "*the blessing of him that was ready to perish :*"—and thus in *saving their country* from the dangers with which, in these "perilous times" it is threatened, they would *save themselves and the Church of England* from the fatal effects of that storm which is even now thickening and gathering around them.

It is under a conviction of the truth of these observations, my Lord, that, as the resident curate of a populous country parish, I have felt myself called upon to make every exertion in my power to bring about a *practical reformation* in the mode of *administering* the Poor Laws in my own village :—and it is because my exertions, in this cause, have been hitherto prospered to a degree, *far beyond my most sanguine expectations,* that I seek to direct your Lordship's attention to my plan, and, through the influence of your name, to promote throughout the kingdom, the adoption of similar measures for effecting the same objects.

It is perfectly unnecessary, my Lord, that I should trouble you with any explanation of the plan which has been adopted here, as the accompanying paper* will speak for itself. I may be allowed however to say a few words on the *means* which were used to bring it about, and on the *result* which has followed from it.

---

* See Appendix I.

My first step was to call individually on the different land-occupiers, at their own houses; and, by such arguments as suggested themselves to my mind, at the time, to point out the *evils* of the present practice of paying the poor for their work (or rather for their *idleness*) out of the Poor Rates, either in whole or in part: and the *benefits* which might be expected to result from their being constantly employed and paid by the farmers themselves. There was no difficulty in producing conviction on these points; and a general approbation of the principle having been thus obtained, a vestry meeting was convened, which was attended by a large number of the most respectable inhabitants. To this meeting was presented a paper headed " Proposals for bettering the condition of the Labouring Poor in Wimeswould, and also for relieving the farmer from the extreme pressure of the Poor Rates," and embracing the principle contained in the first five paragraphs of the accompanying document,* embodied in the form of six resolutions. These resolutions having been read over, were afterwards proposed, seriatim, for adoption, and being *carried unanimously*, were signed by the chairman of the meeting.

The following declaration was also signed by the different occupiers.

" We the undersigned owners and occupiers of land in the parish of Wimeswould, do hereby so-

---

* For which see Appendix I.

lemnly bind ourselves, and engage to employ constantly the number of labourers allotted to us according to the rate payable by us respectively, and to pay them for their work fair remunerating wages ; (provided that no considerable rate-payer in the parish decline signing this paper.) "

No attempt, as your Lordship will observe, has been made to establish a "uniform rate of wages to be paid for labour ; "—an attempt most justly reprobated, as alike impolitic and illegal, in the proclamation issued from the Home Secretary's Office, on the 8th instant.

This matter has been left to adjust itself according to those general principles which, in spite of all efforts to force things out of their natural course, must eventually prevail.

With regard to the *result*—but it may seem almost absurd to talk of the *result* of a plan *two days old :* nevertheless highly important results have already followed.

Previously to the adoption of this plan, there prevailed a widely-spread and deep-seated spirit of discontent, the natural effect of the oppressive system which had obtained in Wimeswould, and under which the poor were groaning. This was well known, although nothing approaching to an overt act of riot, or even of sedition, has been at all committed in the village. We were most earnestly desirous of affording all needful relief, by our own voluntary act, before any symptoms of insubordination manifested themselves, that there

8

might not be the least appearance of our being " under the influence of threats and intimidation." *

This our object has happily been effected—on Monday evening (13th instant) the labouring classes were invited to attend a meeting to be held in a large room in the village, that they might be informed of the measures which had been entered into for their relief: and it would have delighted your Lordship, or any other friend of the poor, to have witnessed the exceeding good order, and good feeling manifested by the men—whilst the paper containing the regulations of "THE WIMESWOULD ANTI-PAUPERISM FUND," &c. &c. was read to them, and commented on. One gentleman who spoke on the occasion, towards the conclusion of the meeting, having intimated that it was desirable that there should be some decided mark given of that approbation which he could already read in their very countenances—the poor men, one and all, immediately stood up, and held up both hands: and after the meeting was concluded the gratitude they expressed was unbounded. Nothing can ever efface from my mind the exquisite sensations which I enjoyed, when on leaving the chair, (to which I had been called by the meeting) I was thronged and crowded by the poor fellows who eagerly pressed forwards to shake me by the hand in token of their thankfulness.

---

* See Proclamation from the Home Secretary's Office, dated December 8, 1830.

Who can for a moment question, my Lord, whether peasants with hearts like theirs would not make industrious, faithful, and contented labourers, if they were but treated like MEN?

Even within the short time which has elapsed since the meeting, those valuable qualities, economy and fore-thought, have begun to shew themselves. This very morning (Dec. 14.) a labourer who was present at the meeting last night, asked whether the men might not be allowed to contribute (out of the savings which they hoped to have to spare when fully employed and fairly paid) towards the fund from which they were to be relieved in time of sickness. Thinking that, if this were permitted, there might arise in the men's minds an idea of RIGHT in the proceeds of the fund which might hereafter prove detrimental to that perfect control which the TRUSTEES *ought* to have over it, I recommended, as a better plan, that the money should, from time to time, be deposited in the Savings Bank, and offered my services to receive, and deposit monthly, such sums as should be put into my hands for that purpose.

I mention this fact merely as affording a clear demonstration, that HOPE is the parent of ECONOMY, and IMPROVIDENCE the natural offspring of DESPAIR.

One suggestion more I would add, which relates to that part of the plan * in which rewards are held out

---

* See the Eighth Regulation of the Wimeswould Anti-pauperism Fund, given in Appendix I.

to creditable young men on their first marrying, after twenty-five years of age. If, in addition to the reward *there* proposed, there were added permission to occupy a small piece of *common land* (say an acre or half an acre) at a mere nominal rent, a very great additional inducement would be held out to young men to abstain from those early and improvident connections which, of late years, have been the very bane of the agricultural districts.

By the consistent and persevering adoption of this system of rewards we might expect, at no very distant period, to see a counterpart of *the happy days of old England*, when there was a constant reciprocity of good-feeling and affection between the cultivator of the soil, and his employer. It is not indeed too much to hope that we might succeed in reviving, before the race has become quite extinct, that ancient and honourable class of agriculturalists, the YEOMEN, who were alike the glory, and the strength of " the olden time."

Whether there exists at present sufficient power in the hands of parish officers to carry into effect such arrangements, I am not aware;—but there can be no doubt, I apprehend, but that it is competent for Parliament (if in their wisdom they shall see good) to vest such a power either in overseers or in special commissioners appointed for the purpose.

All that I have to request of your Lordship is, that if this plan which I have taken the liberty of laying before you, shall appear to you and to the rest of

His Majesty's Ministers in itself practicable, and in its ultimate effects likely to be beneficial to the country at large—you will be pleased to give it the whole weight of your extensive influence.

Might not *a liberal per centage premium* be offered to all parishes establishing " ANTI-PAUPERISM FUNDS ? " We have had many precedents for encouraging, in this manner, the benevolent efforts of individuals in times of extraordinary depression in the *manufacturing* interest— Why not afford the same encouragement to the *agriculturist?*　　＊　　＊　　＊

＊　＊　＊　＊　＊　＊　＊　＊　＊

With every apology for the length of my communication, I beg your Lordship to believe, that should any part of my plan be approved of and adopted by his Majesty's Ministers, it will afford me great pleasure to have been, in any degree, the means of bettering the condition of the poor, and restoring tranquillity to the country ; but should it, on the whole, appear impracticable, or ill-adapted to the present exigences of the nation, I shall at least enjoy the quiet satisfaction of having intended well.

I have the honour to be,

My Lord,

Your Lordship's obedient humble servant,

WILLIAM MILNER FARISH.

APPENDIX I.

TOGETHER with the foregoing letter was sent a printed copy of the annexed Regulations of the Wimeswould Anti-pauperism Society, accompanied by this circular:

"His Majesty's Ministers *in general*, and the Right Honourable the Home Secretary *in particular*, are earnestly requested (if they approve of the annexed plan for ameliorating the condition of the working classes) to promote, by all the means in their power, its adoption within the sphere of their influence."

W. M. FARISH.

WIMESWOULD ANTI-PAUPERISM SOCIETY.

THE WIMESWOULD ANTI-PAUPERISM SOCIETY has for its ultimate object the reinstating the industrious poor in honorable independence:—this object is sought to be effected by means of *rewards*, to be paid out of a FUND raised for that purpose, by voluntary subscriptions.

It is necessary, however, that some *practical amendment* should be previously introduced in the *administration* of the Poor Laws: the leading principle of the amendment which it seems desirable to establish is,—that no man capable of doing a day's work should receive any parochial relief whatever, (whilst in health) except in the shape of wages for work actually done, and that the quantum of wages should be regulated by the quantum of work.

Those poor who are incapable of working, should be the only objects of parochial relief, and the support afforded *them* should be administered as heretofore.

The means of bringing about this change are :—by the division of the poor into *three* classes, the *first* consisting of good steady workmen, the *second* of infirm persons and indifferent workmen, the *third* of aged or unhealthy persons, incapable of doing any work at all : by the farmers and occupiers of land unanimously agreeing to employ the *first* class, and as many as may be of the *second*, on their land, (*each taking a certain number according to the rate which he pays,*) and giving them *fair remunerating wages* for their work.

Such of the *second* class as can find no private employers, should be employed by the Overseer of the Highways, or other Parish Officer, on some public work, and be paid either by the *day* or the *piece*, according as the Officer shall think them *unable* or *unwilling* to do a good day's work.

By these means many would become altogether independent of parish relief; and one object of the Fund of the Society is, by affording them timely aid in case of sickness, to remove the necessity of applying again to the parish for relief; which would, as it were, break *the charm of* INDEPENDENCE, and render a man indifferent as to making future applications. For the further encouraging of this object, annual rewards are offered to all men in the labouring classes who for one whole year support their families by their own industry without parish relief. (*See regulation 7.*)

Another object, which is sought to be effected by this Fund, is the prevention of *unreasonably early marriages amongst the poor.* The method of applying the Fund to this object is by offering a handsome reward to be paid on his wedding day to any young man belonging to the Parish of Wimeswould who shall be married, for the first time, after having attained the age of twenty-five years—provided he have in all respects conducted himself with credit, industry, sobriety, and honesty. (*See regulation 8.*)

REGULATIONS.

1. That the Society be denominated the "WIMESWOULD ANTI-PAUPERISM SOCIETY," and that its FUND be vested in the hands of three or more Trustees, to be nominated by the COMMITTEE.

2. That the COMMITTEE consist of Subscribers of one pound and upwards.

3. That in the *disposal of money* for objects *other than those specially contemplated in these regulations*, every member of the Committee subscribing from *one* pound to *five*, have *one* vote; from *five* to *ten*, *two* votes; and so on, in like proportion;—but that in all other matters, members of the Committee have only one vote each.

4. That the Fund be deposited by the Trustees in the Loughborough Savings Bank.

5. That the objects for which the Trustees are empowered to draw out money from the said Fund, be the following :—*First*, For the assistance of the industrious poor, in time of sickness, who abstain *entirely* from receiving parish relief, either then or when in health (wages from the Overseer for work actually done, not being

considered as parish relief). *Secondly,* For the bestowing of annual rewards on the industrious poor, who having a family of two or more children, bring them up creditably, and during the past year have received no parish relief under any circumstances. *Thirdly,* For the bestowing presents on young men at their first marriage, who being not under twenty-five years of age, and never having had any illegitimate children, have in their general deportment conducted themselves with industry, sobriety, and honesty.

6. That the sum of money given by the Trustees to any poor man on the ground of sickness, be generally somewhat *less* than he could earn when in health, and fully employed, and *never* more, except by the express vote of the majority of the Committee, regularly convened to consider the case. All poor persons applying for relief on the plea of sickness, must bring to the Trustees a written certificate of their inability to work, from the Parish Surgeon. It is desirable that sick men receiving relief, be visited at least once a-week by one or other of the Trustees.

7. That the rewards for bringing up a family be given on the First of January every year (unless it fall on a Sunday, and in that case, on the day after), and that they be regulated on the following scale, which it shall be competent for a general meeting to raise, if the funds will admit of it :—Every man who by labour shall have creditably supported a family of two children (the eldest under twelve years of age) for the year preceding, without being in any way chargeable to the parish, shall receive 5s., and an additional shilling for every additional child under twelve years of age, so brought up. And also, that on the first time of any man's becoming entitled to this reward, he be also presented by the Trustees of the Fund with a *medal,* bearing a suitable inscription and device, as a mark of their approbation of his good conduct. An exact account will be kept in the records of the Society of the names of all persons rewarded, and of the circumstances under which they have deserved this honorable distinction. And that all persons laying claim to any *reward,* give at least one week's notice to the Trustees of their intention, and inform them of the grounds on which they rest their claim.

8. That the reward which the Trustees are entitled to pay to each young man on his first marriage (provided he be not under *twenty-five* years of age, have not been the father of any illegitimate child, and have in other respects conducted himself with industry, sobriety, and honesty) be *ten* pounds, or if the funds will allow it, *fifteen* pounds.

9. That the support and rewards offered in the 6th, 7th, and 8th regulations, be given *only* to LABOURERS and FRAMEWORK-KNITTERS *belonging to the Parish of Wimeswould.* But that all persons who, *after the thirty-first day of December,* 1830, obtain settlements in this parish, *otherwise than by birth,* be not considered as *Parishioners* by the Trustees of this Fund.

10. That the Trustees have no power, on their own authority, to draw out or expend the money of the Fund for any other than the three purposes above specified (except to defray the necessary expenses of management); and that if any circumstances arise which render it expedient to apply any part of the funds to any other purpose, it shall be necessary for the Trustees to obtain the sanction of the majority of the Committee. There must be at least one third of the Committee resident in Wimeswould present, to form a quorum, and one day's notice given. At any meeting convened under these circumstances, Trustees *may move and second resolutions*, but not have the privilege of voting.

11. That if any difference of opinion arise among the Trustees in the administration of relief, the bestowment of rewards, or other business to be transacted by them, the decision of the majority stand in ordinary cases; but it shall be competent for the minority to appeal to a Committee, (whose decision shall be final) if there appear urgent necessity for this step. But, that the Committee have no right to interfere with the Trustees, except when appealed to, unless it be evident that the Trustees are departing from the principles laid down in these Regulations.

12. That on some convenient day in the last week in December there be convened annually a meeting of the Committee, before whom the accounts of the Trustees shall be audited.

13. That at the audit-meeting, the Trustees may be re-elected, or new ones appointed, as shall appear good to the majority of the Committee: and that every Trustee, on accepting his office, do sign a written declaration that he will faithfully, and to the best of his ability, administer the money of the Fund according to these Regulations. All votes of Trustees, for their own or each other's appointment to office, to be cancelled, and the election to be determined by the remaining votes.

14. That a Minute Book be provided, in which all the public transactions of the Committee and Trustees, and all important communications relative to this Society, be entered.

15. That in the event of this Fund being through any cause done away with, the Trustees for the time being be required to give in an exact account of the balance in their hands, which shall be divided amongst the Subscribers as nearly as may be, in proportion to their Subscriptions. And that in the event of any share being unclaimed by the *death* of a Subscriber, the sum due to the deceased be paid by the Trustees to his Executors. If a Subscriber be merely *absent* from the place, the Trustees shall inform him, and send him the money if he require it; and if not, apply it according to his direction. No *individual* Subscriber shall be permitted to withdraw money once given to the Fund.

16. That there be vested in the Committee a power of making such by-laws as circumstances may require.

17. That Subscribers be requested to signify in writing their assent to these Rules, according to the annexed form :—
"We, the undersigned Subscribers to the 'WIMESWOULD ANTI-PAUPERISM SOCIETY,' hereby agree, in all matters of dispute which may arise out of the business of the Fund, to appeal to these Rules as authority: and if there be no Rule bearing on the point in dispute, to submit to the decision of the majority of *votes* at a general meeting."

APPENDIX II.

VISCOUNT Melbourne was pleased to direct the following reply to be forwarded to the Author, from the Secretary of State's Office.

COPY.

Whitehall, 17th December, 1830.

SIR,

I am directed by Viscount Melbourne to acknowledge the receipt of your letter of the 13th instant, with its inclosure, containing a Plan for the Improvement of the Condition of the Agricultural Poor. I am to return you his Lordship's thanks for this communication, to which his Lordship will not fail to give his attention.

I am, Sir,
Your obedient servant,
S. M. PHILLIPPS.

The Rev. W. M. Farish,
Wimeswould,
Loughborough.

COMBE AND SON, LEICESTER.

LETTER

TO

Sir THOMAS BARING, Bart. M. P.

&c. &c. &c.

ON THE CAUSES WHICH HAVE PRODUCED THE

PRESENT STATE

OF THE

𝔄𝔤𝔯𝔦𝔠𝔲𝔩𝔱𝔲𝔯𝔞𝔩 𝔏𝔞𝔟𝔬𝔲𝔯𝔦𝔫𝔤 𝔓𝔬𝔬𝔯;

TO WHICH ARE ADDED

PRACTICAL HINTS

FOR

BETTERING THEIR CONDITION.

———

WITH A DRAWING AND PLAN FOR A DOUBLE COTTAGE.

———

By THOMAS POSTANS, Esq.

MICHAEL STAUNTON,
No. 1, Craven Street, Strand, London.

1831.

PREFACE.

====

THE following pages were written in the autumn of the last year, at a season when disaffection was manifesting itself by acts of incendiarism, and when the dissatisfied labourer, encouraged by the sad example thus set him, sought by clamour and lawless conduct to obtain an encrease in the rate of his wages. At that time, the author of this short letter experienced considerable difficulty in maintaining his desire to avoid the introduction of politics; he trusts he has succeeded.

Fortunately for the country and its peasantry, the power of the law, and the dictates of humanity have been happily blended to diminish those symptoms of outrage and dissatisfaction which had shown themselves to so lamentable an extent.

During the period of excitement the writer, for certain reasons, was induced to withhold the publication of his letter, although written at the time with a view to point out some mode of relief. It is now put forth with an humble hope that it may answer the expectations formed of it by many friends of the author who have solicited copies of the letter and plan. If his endeavours to do good should be less fortunate than he could wish, he will have much to lament; should they be more fortunate than he could expect, the merit will be due both to those who have caused the publication of his plan and to those who from motives of humanity or interest may hasten to carry it into effect.

April, 1831.

Note.—The better to explain the mode for constructing the tank,—read after the word " each" in line 15 page 18—

as an opening between the two smaller tanks for the water to flow over the second in a filtered state into the large one for use.

LETTER

TO

SIR THOMAS BARING, BART. M. P.

&c. &c. &c.

SIR,

    THE suffering and disaffection at present so generally pervading the country, the urgent necessity for the immediate application of some effectual remedy, and a conviction that whatever can in any degree effect that desirable object will obtain a ready consideration from a benevolent mind, have induced me to lay before you my sentiments as to some of the causes of the present distressing condition of the agricultural labourer, and to suggest such remedies, as have occurred to me from careful observation and reflection, for immediately improving his circumstances, and gradually establishing him in comparative comfort and respectability—submitting the whole to your superior judgment and discrimination.

A 2

Thirty-five years ago the agricultural labourer possessed a home to shelter him, a family to comfort him, and food to sustain him. In most cases he was either a resident on the farm where he laboured, or lived in a cottage, in a neighbouring village. Where he was without the reach of coal he gathered wood, furze, or turf, with little or no molestation, for his fire. His family were then allowed to glean the scattered ears more liberally than now,—his garden was indeed small and but ill cultivated. The value of the potatoe was neither so well known nor so highly appreciated as it is at present; and the idea of subsisting upon potatoes alone, as an article of food, was not entertained by the labourer of England. Bread was made at home, which, though coarser than that in present use, was not on that account the less nourishing food for the labouring man. In times of distress, bread and water sustained him at his last extremity.

I recollect that in the year 1795 the common wages paid to a labourer, situated as I have before described, were only 7s. a week, and corn, at that time was about the present price, or higher.* With

* The average price of wheat in the years

1790......£2	6	8	1796......£3	17	4
1791...... 2	13	0	1797...... 2	13	1
1792...... 2	2	4	1798...... 2	9	8
1793...... 1	13	8	1799...... 3	7	6
1794..... 2	11	0	1800...... 5	13	7
1795...... 3	14	2			

wages so much lower than at present demanded,—
without ability to cultivate his garden with such
advantage as "increased skill now teaches," with
corn as high then as it is now, it is of importance
to shew how it then happened that the labouring
man was more industrious, much happier, more
contented, and infinitely more moral than at present.

1st. He had his cottage at a moderate cost, he
had not far to go to his daily labour, and in most
cases had the means of feeding his hog.

2d. It was the general practice to allow two or
three pints of beer or cyder a day (and more in
laborious work) which the farmer could better afford
to give from his store, than he can now afford to allow
money for getting it ; whilst the labourer had no distance to fetch it, as at present, and it was wholesome.

3d. Almost every cottage had its manufactory
carried on in spite of the winter's blast and the
darkness of long nights. The carding of wool
and the spinning of yarn were daily occupations of
some members of the labourer's family, whilst others
were employed in knitting the yarn into stockings,
gloves, and muffs. The manufactures of such an
industrious family were frequently bespoke, and if not
so, always readily disposed of at the next market.

Such were the engagements of a cottager's family
in winter. In spring, setting beans, when all the
family were employed, earning each from 4*d.* to 1*s.*

per day ; and in summer, their employment in harvesting and gleaning, made a perfect year of gain, adding continually to the stock of wages earned by the husband, whilst he drew easily on the resources of the farmer, and escaped the degrading necessity of relief from the poor rates. Not unfrequently, the single man, or the grown up son, boarded with the family, and throwing in his little stock of gain to the general fund contributed to the increase of domestic comfort.

Such, at the period referred to, was pretty generally the condition of the agricultural labourer. His cottage was his happy home, the farmer was his friend, the parson his teacher; the church catechism supplied a code of religious and moral instruction for his children. In times of adversity he bowed to circumstances, and strove to live and die contented. I shall now briefly refer to some of the causes which have mainly contributed to alter his condition, and have reduced this once useful and contented member of the community to the state of an idle, oppressed, dissatisfied, turbulent pauper.*

1st. The gradual increase in the price of corn and of the necessaries of life during the progress of the war, without a commensurate or regular advance in the price of labour employed on land, was one cause.

---

* Written during the late excesses.

2nd. The progressive throwing together of several small farms into one; and as this was done frequently under the superintendence of some fashionable London Surveyor, it was not consistent with his notions of good taste, or his idea of agreeable scenery to allow the humble cot to occupy its old situation to disfigure the fair face of the whole domain, and therefore the cottager was ordered to quit and his cottage to be pulled down. This pretender to taste and knowledge, as indifferent to the wants of the labourer as he was ignorant both of the real value of the land, and of the utility and advantage of providing a habitation for the husbandman, could not have been expected to act otherwise than merely with a view to please his employer. In the division of any great estate the same description of employee, equally ignorant of the real value of the land entrusted to his partition, often succeeded in obtaining rents for the landlord from the farmer in times of improving agriculture, unequalled prosperity and inconsiderate extravagance, without any regard being shewn by either party, to the permanent interest of all,* and it is, therefore, not surprising that all provision for the ac-

---

* I remember to have heard one of those Gentlemen boast, that he had let for a certain Baronet in Sussex 50 farms, though it is well known he had been employed all his life before in parish affairs and house agency in London, and I have reason to know that he was quite ignorant of what was loam sand or gra-

commodation of the labourer in these cases was either
wholly omitted, or perhaps not thought deserving
of the least consideration ; and it also became the
practice, in many cases, to withhold permission to
glean the scattered corn, which, as it became more
valuable, was raked with greater closeness and
care.

In times of war, when high prices were in some
measure provided against by an increase of wages,
when employment was always to be obtained, and
when the sons of the labourer found occupation in the
navy and army, this change in the condition of the
labourer did not bring with it any immediate inconvenience to be greatly complained of, or much
felt : ultimately, however, it proved the source of
many evils, and may justly be reckoned another
cause of his present unhappy situation.

3d. The enclosure of waste lands and commons,*

---

velly soil.   Thus, the fate of 50 families, and their dependants,
was placed in the hands of perfect ignorance.

Another lamentable instance was, where a man who had been
all his life a hot-house gardener, was employed in one of these
agencies upon a Nobleman's estate.   The Nobleman, or rather
the Lady, sent this man down to value and let the land, and to
cut down and sell the timber; such was his ignorance and folly,
that the growing timber down to 20 years' growth and under was
sold, and so much damage done to the estate, that it was necessary for the trustees to interfere, by legal measures, to put a stop
to it ;—the lands were let at double rents, and many industrious
families turned out, and others ruined.

* I have some doubt as to the common rights being beneficial

when carrying into effect, gave activity and employment to the labourer; and when his hands were occupied and his wants supplied, he felt not the evil, he saw not the consequences of this passing away of his rights, in a degree that could make him clamorous for their preservation; and thus was formed another source of future evil to the labourer.

The poor husbandman, living by his daily toil, receiving the wages of his labour, but driven from his cottage and his garden, took up his abode in the outskirts of some town; became, perhaps, the inmate of another class of labourers; drew his supplies from bakers, publicans, and chandlers' shops; his wife and daughters became idlers; his children became contaminated from bad example, and a general demoralization followed; so long as employment and high wages were readily obtained, the unconscious husbandman foresaw not the coming misery of his altered condition.

When war ceased, when disbanded soldiers rejoined their families, when hands grew plentiful, when employment became less and wages decreased, then, and then only, did the husbandman and the labourer feel their misery. But strangers alike to

to the poor.—The poor of this class were not the most moral or the most comfortable, but somewhat independant, and generally idle; and the chief advantage of commons was taken by the adjoining farms.

the cause and to the remedy, the cry of want resounded through the parishes to excite commiseration, and to solicit employment and provision, but in vain. The parish workhouse and the poor rates were the only preventives of starvation.

The farmer, now impoverished by reason of his thoughtless expenditure in times of prosperity, and reduced in his circumstances by the sudden and ruinous fall in the value of his produce,* was unequal to sustain the position he had taken under high prices.† Unable, therefore, to pay his high rents, his tithes and his taxes; unable to support labourers, whose interests had been severed from his own, when prosperous times elevated him above them, he was alike unprepared to contribute to the poor rates, to give the husbandmen employment, or to reinstate him in his proper place.

A time of poverty and distress on the one hand was thus brought about, and pauperism and a state of degradation being produced on the other, a whole train of evil consequences followed in succession. The husbandman, poor and demoralized, became dissatisfied and turbulent; his condition was, per-

---

* About the year 14-15, the seed wheat cost 100s. the quarter, and the produce thereof fetched little more than 50s.

† It should be remembered that out of this prosperity have arisen our improved roads; facility of conveyance of all kinds; the improved science in agriculture; and perhaps, too, almost all our internal advantages.

haps, not sufficiently commiserated, nor the causes of it duly considered.

Thus far have I endeavoured to bring under your notice the once comparatively happy condition of the labourer, and the causes of his decline to a state of privation, demoralization, and hopelessness, which has rendered him an easy prey to the machinations of disaffected and turbulent men, exciting to violence, and to the perpetration of acts unfortunately too well known to require to be more particularly mentioned. To raise him from this wretched condition is the main object of this address, and I proceed at once to mention in detail the means which (should they be adopted) will, I trust, go far to remedy many of the evils, and gradually restore him to regular industry and comfort.

To replace the husbandman to his cottage, is, perhaps, of more easy operation than to reinstate him in his habits of attachment and duty, as regards his sense of his dependence on his employers, and the respect due to them. *But as the first must be done before he can feel that the second is due from him*, it shall be my endeavour here, from practical experience, to lay down a plan for locating the husbandman on the soil he is to cultivate, and thus to reunite in association and mutual interest the farmer and the labourers ; that the tillage of the land and the production of the soil may contribute to the benefit of the farmer, the improvement of the labourer, the advantage of the proprietor, and the general good.

In looking at the good to be effected by the erection of cottages and the appropriation of land for the occupation of the poor, two distinct plans are presented, or rather two methods of arranging this purpose enter into my contemplation ; namely,— the construction of a cottage, with a due share of ground, on farms for the occupation of the labourer employed on them ; and the erection of cottages on waste lands, with an allotment of the soil.

As I am deeply impressed with a sense of the superior advantages of restoring the labourer to his cottage on the farm, the reasons by which I would be governed in promoting this purpose, the method of constructing the cottage, the selection of the site, and the extent of the ground, shall have the first place.

It is necessary to premise, that the farmer himself must be sensible of the advantage to him. The honest labourer, on his part, will soon learn how to appreciate his share in the improvement contemplated. These two parties may reasonably be expected to concur ; but much, of course, must depend on the right feeling and co-operation of the landlord in promoting this plan, with the advantages of which all landlords may not be practically acquainted ; but I trust that they may be prompted to adopt a suggestion which may appear consistent with their kindliest feelings and their best interests.

Where leases interfere, the landlord and the tenant may arrange.

Under yearly tenancies, the landlord can himself effect the purpose, the tenant in possession not objecting.

These preliminaries adjusted, and it being further determined how many labourers a farmer can employ in the ordinary business of the farm, apportioning a given number of men to a given quantity of land, the parties will be prepared to fix upon the sites. These should be marked out according to circumstances, so as neither to huddle the labourers together in one distant corner of the farm, nor to bring them too near to the house. Half an acre of land is the quantity I would propose ; it is as much as a man can attend to, and is not so much as will make him independent of the farmer, *which he ought never to be.* Where the situation will admit, it should slope towards the west, as affording a much better aspect than the south for natural produce, and as being more sheltered from the eastern blast, and the summer drought. It should be open, not surrounded with trees ; the soil should be friable, and of the best quality the farm will afford. There are few farms which do not admit of such a selection, and which may not supply clay, or chalk, or flint, or other material for the cottage, without any great inconvenience, and without much enhancing the expense of constructing it.

With respect to the cottage alone, and without looking to the permanent comforts of the labourer in his garden, a clay soil would furnish the greatest part of the material for building it with, and therefore it might cost somewhat less to construct the cottage on the clay soil; but the poor man could not afford to pay so much annual rent for it as if it were situated on a sandy loam, or other good friable soil, from which his sustenance could be more plentifully and more easily obtained; if situated on a sub-soil of clay under a friable surface, every object is attained.

The double cottage seems to present many leading points desirable to be gained, viz. economy and convenience, a good appearance, and a neighbour, and will yield the best return upon the smallest expenditure. See *the plan.*

To construct a double cottage upon this plan, where there is clay on the spot, and where stones can be found for the foundation, and where alders, oak, ash, or even poplar poles can be supplied for the roof, will cost about £35., and each tenant of the cottage, having his half acre of garden, could afford to pay from £3. to £4. a year for it.

It would be best, where practicable, to choose a spot for building where there is a clay sub-soil; it would save carting, and a pond might be formed

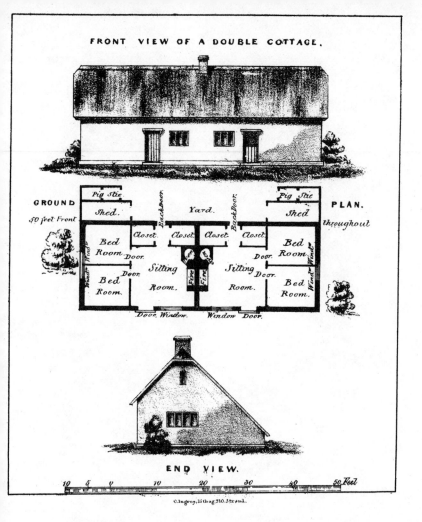

FRONT VIEW OF A DOUBLE COTTAGE.

GROUND PLAN.

50 feet Front   throughout

Pig Stie · Shed · Back Door · Yard. · Back Door · Pig Stie · Shed

Bed Room · Closet. · Closet. · Closet. · Closet. · Bed Room

Door. · Sitting Room. · Fire · Fire · Sitting Room. · Door.

Bed Room. · Door. · Door. · Bed Room.

Door. Window. · Window Door.

END VIEW.

10 5 0 10 20 30 40 50 Feet

C. Ingrey, lithog. 310. Strand.

The Partition between the Bed Rooms may be
carried to the height of the Walls, and over, a loft lighted
from a small window in the end   this loft will be very
useful for drying vegetables, and for holding many articles.
this part of the Building is optional.   The Shed and the
pig-stie as convenience may direct.   The Closets as necessity
may require.   The Oven opening in the Chimney side or
as it now is, as the builder may advise.
Although the above plan is considered perfect any altera
= tion or omission that may be suggested can easily be
accommodated

where the clay would come out, which, by land-
drains and the surrounding ditches, might be fed
with sufficient water to supply the cottage. If on
a clay soil, the foundation need not be laid more
than from six inches to a foot below the surface,
and about eighteen above, (8 course of brick or
stone,) as it would be best to have six inches more
of earth or clay rammed round, and sloping from
it after it is done, to keep off the eaves-drop-
pings, so that there would be a foot below and a
foot above ground of a foundation to receive the
clay. Gravel, or small flints *grouted*,* make an
excellent foundation. A double cottage, after the
foundation is made, would require about 35 or 40
loads of clay, and two waggon-loads of soft straw,—
if the straw be half rotten, so much the better. The
clay must be placed on solid ground, in a round
heap, about two feet thick; it is mixed by riding a
horse around and across it, while a person is shak-
ing the straw (a fork-full or two at a time) and
throwing the water over it, and a second person is
throwing the stuff in, so as to keep the heap in
form. This heap should be kneaded, or stamped
rather, over and over again; the goodness and
strength of the composition depend entirely on this

---

* " Grouted" is a term understood by all builders, and means
lime-wash thrown in upon any rough hard materials, such as
gravel, small flints, broken bricks, &c. which when dry, becomes
one of the hardest substances that can be formed.

working up ; it will require two days to do it well, and after being mixed, should stand a fortnight, to set properly. In this time the door and window-frames should be made, that they may be fixed in by the clay. At the end of a fortnight, the clay is worked over again, a piece at a time, in the same way, taking about as much of the heap as will do a course on the foundations from 12 to 18 inches high, and a foot thick. If the weather should be fine and hot, begin, and a second course may be placed on in about a fortnight, and so on till at its full height. It would take five or six loads of straw to thatch it from 12 to 15 inches thick ; the thatcher charges about 4s. per square (100 feet) for laying it on. A coat of good straw would last from 25 to 30 years, without repairs. It is the best way to mix one-third chalk with two-thirds clay, to form a very solid composition for building; but where chalk and clay are scarce, (or when marl is good,) a mixture of one-fourth, or even one-fifth chalk would make a substantial wall ; and so where chalk is plentiful, and clay less so, the chalk might form the principal part of the mixture. Where chalk may be found, it is generally used with the clay ; though I have known walls made entirely without it, which have lasted sound a great many years.*

* There is a difference between Suffolk chalk and that found under the light soils of Kent, in point of strength, and between

Individuals who have not seen this process, may not perhaps exactly understand it from this description,* although it is as near as can be to the method. It is far better to thatch than to slate, as the thatch projects and gives shelter to the walls, as well as warmth to the inmates ; and whitewash will give an air of cleanliness, and at the same time form a coat for the preservation of the clay from wet.   The clay walls, if built of a well prepared material, and constructed during the summer sun, will harden with time, and last a couple of centuries; particularly if care has been taken to put on the first thatching as late in the autumn as need be, but before the setting in of wet weather.†

I believe I have now touched upon all the material points relating to these cottages, except as regards water.   If water cannot be obtained within 20 or 30‡ feet of the surface, the expense of a well

the clay and marl of one county and another. The Suffolk clay, where good, is very full of chalk stones, which, when properly mixed for building, will dissolve in the composition. I really think that a substantial cottage might be made that would last at least a century, with almost any kind of loamy or clayey soil. The floors to be of the same material as the walls.

* It would be easy to have a person from Polstead, if required, who would go through the whole process.

† It is surprising to one who has not seen these walls, how perfect and hard they are after 20 or more years standing ; no one would suppose them to be made of any such materials.   No house is warmer, or more conducive to health.

‡ Wells of 20 or 30 feet, too, are seldom to be depended on in

B

would be too great, and I will endeavour to shew how this may be provided for in a great measure, if not altogether.

Let a tank be made of the same material as the walls of the house (bricks with cement may be better, but the materials I mention would do) large enough to contain about 10 butts of water, more or less, (this is not a large tank) place it at the lowest part of the ground to be occupied, and just above it a small tank, which will hold about 18 to 24 gallons; and above this, another to hold about 36 to 54 gallons,* having a cross wall to separate them,—(and this wall should be of brick or stone, but stone and the clay mixture might do) and a communication within about a foot of the bottom of each. Turn all the water from the ground above, off the roof of the cottage, or otherwise, as the ingenuity of the labourer may suggest, into the upper tank, having filled both these small ones with gravel of the best he can get, free from loam or clay. The water passing into the first, will, if properly constructed, come out of the top of the second, and run into the large tank in a filtered state, and in the large tank will keep sweet and clean for any length of time, be cool and

dry summers, as they are generally supplied by soakings through gravels, which depend upon the quantity of rain that may fall ; and while the tank and the pond may overflow from a passing shower, such wells would derive no supply from it.

* Or 2 tarred casks sunk would answer well.

wholesome to drink in summer, and soft for washing. The gravel will, in the course of time, get
foul, it must then be taken out, washed clean, and
replaced. Thus the filtration will go on without
any trouble or expense.*

The clay, the stones, the chalk, the timber, and
other materials, can be got together in winter or
spring, and the person about to build upon this plan
will use his discretion in the selection of his woods
for the roofings, the frames of the doors, &c. but I do
not calculate the cost of the double cottage to
exceed £40; whilst I look to the ability of the
labourer to pay £3 or £4 a year for one-half of
the double cottage, with half an acre of ground
attached.

The cottager should be instructed to adopt the
following divisions in the cultivation of his ground
for the advantageous change of his crops :

One-third wheat.

One-third potatoes.

One-third beans, peas, cabbages, leeks, and other
vegetables.

---

* Should it happen that, from a long dry season, the cottager's
stock of water is exhausted, he may, from these advantages, re-
plenish his tank from the nearest water course or pond, though
impure, and still go on with his filtered water till rain come.
This advantage is at present enjoyed at a farm-house situated on
the top of a hill in a chalky country, where great inconvenience
had previously been experienced.

The wheat under spade and hoe culture will produce an average of 8 sacks to an acre, or 5¼ bushels* to his 6th part, which will produce him 100 loaves of 4lb., or 4 such loaves per week for 25 weeks, between Michaelmas and Lady-day.

Good ground, with good culture, will yield him on his 6th part of an acre 80 bushels of potatoes,† 40 bushels of the best for his family use will give 6lbs. a day throughout the year ; and the inferior, with the surplus beans and other vegetables, will enable him to maintain 2 pigs in a year, one at a time.‡

Thus, paying £3 a year, he would get for 2*d*. a day, his cottage and its comforts—bread enough for half the year, potatoes for the whole year, his vegetables and his bacon.

---

* Wheat has been raised upon allotments of land at Tytherton, in Wilts, upon Lord Lansdowne's estate, by poor people, at the rate of 14 sacks per acre, and I am assured a much larger quantity. The production of wheat by this method of spade and hoe culture is of three-fold advantage to the poor man, viz.:—It teaches him œconomy in its whole process;—it furnishes him with a little straw for his pig, &c. and it changes his crops judiciously.

† I have here only given the usual quantity of potatoes grown upon good land, with the best field culture. In Essex they grow more.

‡ It may be supposed the garden will want a supply of manure ; and, certainly, when it is to be had easily, it will amply repay its expenses. The cottager, however, with his pig and good management, will do well enough in that respect. It may here be remarked, that land generally will rather improve than otherwise, where it receives back again the equivalent or produce in manure for what it yields, and here all is consumed at home.

Such, with common providence, and ordinary industry, would be the effect of the cottage system upon
the labourer ; except therefore he should be deprived
of health and of friends, or overtaken by age, he
would not have occasion to resort to the poor rates
for relief.

His interest will be more settled, his morals less
endangered, and his connexion with the farmer fixed
upon a basis of mutual dependence.

Such then is the system I would earnestly recommend to be taken into consideration forthwith.
Although circumstances may not now admit of restoring the domestic manufacture, (yet I think, in
some degree, that might be done,) much out-doors
work is supplied in the garden, and many opportunities may call for the employment of the wife and
children in planting beans in the spring, in harvesting, &c. on the farm, at a rate of wages easy to the
farmer.

Desirable as this plan would seem, yet like all
other plans for the benefit of mankind, it will, no
doubt, have objections started to it ; and must itself
be imperfect, without having regard to the pecuniary
provisions for carrying it into effect.

The farmer cannot, in this case, be expected to bear
the expense of building, except he hold a long lease,
and construct a cottage as London builders do their
houses, to last just for the term of a lease.

Looking, therefore, to the landlord as the person

from whom all the advantages should generally spring, it is necessary to show the benefit to be derived by him in adopting the plan.

There is a very good pattern for these cottages in some double ones at Polstead, a farm in Suffolk, some of which were built 16, and some 22 years ago, and have always let at £8 a year each. Now, in order to give full scope of calculation to cover all contingencies, I will say that the double cottage upon the plan proposed, shall cost . . . £50*

The interest on which at 4 per cent. is . . 2

Add the rent of the acre 1

Annually sunk as interest and rent . . . 3

The cottage when constructed to let at per annum, with the acre of ground . . . 8

Deduct to repay rent and interest annually . 3

Will give an annual surplus of 5

which, if applied as a sinking fund, would pay off the £50 in less than 10 years, and leave the improvement to yield the additional rent as an increased value of the farm, to the extent of £8 per annum as long as the cottages let at this rate—the original outlay and interest thereon having been repaid. The expense of repairing the cottage would be trifling, and it would not require thatching in less than 30 or 35 years.

---

* This is far above the necessary cost in ordinary cases; it need not exceed £35 to £40.

The farmers complain of the want of these cottages, and the labourer complains that he has to toil from one to three miles in all weathers to his labour.

To the landlord or farmer erecting such cottages, having other and important objects in view, a high rent, or the encrease of the sinking fund, must be only of secondary consideration. The cottage can be charged with advantage but £3 per annum ; and this I should propose as the maximum of rent,* when the prime cost, &c. has been returned.

It would be advisable not to allow the power of removing the labourer to vest solely in the farmer ; but, nevertheless, it might be always right to attend to his reasonable representations, and to allow him to receive the rents. The detail of these arrangements must be left to the parties interested.

The principle being admitted, and the advantage allowed, nothing can stand in the way of effecting so great a good but the requisite arrangements between the parties, and the providing of the necessary funds. The poor rates would be so materially reduced, the stock and produce of the land so greatly increased by additional labour bestowed upon it, the convenience of the farmer and the comfort of

---

* Many useful arrangements may be made as to rent, and if the sum could be reduced to one shilling per week, there would be advantages in it, and one in particular would be a short account and certain payment.

the labourer so promoted, and the interests of the landlord so consulted, that one can scarcely anticipate an objection to any measure that could tend to effect this great national object of resettling the labouring classes.*

When the landlord is not disposed to advance the money or to remit it in the tenant's rent, where the tenant on lease does not feel confidence or strength enough, where could be the objection, if all parties would agree, to remitting the poor rates on such farms as adopt this plan, in proportion to the number of men housed or employed on such farms for the next twelve months, and out of other poor rates assessed to pay the wages of the men, whilst employed in constructing these cottages.

If government would receive this plan as a beneficial one, it might be so modified as to meet all cases; and money might on some occasions, under an act of parliament, be borrowed on the credit of the poor rates, and be applied on loan, to be repaid by the rent for a given number of years. I throw these hints out rather for consideration, and as supplying some chance of means for effecting the object under some circumstances, as I am not prepared to digest any part of a pecuniary plan of relief. It is quite clear, however, that the increasing scarcity of

* I calculate that, ultimately, the farmer, under this system, will be enabled, and see that it is also his interest to keep more labourers than he does at present.

money with the farmers must tend to embarrass all efforts at improvement; and whilst so many suckers draw off in too great a proportion from the country the comparatively small part of the circulation that finds its way there, little will be left to be applied to any permanently good purpose; and thus all attempts at amelioration must be vain, when no means can be found to effect it. But I am most respectably informed, that if the farmers were allowed to take the poor from the workhouses in the Hundreds, they could maintain them themselves for one-fourth of what they are charged for their maintenance therein.

If these cottages are to be built, the building will give employment to many persons; but one great benefit will be conferred, if their wages are paid out of a fund provided by the landlord, or any capitalist (not being the farmer) who has to draw his funds from London.

With reference to the second point of building cottages and alloting land.—The same mode of construction can be resorted to; but I must say, that I should deprecate any measure that may have for its object to settle an independent description of peasant upon allotments of public land. Either he must be free from control, enterprising and daring, which he would be upon a small portion of such tenure, or he must be set up as an independent petty farmer, and as such would be a perfect nuisance to all around him. It would be impossible, I conceive, to make him otherwise, and no hope could be entertained of controling him; it would be far better for farmers to take on ~~double the~~ _a greater_ number of cottages and cottagers their need would require, and pay them ~~half or~~ three parts of the year, _or more_ their amount of wages, leaving them to shift as well as they could when there was not full employment for them; and this they might do with their own exertions and the advantages here contemplated.

If these allotments of waste lands take place at all, they should be made to farmers in reduced circumstances, who have lost their farms, in portions of not less than from 60 to 100 acres. These men should be of good character, with respectable and industrious families.*

---

* These may, no doubt, be so located with many advantages. Their whole buildings may be of the same material as the cottages, care being taken that the barns have plenty of holes left in their walls. Their floors may be of the same. Small span of roof must be observed. Many hundreds of acres now in the hands of Government do no more than clear their expenses. The young oak timber in the Government wood near Rochester, is cut down at 20 years' growth and under, and I am told this is done to pay the expenses of surveyors, stewards, woodmen, &c. Here then is an excellent opportunity to try the experiment. With wood, clay, chalk, and good land, much may be done here; and the small rent which the Government may put on it, (say after the first 7 years) would give an advantage to all parties; and there are persons disposed to make this experiment.

Funds should be provided them on loan out of the public stock, which they should undertake to repay with interest, paying no rent for the land for a given number of years, and providing themselves the requisite cottages for the labourers, whom they could hold as their tenants.

I do not agree with the plan of large assemblies, as in dormitories, for these create expense, dissatisfaction, and disturbance :—nothing can be so cheap, so easy, and so convenient to all parties as locating the labourers upon the farms where they are wanting, and where they used to be; and I trust this will be seen and acted upon by all those who are deeply concerned in it without delay. If the work is not proceeded with in the summer season, but is left until the approach of winter, in order that no time should be lost, the ground should be *early* marked out, and dug up to take the winter's frost; the poles cut for rafters, and the clay and chalk carried to the spot during winter, as it will work much better for being weathered. Now if this is not done, a season will be lost, and if the seed-time is lost, the harvest must be lost also, and you cannot house the poor man by the next winter. No doubt parishes would help the poor man to prepare his ground and seed it; this would go a long way in effecting the object. His beans and potatoes should be planted in March, wheat must probably wait untill the next autumn, but then he may have the more potatoes and beans, as both are good preparations for wheat; all the rest may be left to himself.

I have made these observations solely with a view to be useful in these times of excitement and suffering. They are the result of my own experience, which has not been inconsiderable, and also of information derived from intelligent men in different parts of the Kingdom, possessing practical knowledge in such matters, and well acquainted with the state of the country, who all agree as to the course recommended in this letter ;—that the only sure and effectual remedy for the present disaffection and suffering, is to restore the labourer to his home on the land which he cultivates. Impressed with this opinion, I have suggested such measures as seemed to me most likely to facilitate the attainment of an object so desirable. If they prove in any degree useful, I shall have obtained my wish.

I have now only to express the sincere satisfaction I feel in submitting these observations to you, who, following the steps of your honoured and revered Father, have never pulled down the poor man's dwelling, without previously providing him with a better, and have made his bodily comforts, and moral and religious instruction, the objects of your solicitude and care. By the exertions of an advocate so mild, so powerful, and prudent as yourself, the happiest results, under the blessing of Divine Providence, may be expected for the poor man's cause.

Most respectfully,

I have the honor to remain,

Sir Thomas,

with gratitude and esteem,

Your obliged and obedient humble servant,

THOMAS POSTANS.

Printed for Michael Staunton, 1, Craven Street, Strand, London.

ALLOTMENTS OF LAND

A LETTER

TO

LANDED PROPRIETORS,

&c. &c.

Price Sixpence.

ALLOTMENTS OF LAND.

A LETTER

TO

LANDED PROPRIETORS,

ON THE

ADVANTAGES OF GIVING THE POOR

ALLOTMENTS OF LAND.

BY

MONTAGU GORE, Esq.

LONDON:

JAMES RIDGWAY, PICCADILLY.

M.DCCC.XXXI.

A LETTER

TO

LANDED PROPRIETORS,

&c.

GENTLEMEN,

I SHALL make no apology for addressing you on this occasion, further than by remarking, that my object is to impress on your
minds the wisdom of a measure, which, I believe, to be no less requisite for your own
interests, than conducive to the welfare of the
peasantry. It will be admitted by every one,
and is incontestably proved by official returns
that there is, at present, a great surplus of
labour beyond the means of present employ-

A 3

ment; and emigration, and other plans, have been submitted to the public, as being likely to equalize labour to the demand for it

Into a consideration of these proposals, it is not my present purpose to enter; but to endeavour to point out to you the wisdom, the expediency, the policy, of granting allotments of land to the labourers, and thus doing an act *in itself good;* and which will come in aid and assistance of other projects

The first great advantage of this plan appears to me to consist in its certain tendency to diminish the amount of poor's rates. It is the poor's rate which is the curse that at present preys on the vitals of agricultural prosperity; which diminishes the Landlord's rent, and debases the character of the peasant. But give the labourer half an acre of land, and allow him reasonable wages, and you will find your own incomes freed from a burthensome charge, and the parish pauper converted into an industrious peasant.

It is not only by an increase in his *pecuniary* resources that the condition of the peasant will be improved ; his character will be elevated ; his pride, his honest pride, will make the man who can cultivate a bit of land for himself, to scorn dependance on others.

Secondly ; this plan secures property more effectually, than any other that can be suggested. It secures it by giving the peasant " a stake in the hedge ;" by giving him an *interest* in the maintenance of public order ; by attaching him to his superiors.

It is my firm belief that there exists not on the face of the globe, any class of men, who are so naturally inclined to obedience and respect for superiors, as the English peasantry.

Cultivate their affections, improve their understanding, and enable them to see through the flimsy sophistry of demagogues ; and what is of more importance, by your *acts*, give the lie to their *statements*; by your *kindness*, give the lie to those who represent you as *neglectful* of their *interests*; by your *sympathy*, give the lie to those who say you are *callous* to the *afflictions* of the people; and you will secure to yourselves the support of a class of men who will defend your interests, during any political catastrophe. Enlist on your side the bold peasantry of your country, and you may defy the utmost efforts of faction, and rest safe from its attacks. Well has one of our poets described their valour, and bravery.

> " Sober he seem'd, and sad of cheer,
> " As loath to leave his cottage dear,
> " And march to foreign strand;
> " Or musing who would guide his steer,
> " To till the fallow land."
> " Yet deem not in his thoughtful eye,
> " Did aught of dastard terror lie ;
> " More fearful far his ire,
> " Than theirs, who, scorning danger's name,
> " In eager mood to battle came,
> " Their valour, like light straw on flame,
> " A fierce, but fading fire."

But it is not so much to their courage, if called on to fight in your defence, as to the establishment among them of quiet, peaceable, orderly habits, that I would direct your attention. The time that might otherwise be spent in the public-house, will be passed in cultivating their little spot of ground, or in the practice of those domestic virtues that content and industry produce. The peasant will feel himself raised in the scale of society; he will feel that he has a character to lose; he will form sober and virtuous habits himself, and impart them to his children. Nor let philosophers be apprehensive, that if the comforts of the poor are increased, population will increase too rapidly. At present, the ignorant and uninstructed labourer puts no restraint on his passions; he knows that the parish must support his progeny, and is reckless of consequences; but when his character is improved, he will scoff at the idea that his family should ever beg that bread from charity, which he will feel his own and their industry ought to procure for them. He will be proud to think that he is independent of parochial relief, and this feeling will enable him to master his passions and appetite.

On considerations of interest, then, is the plan worthy your notice; and, surely, if it merits the sanction of your reason, it cannot but be grateful to the best feelings of your hearts. How delightful will it be for you to have revived the days of your sires of old, when the English Country Gentleman was surrounded by those who had lived on the property for generations, and had not been compelled to seek precarious subsistence far from their native villages. What more smiling than the aspect of a country thus cultivated! What more grateful to the patriot, than the sight of a people thus employed! All men, I know, cannot expect to partake of this enjoyment; and as I commenced by stating, this plan should not be considered as *superseding,* but as *aiding* emigration and other projects. For what would avail emigration, unless you took measures to improve the character and condition of those who remained behind, and to prevent the recurrence of the evil it is designed to remove?

It would require a volume, if I should attempt to narrate all the instances in which this plan has succeeded. On an estate in Wiltshire, belonging to, I believe, Mr. Heneage, the plan has been attended with the very best effects; it has put a stop to poaching and other crimes; and when the disturbances broke out last winter, the labourers came in a body and tendered their services.

I may mention, as proofs of its success, two instances on property belonging to myself. In the parish of Barrow, in Somersetshire, allotments of land, to the amount of half an acre to each person, have been made, and a more sober, steady, and honest set of men, are not to be met with, than the occupiers of these allotments. In the parish of Orcheston, in

Wiltshire, the labourers have not allotments of land; but a system has been pursued there by an intelligent tenant of my own, and by other farmers, which merits attention.

Every labourer is allowed to have as much land on the farm as he can find manure for; the manure is carted to the spot for him; and he has only the trouble of digging and planting the potatoes, which are carted home for him. The succeeding year a fresh portion of ground is allotted to him; and thus the land is benefitted by undergoing this process, and the labourers all have the means of comfortable subsistence. Now, mark the consequence! When the disturbances broke out last year in Wiltshire, not a single labourer from this, or the adjoining parishes, was implicated in them.

What, let me ask, are the probable consequences to be looked for, if allotments of land were generally made? Is it not rational to conclude, that there would be a general spirit of good will, of order, and peace, spread throughout the land?

When I say *generally*, I am not prepared to say, that any system of this kind is required in the North of England, where the labourers seem to be in more comfortable circumstances; but in the South of England, there can be but few places, where the system would not be attended with great advantages.

I trust, not only that individuals, but that parishes, will adopt this plan; let it be coupled with parochial schools, and let peace, intelligence, and comfort, be attainable by the industrious and diligent!

I would wish to call your attention to the *practical* nature of this measure. Every man has his favourite nostrum for the mitigation of the prevalent distress; but, I fear, the generality of such schemes would only end in disappointment. But *this* system has been *tried;* it has been *tried* in a *variety* of circumstances; it has been *tried* by individuals quite unconnected with each other, and has been uniformly successful. It is an *intelligible* plan; every one can comprehend it, and understand its nature.

My object in writing these few pages, is to impress on your minds the propriety of adopting it on a larger scale; of making it general through this part of the kingdom; and to point out the wisdom of its being followed by *parishes.* And I entertain an hope, that this system will, in a considerable degree, remove the evils which the misuse of the Poor Laws has engendered; promote the interests of the landholders, and contribute to the moral and physical improvement of the peasantry.

Tilling, Printer, Chelsea.

A LETTER

TO THE

MARQUESS OF SALISBURY.

———

Second Edition.

THE

POOR MAN'S BEST FRIEND;

OR,

LAND TO CULTIVATE FOR HIS OWN BENEFIT:

BEING

The Results of Twenty-Four Years' Experience.

IN A LETTER

TO THE

MARQUESS OF SALISBURY,

AS GIVEN IN EVIDENCE BEFORE

THE HOUSE OF LORDS' COMMITTEE ON THE POOR LAWS.

———

BY THE

REV. S. DEMAINBRAY, B.D.,

Chaplain in Ordinary to His Majesty, and Rector of Broad Somerford, Wilts.

———

Second Edition.

———

LONDON:

JAMES RIDGWAY, 169, PICCADILLY;

JAMES PARKER, OXFORD; AND W. B. BRODIE, SÁLISBURY.

———

MDCCCXXXI.

LONDON :

PRINTED BY T. BRETTELL, RUPERT STREET, HAYMARKET.

TO THE

MARQUESS OF SALISBURY,

*Chairman of the House of Lords' Committee on
the Poor Laws.*

———————

MY LORD,

THE great advance in the prices of every article
of agricultural produce during the last war, occasioned the employment of a very large additional
capital on agricultural pursuits; lands were enclosed and cultivated which had never previously
been thought worthy of cultivation; farms were
enlarged and eagerly engaged by a new description
of farmers, who, embarking a larger capital, and
deriving greater profits from it, considered themselves entitled to live in a superior style of comfort. It is, perhaps, hardly fair to complain that
such farmers lived out of their station; many of
them were persons of better education, and of a
class superior to the old-fashioned farmer, who
lived with his workmen, partaking of almost the
same food and labour. The only point of view in

which I wish, at present, to consider the subject,
is the effect produced, by this new system, on the
condition of the agricultural labourer. No longer
boarded or lodged in his employer's house, the tie
of mutual interest was loosened; he worked for
this or that master indifferently, but with little
real attachment to his employer. After his day's
labour was over, he had to seek his comforts elsewhere; and, if well disposed, and not spending
his earnings at the ale-house, he was induced to
marry, to have a home to which he could resort;
encouraged to do so by the certainty that the
parish would provide for his family, and that his
pay would increase with their number.

In every other station of life there is some spur
to exertion, in the hope of bettering one's present
condition: the mechanic can rise to be a master in
the trade of which he is only the journeyman; the
manufacturer, by his attention and usefulness, may
obtain offices of higher trust and emolument; but
the agricultural labourer has no such encouraging
incentive; whatever his prudence or industry may
have been in his youth, he has nothing, to which
as his strength declines he can look forward, but
a dependence on parochial relief. Even if, by inheritance, or by any extraordinary exertion, he
acquires a small property, the system of paying
from the poor-rates a portion of the labourer's
wages, or, what is the same thing, the paying the
labourer from these rates in proportion to the

number in his family, operates silently, but steadily, in depriving the poor man of his little property. If he be the owner of the cottage, or of the acre or two of land, he has no legal claim on his parish as long as he retains it; and therefore, when burthened with a family, must part with it, before he can obtain a fair remuneration for his labour, or that part of it which is avowedly paid from the poor-rate ; and, while his honest pride is struggling against resorting to the parish pay table, he is often in a worse condition than the actual pauper. If to this we add the effect of enclosing commons and wastes, on which the poor man formerly enjoyed certain privileges and indulgences, we shall be forced to acknowledge, that, during the last half century, the situation of the labouring, and particularly of the agricultural classes, has been much deteriorated, as well by the circumstances of the times, as by the mode of administering those laws originally intended for their benefit.

In a short pamphlet, entitled *The Case of Labourers in Husbandry,* published in the year 1795, by the Rev. David Davies, Rector of Barkham, Berks, I find some remarks so appropriate to the present subject, that I must beg leave to insert them :—"Sound policy," says the author, "requires,
" that as many individuals as possible, in a State,
" should have an interest in the soil, as attaching
" them to the country and its constitution ; but,

" instead of giving to labouring people a valuable
" stake in the soil, cottages have been progressively
" deprived of the little land formerly let with them,
" and all their rights of commonage have been
" swallowed up in large farms, by enclosures.
" Thus an amazing number of people have been
" reduced from a comfortable state of partial in-
" dependence to the precarious state of mere hire-
" lings, who, when out of work, immediately come
" to the parish."

If such a remark could be applicable to the labouring classes in 1795, how much more forcibly does it apply to those of the present moment? Since that time many hundred enclosures have taken place; but in how few of them has any reserve been made for the privileges which the poor man and his ancestors had for centuries enjoyed? The commons and wastes enclosed have been, in general, engrossed by large farms, with hardly a nook or corner reserved for the poor man's cottage. And even if some small portion had been reserved for him, how soon must the mode of administering our poor laws, above described, have stripped it from him?

The same author informs us, that Bacon, in his history of Henry VII., praises an enactment, that
" All houses of husbandry, with twenty acres of
" ground to them, should be kept up for ever,
" together with a competent portion of land to be

" occupied with them, and in no wise to be severed
" from them—this did of necessity enforce that
" dweller not to be a beggar."

I must likewise add that, by the 25th Hen. VIII.,
c. 13, it is enacted, that (for preventing many
farms being accumulated into few hands. and for
the encouragement of tillage) no person shall have
above two thousand sheep at one time, on pain of
forfeiting 3s. 4d. for every sheep above that number. And, for the same reason, no person shall
take above two farms with houses thereon ; nor
shall any person have two, except he dwell in the
parish where they both are, on pain of 3s. 4d. a week.

From these and similar enactments, it appears
that the legislature of this country has, from time
to time, interfered, to protect the smaller farmer
from the encroachments of the larger*.

But it will be more important to our present
purpose, to be informed of our ancestors' opinions, at
the period from which we date the origin of our poor
laws. In the 31st Elizabeth, c. 7, an Act passed
to prevent any cottage being built in the country,

---

* There is a natural tendency to property being engrossed
by the few to the injury of the many, which some governments
have thought it necessary to counteract. The Mosaical law
prevented any permanent alienation of property : once in fifty
years every thing was restored to the family of the original
proprietor (Lev. xxv. 10). The frequent struggles in Rome
for an Agrarian law, sufficiently mark the importance there
attached to a more equal division of landed property, and to the
raising the poorer classes, by these means, above immediate want.

without four acres of land being attached to it; a sufficient proof of the attention then paid, by the legislature, to the annexing land to the poor man's cottage. This Act continued in force for nearly two centuries, not having been repealed till the 15th Geo. III., c. 32, the preamble to which deserves particular attention. In this it is stated, that the 31st Elizabeth had laid the industrious poor under greater difficulties to procure habitations, and *tended very much to lessen our population.* If a tendency to lessen population was the evil then intended to be removed, a much greater evil has arisen, from not regulating and proportioning the increase of population to the means of employment and subsistence. Had the Act of Elizabeth been modified, instead of repealed—had even the *single* acre been reserved for the poor man's cottage, we should not, perhaps, at the present moment, experience the same superabundance of agricultural labourers dependent on parochial relief.

That some inconvenience was felt from this repeal, even during the reign in which it took place, can hardly be doubted, when we find an Act passed in the 59th Geo. III. to enable parishes to take twenty acres of land on lease, or by actual purchase, for the employment of their poor. This Act, though in a certain degree salutary, has not been attended with any extensive benefit, and probably, because it did not return to the true spirit of the Act of Elizabeth. The 59th of

Geo. III. directed the land to be cultivated *on the parish account:* the Act of Elizabeth attached the land to the poor man's cottage, *to be cultivated for his own benefit.*

The 59th George III. passed soon after the conclusion of the last war, when the flood-tide of agricultural prosperity had ebbed back to its natural level, and when the change in the value of stock and produce pressed so severely on the farmer, however much his rent was reduced—at such a moment, when most farmers were failing, each parish was, by this Act, enabled to undertake farming with their unemployed poor—a pitiful expedient!—the working for the parish would not increase the quantity of labour with which the labour market was then so overstocked. The desirable object was, to find additional and useful labour. But, by a mistaken and short-sighted policy, it attempted a palliative, where it ought to have sought a cure; it attempted to give a temporary relief to the rate-payer, when, by giving the land to the poor man, to cultivate for his own benefit, it would have raised him above the necessity of receiving parochial relief; it would have much increased the quantity of labour—the great desideratum, and would thus have *permanently* reduced the parish rates.

If the power granted to parishes, under the 59th Geo. III., of taking land for the employment of their poor, was so far extended, as to enable them to let the same to their industrious poor;

and if the quantity of land the parish was authorized to take, was duly proportioned to its size and population, we should return, in part, to the spirit of the Act of Elizabeth ; and, I sincerely hope, much of the present distress among the agricultural labourers would be prevented, and not only the parish rates essentially relieved, but the home market of our manufacturers much extended by the more flourishing state of the agriculturists.

I presume not, however, to dictate the mode in which so desirable an effect may be produced ; my object, in these statements, is to prove that precedents are not wanting for a legislative inter-ference in subjects of this nature ; and I humbly conceive that, if an Act could be passed to autho-rize and encourage, if not actually to enforce, an allowance of a small portion of land to each agri-cultural labourer, it would do more, to tranquillize and satisfy that description of persons, than any other measure that could be adopted.

> " A time there was, ere England's griefs began,
> " When ev'ry rood of ground maintain'd its man."
>
> GOLDSMITH.

It may appear presumptuous, in so humble an individual as myself, to publish an opinion on a subject, to which the committee, over which your Lordship so ably presides, has directed its particular attention ; but as the decision, to which your Lordships may come, cannot be acted on till after the recess, I trust that a plan which can be carried into immediate effect—which not only every land-owner, but every farmer can put at once in execution, will neither be uninteresting or unacceptable to the public. Their attention has latterly been much directed to the subject of letting small portions of land to the poor. In the *Quarterly Review* for Midsummer, 1829, this system was very ably and strenuously advocated, and the parish to which I shall have occasion presently to more especially advert, was mentioned in that article as having tried that experiment with success. For though since this Review was published the public attention has been more particularly directed to it, and the press has almost daily teemed with its recommendation, it must not be forgotten, that, towards the close of the last century, and at the beginning of the present, many benevolent societies were formed for benefitting the condition of the poor, most of which recommended the poor man's having a garden or potatoe ground. Mr. Estcourt, the father of the present member for the University of Oxford, successfully adopted the plan in the parish of Newnton, Wilts, where, for several years, only two aged parishioners received parochial relief, all the rest having accepted small portions of land at a moderate rent in lieu of assistance from the parish.

But though several persons in the intervening time have tried the experiment with success, and particularly since the article in the *Quarterly* above alluded to; yet, as there must be many who, with the sincerest desire of benefiting the poor, and the most ample means of effecting it, still doubt its general practicability, I am induced, at the recommendation of some zealous friends to the system, and whose opinions I highly respect, to publish a statement of the actual profits derived by the poor man from spade husbandry during the present year, 1830, in the parish of Broad Somerford, Wilts, where the experiment has been under trial for full four-and-twenty years.

It is a statement which was drawn up for the information of the Lords' Committee, and according to your lordship's direction, by my son, a solicitor, at Highworth, Wilts. It arose out of the evidence which I had the honour of giving to the Committee, and will, I hope with a little attention, be as intelligible to general readers as it is strictly accurate in its details. It was delivered to your Lordship's Committee on the 16th of December, and I publish it with as little delay as possible, because it is important that no time should be lost in finding employment for the ablebodied labourer; and if this employment can be made satisfactory to the person employed, and thus convince him that attention is paid to his real and permanent interest, it must have a powerful effect in restoring general confidence and tranquillity.

At the present moment, several parishes have engaged to pay their labourers a rate of wages which it will be extremely difficult for them to continue. The farmer, having joined in making the engagement, cannot depart from it with honour, or without perhaps exciting fresh disturbances. How is he then to extricate himself from this difficulty? I earnestly recommend him to try the effect of offering the poor man, at a fair but moderate rent, a quarter or half an acre of good land, to cultivate for his own benefit. Labour must be found for the poor man, and it must not be of that degrading kind which, from its avowed inutility, was felt as an insult, and which, in the present feverish state of society, would not again be borne. It must be useful labour; and if it be for himself, it will be cheerful and contented labour.

But how is the poor man to support himself while cultivating his quarter or half acre? In his present depressed state he will, in some cases, perhaps, be unable to do so without parochial assistance. At the outset some aid may be necessary; but not more than if he were one of the supernumeraries, scraping roads, dragging about loaded waggons, fetching bricks from a distance, or any of those ill-judged and irritating expedients for creating artificial labour. But with this difference, that if he works on his own land, for his own benefit, he will be well disposed and contented, and will probably consent to work on it at the same rate of wages he was accustomed to receive previous to the late extorted advance; in which case the parish would at once feel the benefit of the arrangement in reducing their rates.

But it may be said, how can each parish find land for the poor to occupy, in the manner suggested? By the 59th of George III., before alluded to, they are authorised to take twenty acres for the employment of their poor, which might be divided into lots proportioned to the wants of the parish; and, instead of the poor working on it on the parish account, let them do so on their own. If the obtaining such a quantity of land be difficult, and if it would lead to unavoidable delays, let each landed proprietor,—let each farmer, though only a rack-renter, supply the quarter or half acre to his own labourers, at the same proportionate rent which the former receives, or the latter pays. I urge the immediate adoption of this plan, because the circumstances in which we are placed are urgent; and I know of no other mode which could, with so little difficulty, be put in execution, or which would so immediately restore general harmony and tranquillity. But I urge it, not merely as a temporary expedient, but as a permanent system, as one best calculated for bringing back the agricultural labourer to his proper station in society, and replacing *a bold peasantry, their country's pride.*

It is with great pleasure that I learn, from the public newspapers, that some parishes have recently

adopted this plan; and I particularly rejoice that
one in my own immediate neighbourhood, Calne,
has come to this determination ;—I congratu-
late them on having done so, not doubting of its
favourable results. But as the experiment has
hitherto been tried chiefly in small agricultural villages, and it may be supposed not equally suited to
towns of the size of Calne, I must mention that, in
the spring of the present year, having, through the
kindness of Mr. Selwyn, obtained about eight acres
of land in the immediate vicinity of Richmond, in
Surrey, for the purpose of letting as gardens for the
poor inhabitants, I have had such numerous applications for it, that I have been obliged to subdivide it
into ninety-five portions, all of which were cultivated
in the best manner, and rendered highly productive
in potatoes, and every species of garden-stuff, and
for which the rent has already been punctually and
thankfully paid, at the rate of nearly five pounds
an acre ; and, though not really due till the year is
completed, it has been paid at Michaelmas, as
the tenants were considered better able to pay it
then, than at the conclusion of a long winter.

I mention this latter instance as a proof of the
eagerness of the poor everywhere to obtain land ;
here mechanics of every description were converted
at once into expert gardeners. Healthy exercise
in the open air, after a day of confined labour, was
a real relaxation : and it was a gratifying sight to
witness them, at the close of a summer's evening,

surrounded often by their wives and children, at their cheerful labour.

But I advocate the system principally as it relates to agricultural villages, and will therefore proceed to state the circumstances which led to its adoption in my own parish in Wiltshire.

In the year 1806, an enclosure was proposed for the parish of Broad Somerford, and a very liberal offer was made to me, as rector, for an allotment of land in lieu of tithes. But, considering it my duty to attend to the interest of my poorer parishioners, I did not consent, till I obtained for them the following conditions, namely, that every poor man whose cottage was situated on the commons or waste lands, should have his garden, orchard, or little enclosure, taken from the waste within the last twenty years, confirmed to him ; and that in case the same did not amount to the half acre, it should be increased to that quantity, by allotting a portion of land (sufficient to make up the two roods, or half acre) to the rector, churchwarden, and overseer, for the time being, who should annually let the same to each poor cottager free of rent and taxes, by which clause the allotment was secured from alienation. The same kind provision was made by the lord of the manor for cottages held of him on lives. In addition to which, eight acres were allotted to the rector, churchwarden, &c. adjoining to the village, for the benefit of its poor inhabitants, to be annually allowed them,

according to the number in their respective families; and thus every man with three or four
children was sure of his quarter of an acre, at the
least. Very great benefit has been derived from
these provisions. It in no way interfered with the
poor man's labour for the farmer; at extra hours,
and on days and half days, on which the farmer
could not employ him, ample time was given for
the cultivation of his potatoe garden. But he did
not long confine himself to the cultivation of only
one kind of agricultural produce; however small
his portion of land, he could subdivide it, and have
his crops in succession; but wheat and potatoes
formed the principal ones: the poor man's mode of
cultivation and manuring for the latter, always
securing him the following year a good crop of
wheat. Indeed, it was the common observation of
the neighbourhood, that the poor man's crop never
failed. Spade husbandry, and the constant and
minute attention of himself and family, secured
him an abundant crop, even when the farmer's
was deficient. In this manner the present generation of labourers in this parish may be said
to have been brought up in habits of early
industry and agricultural intelligence. As some
showed superior skill and industry, or were burthened with larger families, small additional portions of land were from time to time let to them,
as I was able to withdraw it from the hands of the
larger farmers, to whom, at the time of the

B

enclosure it had been let on lease. In the year
1819, a tenant giving up a farm of about ninety-
eight acres of poor land, eighteen acres were
reserved from it for some poor, but industrious
men, who, though they had long witnessed the
former tenant's want of success upon it, gladly
and eagerly undertook it. That land, which,
from the year 1806 to 1819, had never been able
to bear a blade of wheat, and only a scanty crop
of oats. is now equally productive with any land in
the parish. It will be found, in the annexed table,
to have borne, last summer, a larger quantity of
wheat per acre than the land hitherto esteemed
some of the best in Broad Somerford. The wet-
ness of the season was certainly favourable for the
lighter land, and something may be allowed to
this circumstance ; but it is notorious that these
eighteen acres, formerly of marshy peaty land,
now are uniformly and abundantly productive,
under the poor man's mode of cultivation. I
must observe that, on these eighteen acres, there
are five-and-twenty tenants.

But I have yet to produce a much stronger instance of the efficacy of the poor man's husbandry.

In the summer of 1829, a tenant, William
Knapp (I mention names in these statements
that my facts may be examined, if they admit
of the smallest doubt) informed my son, who
has for some time collected my rents for me,
that he must give up, at Michaelmas, his farm

of eighty acres, adjoining the above-mentioned eighteen-acre piece. He stated, that his crops would hardly repay his labour, and that instead of paying his yearly rent of sixty pounds, he requested thirty might be deemed sufficient, in consequence of the unfavourableness of the season. A receipt in full was given for the sum thus offered, and the farm surrendered at Michaelmas 1829. On this occasion, my son wished me to let the whole farm to the poor, in small portions; but I objected, lest the offer of so large a quantity should overstock the market, and lessen its value in the estimation of my poor tenants. But on the day appointed for letting it, there were so many eager and importunate applicants for it, that he was prevailed on to exceed his commission, and let the whole farm to them, in portions of one or two acres, with the exception of fourteen or fifteen acres of sandy gorze or furze land, of much too bad a quality to be rendered profitable to them. Selecting the most industrious and deserving of the applicants, and making them cast lots for their several portions, all were pleased and satisfied ; and this farm of eighty acres, which the preceding year had been thrown up at a rent of 60*l.*, has this year produced upwards of 80*l.* clear of all expenses, from willing, punctual, grateful tenants ; not a sixpence was deficient at the annual audit last Michaelmas.

Whoever has experienced the eagerness of the poor man to rent a small portion of land, and

knows the value he puts upon it, will not be
equally surprised at the regularity of his payment :
but the important question is, did it really answer
the poor man's purpose further than employing his
extra labour, and giving him the appearance of a
little independence, by possessing a something he
could call his own ? It is principally for the purpose of answering this question, that the present
statement is published. The annexed table of
average produce, under the head of Upper Marsh,
will prove what spade husbandry, and the poor
man working for himself, can produce, even on
very inferior soils.

Here is land tithe free, with the poor rates
moderate, which the farmer throws up at 15s. an
acre (a sufficient proof of its very indifferent
quality), yet this land is made productive, and
amply productive, by the poor man's attention and
industry. It was not fresh broken-up land, which
for one or two seasons may produce a crop, but is
soon exhausted ; it had been full twenty years
under the plough, and during that time never in
one single instance had a good crop. Yet, by the
blessing of providence, in the very first year of
the poor man's occupation, it is covered with a
luxuriant harvest, presenting a scene interesting
from its abundance, as well as from the suddenness
of the change. Many visited it out of curiosity, who
can confirm this account; but that it may not be
left to such uncertain evidence, I must refer to the
accompanying table, the particulars of which were

collected from the mouths of the individual poor tenants, whose names are given, that they may at any time be referred to for confirmation. It is not to be supposed these tenants would over-rate their profits, when they spoke to their landlord's steward. Other tenants are apt enough to under-rate their earnings on such occasions, but these honest fellows, I am convinced, told the whole and undisguised truth. If there could have been any temptation to mis-state, it would have had an opposite tendency to that of increasing their profits, and we may therefore rest assured, they are not exaggerated. Yet it appears from the table, that the average produce per acre on these three different portions of land were as follows:—

	Wheat.	Potatoes.	Barley.	Oats.
	S. B. P.	S. B. P.	S. B. P.	S. B. P.
On the strong clay land in a part of the parish, usually considered the best, in the Down Field Farm, average produce per acre	6 3 2	88 1 0	——	——
On the eighteen acre piece, adjoining Upper Marsh, poor land, but eleven years under the poor man's cultivation, by spade husbandry .	8 1 2	84 0 1	——	——
Upper Marsh, the greater part very poor land, and the first year of being under the poor man's cultivation	7 2 3	79 1 3	9 0 0	14 2 0

This statement sufficiently shows the average produce per acre to have been very encouraging; the actual profit per acre will more clearly appear from the table itself. I must, however, remark that, in calculating the price of labour, I have given the amount which the poor man would have paid, had he employed another to do it for him. But the great profit is the employment of his extra hours, and of his wife and children, who can often advantageously supply his place ; the amount of profit is therefore much under-rated. I must likewise add, that the charge of one pound for carrying out his dung is sometimes saved, as, if he recommends himself to the farmer for whom he works, it will often be done for him gratis ; but I have endeavoured, in every instance, to under-rate rather than over-rate his profits.

It remains only that I should say a few words on the construction of the table. In the first column is given the name of the tenant ; in the second, the quantity of land he occupies ; in the following columns, the actual produce of each portion of land during the year 1830, whether in potatoes, wheat, or any other kind of grain. But as the quantity of land is irregular, and the produce will be better understood by reducing it to the acre, the last columns give the quantities which an acre of land would have afforded at the same rate of produce. From these several statements per acre, is easily calculated the average produce per acre, which is given underneath. The remaining calculations for the expense of cultivating, and for rent, &c. will be best understood by inspection of the table itself. The rent I always make free of every rate, and the only penalty for non-payment is the surrender of the land, which, in the course of so many years, I have had occasion to enforce only in one single instance. I must likewise add, that I find it in no way necessary to regulate or controul their mode of cultivation; each man can best understand his own interest, and this freedom has never been abused. In confining them to a particular course of tillage, the one who manures and manages his land best, can often succeed in crops which would be injurious and unproductive on land in worse condition. Every abridgement of freedom discourages improvement.

I must now conclude, with many apologies to your Lordship for my presumption, in thus publicly addressing you; but the situation which your Lordship holds, as Chairman of the Committee, before whom I had the honour of being permitted to give the details, which I now submit to the public; and the table which accompanies them having been drawn up by my son for their Lordships' information, by your Lordship's immediate directions, I hope I may be pardoned the liberty I have taken ;—my sole view in prefixing your Lordship's name having been my earnest wish of drawing a larger share of the public attention to a subject of such paramount importance.

I remain, my Lord,

With the greatest respect,

Your Lordship's

Very humble and obedient servant,

S. DEMAINBRAY.

Rectory, Broad Somerford,
Dec. 21st, 1830.

———◆———

While this was preparing for the press, a just-published pamphlet, on Spade Husbandry, was put into my hands, written by a highly respectable magistrate for the counties of Wilts and Hants, from which it appears, that in parishes immediately adjoining to me the poor-rates, from the enclosures of commons and allotments to the poor, have been reduced considerably more than one quarter, very nearly one third of the whole.

The statement is as follows :—

		AMOUNT OF RATES.		
		£.	s.	d.
In the year ending March 25, 1819,		2074	1	8
Ditto Ditto,	1830,	1424	18	0
Reduction in Rates,		£.649	3	8

I need, I believe, have very little hesitation in asserting the town and tithing alluded to are Malmesbury, and the adjoining village of Rodbourne: and that this reduction in rates has taken place, though, in the mean time, a very large manufactory for broad cloth has entirely ceased, and there is no other manufactory substituted in its place, to give employment to the numerous hands formerly engaged in it. In addition to which, the women and children of the town were much engaged in lace making, which, from the inventions of Urling, is well known to be much on the decline.

The instance therefore here given is complete, of an actual abatement, under very unfavourable circumstances, in the amount of poor-rates; which are universally allowed to be one of the great evils of the present day. But there is another evil, immediately connected with the former, and certainly of equal magnitude, for which the foregoing statements suggest a mitigation, if not an absolute cure; namely, by retaining such of the poor lands in occupation as can be made profitable to the poor man. In the last Spring sessions it was asserted in the House of Commons, on no mean authority, that the poor lands of this country must go out of cultivation;—that they could not compete with the richer lands of Ireland, which steam navigation had brought so much nearer to us. Such an assertion, more than once repeated, by a person, for whose abilities and integrity I entertain the

highest respect, and who, as Secretary for the Home
Department, had the best means of information,
was indeed alarming. If capital is *advisedly* to
be withdrawn from the cultivation of lands on
which so much has been expended,—if any considerable portion of this island is to return to the
unprofitable wastes which many of us can still remember,—what is to become of the population
reared on them, and hitherto employed on them ?
Can the richer lands bear the additional burthen of
maintaining them ? Or, if they could, if manna
dropped down from heaven, to feed the unemployed
multitude, would they not be ill-affected and discontented in this new wilderness ? Is not an ab-
straction of capital from the landed interest now
in the course of progress, and is not a total want of
accommodation to the farmer, from the country
banker, one of the prominent reasons of the present
agricultural distress.

In remedying any deep-seated disorder, it is often
necessary to have recourse to violent remedies,
which, during their operation, are not only painful
but often discouraging. I pretend not to fathom
whether free trade, without general reciprocity,
or whether an annihilation of a paper currency,
will be ultimately beneficial; I only judge of their
present effects; and am therefore too apt to think
a rash confidence in theory, rather than practice,
has guided some of our councils. With the timidity
of age I could wish to tread back some steps, in-

cautiously taken ; and that greater deference was paid to the wisdom of our ancestors ; and I could wish that the words of Montesquieu, in his *Esprit des Lois*, lxxi. c. 18, were more often kept in the view of our legislature :—" The cultivation of the " soil is the greatest of all manufactures, and the " truest source of riches."

AN ACCOUNT of the Produce derived by Poor Men from Spade Husbandry, in the Parish of BROAD SOMERFORD, in the County of WILTS, in the Year 1830.

IN THE DOWN FIELD, WHICH IS STIFF HEAVY LAND.

TENANTS' NAMES.		Quantity of Land.			Potatoes.		Wheat.			Potatoes, per Acre.			Wheat, per Acre.		
		A.	R.	P.	s.	B.	s.	B.		s.	B.	P.	s.	B.	P.
William Tarrant	had on	0	1	34	.	.	3	2	equal to	.	.	0	7	2	1
Jacob Miles	ditto	0	1	0	17	0	.	.	ditto	68	0	0	.	.	.
William Barnes	ditto	0	0	39	25	0	.	.	ditto	102	2	1	.	.	.
Charles Tanner	ditto	0	0	39	27	0	.	.	ditto	110	3	0	.	.	.
William Tanner	ditto	0	2	39	.	.	4	0	ditto	.	.	.	5	1	2
Richard Woodman	ditto	1	0	0	80	0	.	.	ditto	80	0	0	.	.	.
Ditto	ditto	1	0	0	.	.	6	0	ditto	.	.	.	6	0	0
Richard Tanner	ditto	0	1	0	20	0	.	.	ditto	80	0	0	.	.	.
Ditto	ditto	0	2	0	.	.	4	0	ditto	.	.	.	8	0	0
										441	1	1	26	3	3

Potatoes.
s. B. P.
5)441 1 1
88 1 0   Average produce per Acre

Wheat.
s. B. P.
4)26 3 3
6 2 3

Dr.   *The Poor Man in Account with Himself.*   **Cr.**

IN RAISING AN ACRE OF POTATOES IN THE DOWN FIELD.

	£.	s.	d.		£.	s.	d.
To digging an Acre, at 3d. per lug or perch	2	0	0	By 88 Sacks and 1 Bushel of Potatoes, at the average price of 4s. per Sack	17	13	0
Ten Sacks of Potatoes for Seed, at 5s. a Sack, which was the price last year	2	10	0				
Four Days' Work for a Man, at 1s. 6d. a-day, planting	0	6	0				
Ditto for a Woman, at 6d. a-day, to help	0	2	0				
Ditto for a Man hoeing, at 1s. 6d. a-day	0	6	0				
Ditto for a Man earthing up	0	6	0				
To digging up the Crop in a workmanlike manner, so as the Land would be fit to put to Wheat or Barley, without being redug, 5d. a Sack; and take the average of 88 Sacks per Acre, it will amount to	1	16	8				
Expense of hauling Dung	1	0	0				
Rent of Acre, free of all Rates	2	0	0				
	£.10	6	8				
The Nett Profit to the Poor Man	7	6	4				
	£.17	13	0		£.17	13	0

Dr.   *The Poor Man in Account with Himself.*   *Cr.*

IN RAISING AN ACRE OF WHEAT IN THE DOWN FIELD.

	£.	s.	d.		£.	s.	d.
Two Bushels and a Half of Wheat for Seed, at 7s. 6d. a Bushel . . .	0	18	9	By Three Quarters and Two Bushels of Wheat, at the present price of 3l. 4s. a Quarter	10	8	0
To Hoeing in an Acre of Wheat .	0	5	0				
To Weeding same	0	5	0				
To Reaping same	0	7	0				
To Thrashing out Six Sacks and Two Bushels, at 1s. 6d. a Sack . . .	0	9	9				
Hauling Dung	1	0	0				
Rent of Acre, free of all Rates .	2	0	0				
	£.5	5	6				
Nett Profit to the Poor Man .	5	2	6				
	£.10	8	0		£.10	8	0

In the Eighteen-Acre Piece, which has been let to the Poor ever since 1819, and much improved in Quality by their mode of Cultivation.

NAMES OF TENANTS.		Quantity of Land.			Potatoes.		Wheat.			Potatoes, per Acre.			Wheat, per Acre.		
		A.	R.	P.	s.	B.	s.	B.		s.	B.	P.	s.	B.	P.
William Tarrant	had on	0	2	0	50	0			equal to	100	0	0			
Ditto	ditto	0	2	5			5	0	ditto				9	1	2
Charles Giddings	ditto	0	1	0			2	1	ditto				9	0	0
Mary Knapp	ditto	0	1	0			2	1	ditto				9	0	0
Giles Porter	ditto	0	1	0			2	2	ditto				10	0	0
Jasper Porter	ditto	0	1	0	19	0			ditto	76	0	0			
Thomas Turtle	ditto	0	2	0	40	0			ditto	80	0	0			
Ditto	ditto	0	2	0			3	2	ditto				7	0	0
Jacob Miles	ditto	0	1	0	24	0			ditto	96	0	0			
Ditto	ditto	0	1	0			1	3	ditto				7	0	0
John Knapp	ditto	0	0	35	15	0			ditto	68	2	1			
Ditto	ditto	1	0	0			7	2	ditto				7	2	0
										420	2	1	58	3	2

Potatoes.
s. B. P.
5)420 2 1
84 0 1

Wheat.
s. B. P.
7)58 3 2
8 1 2

Average produce per Acre . 84 0 1

Average produce per Acre . 8 1 2

Dr.   *The Poor Man in Account with Himself.*   *Cr.*

IN RAISING AN ACRE OF POTATOES IN THE EIGHTEEN-ACRE PIECE.

	£. s. d.	£. s. d.
The same Expense as mentioned in the Down Field Account, excepting 10s. less for Rent }	9 16 8	
Deduct 1s. 8d. for digging up the Crop, the average being less }	0 1 8	
		9 15 0
Nett Profit to the Poor Man .		7 1 0
		£.16 16 0

	£. s. d.
By 84 Sacks of Potatoes, at 4s. per Sack	16 16 0
	£.16 16 0

Dr.   *The Poor Man in Account with Himself.*   *Cr.*

IN RAISING AN ACRE OF WHEAT IN THE EIGHTEEN-ACRE PIECE.

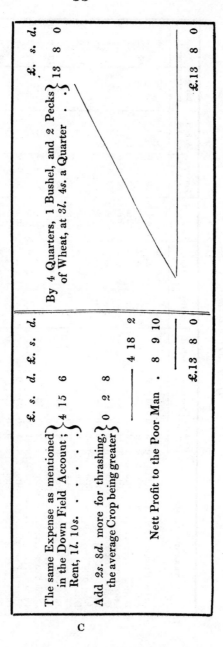

	£. s. d.	£. s. d.
The same Expense as mentioned in the Down Field Account; Rent, 1*l.* 10*s.*	4 15 6	
Add 2*s.* 8*d.* more for thrashing, the average Crop being greater	0 2 8	
		4 18 2
Nett Profit to the Poor Man		8 9 10
		£.13 8 0

	£. s. d.
By 4 Quarters, 1 Bushel, and 2 Pecks of Wheat, at 3*l.* 4*s.* a Quarter	13 8 0
	£.13 8 0

C

In the Upper Marsh Farm, which is poor light Land, and was let to the Poor soon after Michaelmas 1829.

TENANTS' NAMES	Quantity of Land A.	R.	P.	Potatoes s.	B.	Wheat s.	B.	Barley s.	B.	Oats s.	B.	equal to	Potatoes, per Acre s.	B.	P.	Wheat, per Acre s.	B.	P.	Barley, per Acre s.	B.	P.	Oats, per Acre s.	B.	P.
Harry Hindon .... had on	0	3	0	60	0					7	1	equal to	80	0	0							14	2	0
Ditto	0	2	0			6	0					ditto				6	0	0						
Ditto	1	0	0	80	0							ditto	80	0	0									
Giles Porter	1	0	0	40	0							ditto	80	0	0									
Robert Croker	0	2	0			4	2					ditto				9	0	0						
Ditto	0	2	0					5	0			ditto							10	0	0			
John Knapp	0	2	0									ditto												
Ditto	0	2	0							8	0	ditto										16	0	0
—— Wheeler	1	0	0					8	0			ditto							8	0	0			
John Conely	0	2	0	34	0							ditto	68	0	0									
Ditto	0	2	10							8	0	ditto										16	0	0
Jacob Teagle......	0	1	30	50	0							ditto	88	3	2									
Ditto	0	1	0	20	0					7	0	ditto	80	0	0							16	0	0
Thomas Knapp......	1	0	0									ditto												
Ditto	1	0	0			8	0					ditto				8	0	0						
Ditto	1	0	0							10	0	ditto										10	0	0
													476	3	2	23	0	2	18	0	0	72	2	0

Potatoes.
6)476 3 2
79 1 3

Wheat.
3)23 0 2
7 2 2

Barley.
2)18 0 0
9 0 0

Oats.
5)72 2 0
14 2 0

Average Produce per Acre .. 79 1 3 | 7 2 2 | 9 0 0 | 14 2 0

Dr.   *The Poor Man in Account with Himself.*   *Cr.*

IN RAISING AN ACRE OF POTATOES IN THE UPPER MARSH FARM.

	£.	s.	d.	£.	s.	d.
The same Expense, &c. as mentioned before . . }				9	16	8
Deduct for digging up, the average Crop being less . }				0	3	8
				9	13	0
Nett Profit to the Poor Man .				6	4	9
				£.15	17	9

	£.	s.	d.
By 79 Sacks, 1 Bushel, and 3 Pecks of Potatoes, at 4s. per Sack . . . }	15	17	9
	£.15	17	9

Dr. *The Poor Man in Account with Himself.* **Cr.**

IN RAISING AN ACRE OF WHEAT IN UPPER MARSH.

	£. s. d.	£. s. d.
The same Expense &c. as before . . . . }	4 15 6	
Add for thrashing out the average Crop, being greater }	0 1 6	
		4 17 0
Nett Profit to the Poor Man .		7 7 0
		£.12 4 0

	£. s. d.
By 3 Quarters, 6 Bushels, and 2 Pecks of Wheat, at 3l. 4s. a Quarter . }	12 4 0
	£.12 4 0

Dr.   The Poor Man in Account with Himself.   Cr.

IN RAISING AN ACRE OF BARLEY IN UPPER MARSH.

	£.	s.	d.		£.	s.	d.
To Four Bushels and 2 Pecks of Barley, for Seed, at 3s. 6d. a Bushel	0	15	9	By 4 Quarters and 4 Bushels of Barley, at 35s. per Quarter	7	17	6
,, Hoeing-in an Acre of Barley	0	5	0				
,, Mowing same	0	1	6				
,, Thrashing out 9 Sacks of Barley, at 10d. per Sack	0	7	6				
,, Hauling Dung	1	0	0				
,, Rent	1	10	0				
	£3	19	9				
Nett Profit to the Poor Man	3	17	9				
	£7	17	6		£7	17	6

Dr.   *The Poor Man in Account with Himself.*   *Cr.*

IN RAISING AN ACRE OF OATS IN UPPER MARSH.

	£.	s.	d.	£.	s.	d.
The same Expense as for Barley—namely				3	19	9
Add more for Thrashing . .				0	4	7
				4	4	4
Nett Profit to the Poor Man .				4	9	8
				£.8	14	0

	£.	s.	d.
By 7 Quarters and 2 Bushels, at 24s. per Quarter	8	14	0
	£.8	14	0

Printed by T. Brettell, Rupert Street, Haymarket, London.

FINIS.

LETTER

TO THE

LORD CHANCELLOR,

ON

TITHES.

TITHES.

COMMUTATION *versus* COMPOSITION:

THE

RIGHTS OF THE LAITY,

AND THE

RIGHTS OF THE CHURCH,

ILLUSTRATED, AND PROVED NOT TO BE THE SAME;

IN A

LETTER

TO THE

LORD CHANCELLOR BROUGHAM.

BY

MAJOR HENRY COURT,

MEMBER OF THE ROYAL ASIATIC SOCIETY.

LONDON:

JAMES RIDGWAY, 169, PICCADILLY.

M.DCCC.XXXI.

TILLING, PRINTER, CHELSEA.

TO THE

RIGHT HONOURABLE

HENRY, LORD BROUGHAM & VAUX,

Lord Chancellor of Great Britain, &c. &c. &c.

My Lord,

On the Motion of the Archbishop of Canterbury for the Second Reading of the Tithe Composition Bill, your Lordship is represented, in the course of your Speech, to have observed, " If it was fit that some change " should be made, that these secular interests " of the Church should be, in some degree, " relinquished, he would wish to impress upon " their Lordships, and more particularly upon " the Right Reverend Bench, that not the inte- " rests of the community only, but, in an especial " manner, the interests of the Church, required " that the sacrifices should be made; for he " did not think the wit of man ever devised

B

" a scheme so well calculated as that of Tithe,
" to produce ill blood between a nation and its
" religious instructors." It would be committing great injustice, for a moment to suppose,
that the people of England and Ireland do not
excite a more than equal degree of sympathy
and interest in your Lordship's breast, than the
slaves of the West Indies, or the negroes of
Africa; and as the powerful mind of your
Lordship has so frequently, so humanely, and
so strenuously been applied to the means of
alleviation, and gradual abolition of the slave
system in the colonies, a greater confidence is
reposed in the disposition of your Lordship, to
direct your attention and best endeavours to
the removal of that State of Vassalage which is
imposed by the present system of the Tithe
Laws upon the whole agricultural community
of England and Ireland.

You will, my Lord, participate in the gratification which we must all feel, in contemplating
the exemption of any portion of our fellow-
subjects from a debasing thraldom, from which,
by the wisdom, the firmness, and the determination of the people of Scotland, they have so
happily rescued themselves. Our satisfaction
in beholding them released from such ignominy,
is the more peculiarly heightened by the reflection; that they at once offer to us the bright

example of a highly cultivated, moral, and religious people, who cheerfully discharge their obligations to the Ministers of their Church, whilst they faithfully fulfil the higher duties of loyalty and allegiance to the King, and to the laws; who, at the same time, present to your Lordship, to His Majesty's Ministers, and to all classes of His Majesty's subjects, a clear, marked, and undoubted evidence, established by long experience, in precedent of the practicability of the justice, and of the true upright policy, of effectually removing the evils of the present system of Tithe Laws, which the people of Scotland have so worthily and so indisputably demonstrated, can be done on an equitable principle of commutation, without injury to the State, without any danger to religion, and without detriment to the equitable rights of the Church.

It is true, my Lord, that there is a clear distinction between the situation of the slaves in the West Indies, and the agriculturists of England and Ireland ;—the one is the property of his master, and is denied the privilege of locomotion, or the exercise of free will ; the other is free in these respects, so far as circumstances will enable him to indulge such privileges. The distinction, also, exists, as between the individual (the slave) who, by law, is com-

pelled by the mere will of another, (his master
and owner, who feeds, who clothes, who lodges,
and who takes care of him, in sickness and in
health, in infancy, in youth, and in old age,) to
work at any time, place, or manner, for the
benefit of his master; and the man (the subject
of Tithe) who is not compelled by any individual, but by the no less absolute force of circumstances, is necessitated to work for the
benefit of another, (the Tithe-owner,) who is
armed by the powers of the law to take from
him, not only a portion of the produce of his
labour, but, in reality, a portion also of the substance which he may expend in furtherance of
the objects of his labour; who is not fed, nor
clothed, nor maintained in any way by the
other, who may even be totally regardless whether the portion so taken do not deprive him of
the very means of his subsistence.

The owner of the slave in the West Indies
says, that he has a right to his slave, acquired
by purchase or inheritance, sanctioned by the
enactments of the Legislature, and confirmed
by the practice of the most remote antiquity,
and also of Holy Writ; and his plea cannot be
impeached, whatever just objections may otherwise be made to his title of property.

The Tithe-owner may, or may not have acquired his title by purchase, or inheritance;

but it is more than doubtful, whether the right
which he now exercises under the powers of the
law, to a Tithe of the whole produce of the
land, be sanctioned by the practice of antiquity;
and, most certainly, it is not by the doctrine
of Christ, for, as Bishop Newton has said, in
vol. 2. p. 185, of his Works, " The Levitical
" Law being abolished by Christ, the divine
" right of Tithes ceased with it." That such
a law was denounced by our Saviour, is sufficient for our conviction that it was considered
by him to controvert the purposes of his mission
upon earth. We have, therefore, the less reason to be surprised, that the practice of such a
law has been uniformly attended with detriment to religion, and with animosity, contention,
and tumult, among men.

So far, therefore, as undisputed antiquity
may plead a title or excuse in such cases, the
proprietor of the slave, who holds absolute
power over the person ; may assume a preferable
claim to the Tithe-owner, who has only a qualified power over the labour and property of his
subject.

Your Lordship, in continuation of your
Speech, is further represented to have said,
" The Church and the Landlord were partners ;
" one-tenth of the produce of the land was the
" property of the former, just as much as the

" remaining nine-tenths were the property of
" the latter. If it was thought hard by the
" Landlords that the Clergy should step in and
" take one-tenth, it was perfectly competent
" for the Clergy to say, our tenth is as much
" our property as your nine-tenths are yours.
" It was true that the Clergy were sleeping
" partners so far as agricultural labour was
" concerned ; but they had other duties to per-
" form to society, for which their property in
" the land was the legal stipulated recom-
" pence." And in another place your Lordship
says, " The Clergy and the Land-owners
" should go in hand. A Clergyman ought to
" be able to say, You have nine-tenths, we have
" one-tenth, and the right to either is the same."
In this latter quotation of your Lordship's Speech
I most cordially agree; and if it is on this principle that the Archbishop of Canterbury's Bill
is to be conducted, it will be quite immaterial
whether the settlement of the question may
take place in the form of composition for a term
of years, or in that of commutation for per-
petuity; and I should hope in such case, that
every person will accord with your Lordship,
in agreeing to the plans proposed by that Bill.
But your Lordship will permit me to observe,
with all due deference, that this latter quotation
seems to rest on a principle, very much at

variance with that of the partnership mentioned in that which preceded it. What ought to be the case, and what constitute the actual facts of the case, remain to be considered; and it will be my endeavour to place the respective merits of the two positions in such points of view, as will admit of no misunderstanding, and which nothing short of misinterpretation can by any possibility render capable of disputation.

In entering upon this subject, I shall, for the sake of simplicity, consider the landlord and the farmer as one person, which is frequently the case in practice, and which is strictly applicable to this question.

I proceed, therefore, to consider the case as it ought to be, viz. : " The Clergy and the " Land-owners should go hand in hand." " A " Clergyman ought to be able to say, You have " nine-tenths, we have one-tenth, and the right " to either is the same."

In order that the Clergyman should go hand in hand with the Landlord, your Lordship will readily allow that they ought mutually to participate the benefits of the land in their respective proportions; that is, nine-tenths to the Landlord and one-tenth to the Clergyman. This is a clear, unsophisticated, intelligible, and honest hand in hand principle. The only question, therefore, which remains to be settled, is the whole amount of benefit accruing from the land, which may be detailed as follows:—

First,—There is the rental of the land, which the Landlord has acquired either by inheritance or purchase, and which proceeds from the power of the land to yield a natural produce.

In the second place,—There is the profits of the capital or stock vested in the land, at the risk of the Landlord alone.

Thirdly,—There is the profits of the labour employed upon the land, which is also advanced at the risk of the Landlord.

These three items, the rent of land, the profits of stock, and the profits of labour, constitute the only possible sources of benefit to the Landlord, which for simplicity may be comprised under two terms, the rent of land, and the profits of the farmer; and under one denomination the whole benefit accruing from the land will appear, under the title of " PROFITS OF THE LAND," of which the Landlord is to have nine-tenths, and the Clergyman one-tenth, according to the proportions of their respective interests, on the principle of making the rights of the Clergyman and of the Landlord the same, and this OUGHT TO BE THE CASE.

But if the claims of the Church, in defiance of the just and fair hand-in-hand principle of participation of benefits, are to be regulated by the existing system of Tithe Laws; then, my Lord, we may inquire into the nature of the partnership mentioned in the quotation, for an exemplification of those monstrous claims, which have the effect to place the whole agricultural community of England and Ireland in a state of vassalage to the Tithe-owner.

Before I do this, I will take leave to notice, that the Bishop of London is represented to have expressed his entire concurrence with the opinions of your Lordship; and to have observed, that " the rights of the Laity, and " the rights of the Church, were the same. " It was necessary, again and again, to state " that principle." The Bishop of London's objections were confined to the Clergymen, being considered *sleeping partners*, which your Lordship explained, by saying, " That the " law recognised the duties they discharged, " and for their discharge gave them a share in " the PROFITS of the land." After which, the Bishop of London is said to have expressed a hope, that the explanation " would go forth " to the country."

Permit me now, my Lord, to examine into the real merits of this partnership, between the Landlord and Tithe-owner.

The Landlord, we will say, and this at least

will not be disputed, is to have nine-tenths
of his own property in the land; and in consideration of the duties discharged by the
Clergyman, he is to be allowed one-tenth.

The land yields, say food for one cow, for
the quantity is immaterial; and during the
pasturage of this cow upon the land, there
arises a produce of milk, and the production
of a calf, which yield a profit of five pounds.
The Landlord keeps his cow, which he may
keep or sell as best pleases him; but the profit,
which can only arise from the pasturage of
the land, he divides with his partner, as in
duty bound; the Landlord getting his proportion
of four pounds and ten shillings, and the Clergyman his proportion of ten shillings. So far
all is fair and equitable; and the whole natural produce of the land appears in the form of
profit, and the hand in hand principle is duly
supported. But there comes a period of winter,
which renders it unavoidable, that the cow,
to give milk, should be subsisted with hay,
which occasions to the Landlord an expense,
equal to, or more than the value of the milk
yielded by the cow. The Landlord having
no profit, makes no tender to his partner of
any share of the milk. The Tithe-owner, his
partner, makes a demand; the partner, in reply, says, I have had no profit, for I have ex-

pended as much upon the hay as the milk is worth; besides which, you have already had your share, for I have paid you the tithe upon the hay. In reply, the Tithe-owner says, " I " know nothing about that, if it be so; I insist " upon your giving me the tenth of the milk " whilst the cow has been fed at your ex- " pense." " The rights of the Laity, and the " rights of the Church, are the same."

The Landlord then cultivates land; and, in so doing, incurs an expense of twenty pounds for the ploughing, harrowing, harvesting, pur- chase of seed, &c., and the payment of labour; but, by the return of harvest, he obtains a pro- duce to the value of twenty-five pounds. He, therefore, according to the laws of partnership, and his own simple notions of natural right and justice, offers to his partner his proportion of the profits of five pounds, amounting to ten shillings. The Tithe-owner says, My friend, you have committed a great mistake in your calculation, and you have forgotten, that " The " rights of the Laity, and the rights of the " Church, are the same;" I must have, on cultivated land, not only one-tenth of the profits, but also one-tenth of the expense, which you have incurred in producing those profits; and the amount of these will be two pounds and ten shillings, which I must have for my share of the partnership. The Landlord says, I offer to you a just proportion of the whole benefit which I have myself derived from the land; and, surely, you do not mean to tell me, that expense is the same as profit; this would indeed be a strange perversion of reason for your demand. Quoth, the Tithe-owner, Don't talk to me of proportions and reason, but go and consult the law, or rather the practice of the Law of Tithes, and it will tell you, that if you had expended fifty pounds, and you had only obtained a return of twenty-five pounds, I should still insist upon two pounds and ten shillings as my share of the partnership; because, as " I have again, and again, stated, the rights of the Laity, and the rights of the Church, are the same."

Here, my Lord, is no exaggeration, but a simple and indisputable illustration of the relations actually subsisting between the Land-lord and the Tithe-owner under the existing system of the Tithe Laws; and I beg pardon for observing, that it will exceed even the vast capacity of your Lordship's sagacity, to recon-cile such a partnership with any just maxims of law, of reason, or of justice. The maxims of law will, however, decide the question at once, by reference to the definition given of partnership.

" PARTNERS are, where two or more persons
" agree to come into any trade or bargain, in
" certain proportions agreed upon. In order
" to constitute a partnership, a COMMUNION
" OF PROFIT AND LOSS between the parties
" is essential, and this is the true criterion to
" judge by, where the question is, whether
" persons are partners or not."

The rights of the Laity, and the rights of
the Church, are, therefore, unquestionably *not*
the same in their existing relations.

There is no man, my Lord, who entertains
higher respect than myself for your great
talents, and for the exalted purposes to which
they have been applied. But when your Lordship is pleased to assert, that one-tenth of the
produce of the land is just as much the pro
perty of the Tithe-owner, (who makes no exertion, who incurs no expense, and who runs
no risk,) as the remaining nine-tenths are the
property of the Land-owner, I must, with all
humility, beg leave to submit the reason of my
objections to any such doctrine ; and at once
presume to assert, that the Tithe-owner possesses no other right to the tenth of the produce
of cultivated land, than that of a tax imposed
by the Legislature for his individual benefit,
to the individual detriment of the Landlord.

I believe, my Lord, that I speak in the

spirit, and in the justifiable language of the British Constitution, when I say, that every subject of the King possesses a natural inherent right of property in the labour of his hands, in the exercise of his talents, and in the use of his substance, so long as he exercises those rights in conformity with the laws of the land, and without injury to his neighbour; that he has a full, natural, and inherent right to what his labour or his substance may produce; and that, without his consent, no man has a right to infringe those rights, or to participate in their fruits, excepting so far as may be legally demanded of him for taxation, imposed by enactments of the Legislature to meet the public service.

The Tithe-owner, therefore, in being permitted by law to demand from the Land-owner a tenth of the produce of cultivated land, which produce is the result of the labour, of the talents, and of the application of the substance of the Landlord, possesses a right to tax the Landlord, and he has no other right whatever.

When the Bishop of London is pleased to say, " that the rights of the Laity, and the " rights of the Church, are the same," it may be presumed his Lordship does not mean to assert, that the natural and inherent rights of property are the same as the right of taxation.

Property and taxation are converse propositions; as much so, as beauty and ugliness, or light and darkness. As taxation is a necessary adjunct for the protection of property, so will the contrast of ugliness convey stronger perceptions of beauty; and the contrast of darkness will give due effect to the lustre of light. But ugliness, or darkness, have never yet excited admiration; nor will the tithe of the whole produce of cultivated land, which carries with it all the evils of taxation, without any of its benefits, ever be considered to merit being classed with a right of property; nor so long as a Tithe of that exceptionable nature exists, will it ever be acknowledged, " that the rights of the Laity, and " the rights of the Church, are the same."

The right of a man to the property in his labour, his talents, and his substance, is anterior to all law; it constitutes the very foundation and necessity of law. To protect this right, man enters into the social state; to this end laws are framed, and Governments are formed; and according as Governments are perfect, is this right respected, protected, and preserved. Has not, my Lord, the agriculturist the same right to the fruits of his industry and capital, as the manufacturer, or any other class of His Majesty's subjects? Let us suppose, for a moment, that a person came to the manufacturer and said, I am vested with a power by the Legislature to take one-tenth of the produce of your capital and industry, and you must give it to me for my own use ; *it is as much my property as the remaining nine-tenths are yours.* How long does your Lordship suppose that such a demand would be submitted to without remonstrance, and that of no ordinary degree ?

Then, indeed, would be verified the remark of Sir Robert Peel, in the debate on the Reform Bill, on the 27th of July : " Only let the Com-
" mittee think of the influence of the Press and
" Political Associations in the towns, which
" could not be said to exist in the agricultural
" districts. In fact, both the moral and poli-
" tical power of the towns would be out of all
" proportion greater than that of the people in
" the country, who could not so easily combine
" together as those in the towns, and who could
" not therefore act with the same force."

But, my Lord, it is to be hoped, that the time is arrived when justice will be done for justice sake; when no advantage will be found to result from clamour or combination; when the first appearance and evidence of a wrong will be sufficient for the attempt of its corrective, without the aid of combination or even of importunity ; when the congregated force of the towns will be no more availing than the tranquil dis-

positions of the country; when all will be conscious, that every effort is made to render impartial justice, whether to the individuals who
are scattered in the country, or to the more
imposing masses in the towns; and when none
shall be vested with powers to tax their neighbour's industry and capital, for their own personal gratifications.

It will be said, perhaps, that there is no
analogy between the produce of the land and
that of manufactures. That the land has a
natural produce, which is the gift of our benefi-
cient Creator; and that a share of the natural
produce is, in strict reason and justice, appropriated to the purposes of religion. No man
can dispute, no rational man would desire to
detract from such a position; nor in the first
part of the case of the cow, given as above, is it
for a moment questioned. But in cultivated
land,—the gift of the land is that portion of the
produce which is separated as profits;—all the
rest of the produce, is merely the return by the
land to the landlord, of what had actually been
bestowed by the landlord upon the land in cultivation. If I lend a man one hundred pounds,
and he returns it to me, he renders me no benefit; but if he gives me one hundred and five
pounds, he recompenses me, and benefits me
five pounds. This measure of the gift of culti-

c

vated land, it must also be recollected, will always exceed, or, at the least, never can fall short of the natural produce, because, if it did, the landlord would have no motive to incur the trouble and expense of cultivation. The Tithe-owner, therefore, in taking one-tenth of the profits of cultivated land, is assured, that he will participate with the Landlord in the benefits derived by cultivation ; and if there should be no benefit, the land will, with equal certainty, be returned to its primeval state of natural produce. Thus the fair hand-in-hand principle of the participation of benefits will be secured to both parties, without the possibility of injury to either ;—and a Clergyman may then truly say, as he certainly ought to be able to say, " You have nine-tenths, we have one-tenth, " and the right to either is the same." On this principle, and on this principle alone, will " the rights of the Laity, and the rights of the " Church, be the same ;" and, acting on this sacred principle, the explanation may go forth to the country in all the pride and assurance of an honest conviction of the truth of its consistency with religion, and justice, and common sense.

But when a Landlord expends a capital upon farm buildings, in the purchase of stock, and in the payment of labour, with a view to the culti-

vation of the land ; he acts the same part with
the same design as the manufacturer, who erects
buildings and machinery, buys raw cotton, and
pays for the labour of artizans ; and there arises
a strict analogy between the two. And it is
insisted ; that there exists as much reason for
taxing the manufacturing buildings, machinery,
and wages, by taking one-tenth of the manufactured goods ; as there is for taxing the farm
buildings, farming stock, and the wages of labour
employed on cultivated land, by taking the
tenth of the whole produce of the land. The
expenditure in both cases is alike,—the work of
mens hands, and the results in both cases proceed from the same causes,—the exercise of
skill and industry, and the employment of
capital.

To subject men, in either case, to a tax of
such a nature, for the benefit of individuals, is
nothing short, my Lord, of inflicting upon them
a debasing thraldom ; and so long as the agriculturists are exposed to the injuries of such a
system, so long will they be justified, by every
lawful means, to counteract its obviously heart-
rending pernicious effects. And shall it be said
that the Ministers of Religion are to contend for
the continuance of a system, which our blessed
Lord had abolished as inimical to the purposes
of his mission upon earth ?—Impossible.

The Archbishop of Canterbury, on making his Motion, is represented to have been pleased to say, that he had found extreme difficulty of framing any measure of Commutation, consistent with justice or expediency.

Justice, my Lord, is a very simple word, and is easily to be understood. The definitions of it, I find to be, " that virtue by which we give " every man what is his due ; vindicative retribu- " tion ; assertion of right." Justice is of so pleasing form, as to convey to the imagination all the beauty of holiness. With what justice I may have recommended a Commutation of Tithes, I will leave to the impartial decision of your Lordship's consideration of what has already been said.

Expediency, is a word of indefinite import. It is suited alike to the sinner and to the saint. It may be very inexpedient for a man to pay his debts, or to give to another his due ; but it is at all times just that he should do so. With respect to the difficulty represented by His Grace, as arising from the conflicting interests of the Vicar and the Rector, I confess, my Lord, that I do not clearly understand why a great principle of legislation, intended to do justice for the benefit of the whole community, should be deferred until it may be able to reconcile the interests of a few individuals, with the dif-

ferences between hops and wheat, gardens and
corn fields. I think it is but fair to suppose,
that the mutual merits of these partial interests,
might be sufficiently well adjusted in details of
the Bill for Commutation ; and that the less
difficulty would ensue, as those interests more
especially affect men of an enlightened and
liberal understanding, the business and occupation of whose lives it is ;—to study, and to enforce, by every argument and persuasion, that
great principle of moral obligation, " To do
" unto all men as you would they should do unto
" you ;" and who, in their conduct towards each
other, would, therefore, have this obligation ever
present to their minds, as a guide to their
actions.

The difficulty would, however, be effectually
obviated by the Commutation of Tithe on the
fair hand-in-hand principle of the participation
of benefits. Neither the Vicar, nor the Rector,
would be any longer so unbecomingly per-
plexed by the vicissitudes of wheat and hops;
but their respective rights, would at once be
adjusted on a fixed principle of the actual profits of the land, whatever may be the disposal
of its cultivation.

I shall not presume to offer any observations
upon the Composition Bill, because, having
been unsuccessful in all my endeavours to ob-

c 3

tain a copy of it, I am unacquainted with its details, and am ignorant of the principle upon which it may be proposed to guide the Commissioners in the assessment of the value of the estate. The value of an estate can only, it is certain, be represented by the yearly profits arising from it. The essentials of the Bill may, therefore, be said to depend upon this unknown principle.

As the rights of the Lay Impropriators are analagous with those of the Church, out of which they issue, and to which they are appendant, it cannot, for a moment, be supposed, that legislation on this subject can be intended to be partial in its operations; because the arguments which apply in objection to the existing practice of the Tithe Laws, as regards the Church, would derive additional weight, if particularly extended to Lay Impropriation, by all the comparison which may attach to the bees, with the drones of a hive. But the question will still remain, whether it be consistent with justice to adopt a Bill having such a tendency, unless it be accompanied with another to rectify its deficiencies.

With respect to that part of His Grace's Speech, wherein he is pleased to say, that, in the case of Commutation, the whole profit would fall into the hands of the Landlords, on the expiration of existing leases;—I must beg leave, with all becoming veneration and respect for His Grace, to offer my objections to this conclusion.

As the Tithe, under the fair representation of the analysis which I have before given, is partly taken from rent, partly from stock, and partly from the wages of labour; and as, by the Commutation proposed, *no* portion of that which falls upon rent, *nor* of that which falls upon the *profits* of stock, *nor* of that which falls upon the *profits* of labour, is proposed to be abstracted; so, the diminution of Tithe will merely attach to that portion which is so unwisely and so unjustly taken out of the capital vested by the farmer; consequently, the immediate effect will be, only to restore to the farmer that portion of the Tithe now taken, which religiously and justly belongs to himself. This effect will necessarily produce a diminution of the charges of cultivation, or of the cost of production; and universal experience determines, that the ultimate effect of a diminution of the cost of production is to create the possibility of reduction of price; by which, sooner or later, the whole community are certain to be benefitted. There will thence necessarily arise a new balancing principle, which will the more easily adjust the interests of the landlord and the farmer; as the Tithe, under the Commutation, will bear that fixed proportion to the profits of either, which before rested, with appalling uncertainty, upon the devoted head of the farmer; and which sometimes, by the terrors it inspired, caused the contract of the farmer to be at the disparagement of the Landlord; but which, much more frequently, and generally, produced a detriment to the farmer, by discouraging his exertions on the land.

Wherever those terrors operated to the disparagement of the Landlord; it is, perhaps, only fair to presume, that the Landlord will have restored to him that balance of right to which he may justly lay claim, in communion with the benefit to the farmer. But the general result of the Commutation will be;—to cause the new balancing principle to adjust the benefits of the community by a reduction of price;—to adjust the benefits of the Landlord and Tithe-owner by the improvement of the land, and by the extension of the cultivation;—and to adjust the benefits of the farmer, by giving him confidence in the employment of his capital, and the best exertions of his industry, and in enabling him to regulate his contracts with the Landlord, under the certainty of duly providing for his own interests.

Besides, my Lord, I desire to be understood, that in advocating the Commutation which I have proposed, I deliver it on its own merits, as a measure of PURE JUSTICE. And I submit, that, in conferring an act of justice, it is needless to inquire what particular interests may be benefitted.

Standing on the Adamantine ROCK OF JUSTICE, I send forth my fervent prayers to heaven for blessings on my Country, and for the purification of her Church. Looking down, I see the frail BARK of DELUSIVE COMPOSITION shattered against the impervious Rock; whilst the Demon of UNRIGHTEOUSNESS is overwhelmed, and sinking under the waves of " Vindicative Retribution." In the offing, I behold the fair vessel, " ASSERTION OF RIGHT," which is freighted with the sweets of COMMUTATION ; conducted by WISDOM at the HELM, with the Banner of TRUTH flying at her Ensign, and her Streamer at the mast head waving with the motto, " The Rights of the " Laity, and the Rights of the Church, are the same." The noble crew, spreading her sails of CONFIDENCE to the steady breeze of UNIVERSAL APPROBATION, she is impelled along the Sea of DESIRE into the smooth HARBOUR of LEGISLATION. There, casting the ANCHOR of HOPE, and being moored by the LINKS OF

ROYALTY to the ROCK OF JUSTICE, she sends
forth her cargo to the applauding multitudes
on the shore; and TRIUMPHANT VIRTUE, at
the same time, proclaiming the glad tidings of
INDUSTRY UNFETTERED, diffuses universal
joy, by the CONSUMMATION of the GENERAL
WELFARE, CONCORD, PEACE, SECURITY,
and HAPPINESS TO THE STATE.

Having concluded these observations, which
I most respectfully submit to your Lordship's
consideration, I have, in connexion with them,
taken the liberty to annex a copy of the Petition from the Parish of Wargrave, in the
county of Berks, which was presented to the
House of Peers, on the 11th of February last,
by the Earl of Radnor.

This Petition has but few names attached
to it, as no attempt was made to carry it
beyond the precincts of the parish; and, consequently, it will derive no importance from
the aids of combination. But as many of the
Gentlemen who signed the Petition possess
the advantages of a clear understanding, and
intelligence of mind; and as all the Petitioners
are men of respectability, it will, I am persuaded, be considered worthy of every support
which its intrinsic merits may intitle it to receive, notwithstanding that the Petitioners are
few in number, and retired into the country.

At the same time that this Petition was forwarded to the Earl of Radnor for presentation, I delivered a few remarks to his Lordship in support of its prayer, extracts of which I have also appended to this Address.

It only remains for me to offer to your Lordship my earnest apologies for the honour which I have assumed, by intruding these observations upon your attention; and to subscribe myself, with most unfeigned respect,

My Lord,

Your most obedient,

And Humble Servant,

M. H. COURT.

CASTLEMAN'S WARGRAVE,
August 9, 1831.

To the Right Honourable the Lords Spiritual and Temporal of the Imperial Parliament of Great Britain and Ireland.

The PETITION of the undersigned, being principal Owners and Occupiers of Lands, in the Parish of WARGRAVE, County of Berks,

HUMBLY SHEWETH,

That your Petitioners are deeply sensible of the injuries inflicted upon themselves individually and of those resulting to the community at large, by the existing practice of the Laws for the imposition of Tithes upon Lands.

Your Petitioners respectfully submit to your Right Honourable House, that the Highest Authorities of the Law have defined the Tithe to be a *tenth part* of the *increase yearly arising and renewing from the profits of lands:* thus giving to the Tithe, the fair form of a right of property in a proportionate distribution of that increase arising from the profits of lands, which proceeds from the creative powers of the land, through the beneficence of an all-bountiful and all-merciful God, in reward of the industry of man.

But your Petitioners humbly represent that the *practice* of the law, which enforces a delivery of one-tenth of the *whole produce*, exacts thereby a proportion of the increase greatly *exceeding* the distribution allotted by the *principle* by which Tithe is defined; for by no construction of language, nor interpretation of the nature of things, can expenditure and consumption employed in the cultivation of land be considered as *increase*. The farmer who sows two bushels of corn, and who obtains by the return of harvest twenty bushels, will not acquire a greater increase than eighteen bushels, admitting even that the produce can be raised *without* any exertion of labour or charges for cultivation. In like manner, the subsistence of the labourers, and the hay and corn consumed by cattle employed in cultivation, constitute no part of the *increase* arising from *profits*.

Your Petitioners humbly submit their allegations in this instance with the more confidence, by reference to sec. 7. Statute 2d and 3d Edward VI. c. 13, which enacts that no Tithes are due from Servants in Husbandry. But the Tithe of the whole produce necessarily exacts the *tenth* of all its *component parts*; in which, it appears to your Petitioners, must unquestionably be comprised the subsistence of servants in husbandry, who constitute the most material of human instruments in the creation of that produce. The practice of the law becomes consequently obnoxious to an infraction of this righteous and salutary statute. The anomalies of the practice of the law, your Petitioners humbly submit, are also remarkable in reference to this matter; for it provides that no Tithe is due for pasture of horses employed in husbandry, giving, as a reason, that, by their labour, corn is increased. So that when the really useful labours of horses are brought into action, which will necessitate due supplies of hay and corn for their support, they become, in fact, titheable for the whole of the hay and corn which they consume, whilst they are accessary to production, in contradiction of the just reasoning provided for the practice.

Your Petitioners, therefore, with all due deference and submission to the authority and wisdom of your Right Honourable House, will respectfully and humbly submit, that by no possibility can the whole produce be considered as the increase yearly arising and renewing from the profits of lands, that such increase must indisputably and unerringly be represented by the rent of land, added to the profits of the farmer : that the rent of land is a quantity capable of accurate knowledge, or of fair estimation, and that the profits of the farmer will generally admit of near approximation to truth, by taking them as equal to one-fifth of the rent ; after making due allowances for the subsistence of the farmer as wages of his industry, for a fair interest of the capital, which he may vest in his farm, and for a reasonable compensation of his risk, to which allowances he may be considered in rigid truth to be entitled.

Your Petitioners humbly represent that, to the deviations of the practice of the law, from the equitable principle by which Tithe is defined, may be attributed all those vexatious and lamentable collisions, which are not less prejudicial to the sacred interests of religion, than they are inimical to private happiness, and detrimental to the public peace. To the same cause also may be ascribed, the injuries resulting from undue restrictions upon the employment of capital, and upon all those exertions of industry, which would otherwise be directed to the increase of Agricultural production, the development of public wealth, and that consequent increase of public revenue which would best provide for reduction of taxation. Your Petitioners, therefore, humbly submit, that the practice of the law is attended with no less injury to the community at large, than with injustice in its operation towards those more immediately connected with Agricultural pursuit.

Your Petitioners have also to lament, that a just and equitable right of property, as defined by the principle of Tithe, is by the practice of the law converted into an unequal, injurious, and ignominious tax, which is opposed to all acknowledged maxims of justice and policy by which taxation is controlled, and of which more convincing proof cannot be adduced, than by incontrovertibly observing, that it enforces a contribution of the *largest* proportion of the increase arising from profits, from lands which are the *least* capable of affording it. The owners and cultivators of the soil are thus made subject to a system of taxation, which necessity alone could reconcile, even to meet the urgencies of the State ; but which, when levied at the arbitrary caprice of individuals for their own personal benefit, your Petitioners consider it to be no exaggeration, to say, that the whole of the Agricultural community is thereby placed in that *state of vassalage* which is directly opposed to the enlightened design and spirit of the British Constitution, and is totally unworthy the lofty pretensions of men, who, as Britons, have been taught and encouraged to cherish as their birthrights, that purity of justice and that perfect liberty which is only to be circumscribed by those duties of allegiance which they are proud to owe as loyal subjects of the King, and to the dominion of the laws.

Your Petitioners, therefore, humbly express their earnest prayer, that your Right Honourable House will be pleased to take into your early consideration the state of the Laws for the imposition of Tithes on Lands, with a view to such amelioration of the present practice, as by a limitation of the Tithe to a defined proportion of the Rent, will protect the full and fair exercise of the right of property of the Titheowner to the tenth of the increase *yearly arising and renewing* from the profits of Lands ; at the same time, that your Petitioners and the Agricultural community will be relieved of the odious thraldom and grievances inflicted by the operation of that impolitic and unjust tax, which your Petitioners humbly represent to be engendered by the present admitted practice of the law, in the exaction of the Tithe of the *whole produce* of the Land.

Your Petitioners, confiding in the indulgence of your Right Honourable House, will respectfully beg leave to observe, that it has been their anxious endeavour to avoid any imputation of hostility to the Established Church; and they have been the more desirous so to do, from their individual esteem of their Reverend Vicar, whose high character, piety, and talents, have, with uniform kindness of disposition towards all conditions of his parishioners, been directed to the discharge of the charities and usefulness of an enlightened Minister of the Gospel.

Your Petitioners, whilst thus earnestly imploring and resting with entire confidence and submission in the wisdom and authority of your Right Honourable House, for such relief from the present practice of the Tithe Laws as will yield to them a perfect participation in the benefits of the design and spirit of our cherished Constitution, desire to express their firm determination by every exertion in their power, both of person and property, to uphold the authority of the Laws, and to defend the Throne of our beloved King, from every danger which may impend through the evil designs of turbulent and wicked men.

And your Petitioners shall ever pray.

REMARKS

IN SUPPORT OF THE

WARGRAVE PETITION.

Extract from Blackstone, vol. 2. p. 24.—" A second " species of incorporeal hereditaments is that of Tithes; " which are defined to be the *tenth* part of the increase " yearly arising and renewing from the *profits of lands*, the " stock upon lands, and the personal industry of the inha- " bitants."

The increase arising from stock, will evidently constitute part of the profits upon lands; therefore, it was unnecessary to enlarge the definition in the Petition. The Tithes upon personal industry are now strictly limited by law to Special Custom, for Fish caught in the sea, and for Corn Mills.

The definition thus given by Blackstone is delivered, also, in Sir T. E. Tomlyne's Law Dictionary, in Rees's Cyclopædia, and in a Work upon Tithes, recently published, in 2 vols. by Mr. Eagle.

However high this authority may be, the definition is supported by the still stronger conviction of its consonance with common sense, and with the incontrovertible principles of reason and justice.

As in geometry it is considered a sufficient demonstration of a proposition, that the denial, or deviation from the truth asserted, are proved to lead inevitably to absurdity, or impossibility; so, in moral or politcal science, the correctness of a principle may be established with equal certainty, if it be proved that a departure from its injunctions will unavoidably influence the bad passions of hatred, animosity, contention, and a sense of injustice amongst individuals, attended with undoubted injury and calamity to the public interests; and as the evil effects of the Tithe Laws invariably result whenever and wherever the practice of them is enforced in opposition to the justice and correctness of the principle; the authority and propriety of the principle, as marked by the above definition of Tithe, will rest upon conviction, confirmed by experience.

Leaving further argument on this question; let us consider how the definition may be supported on reference to the original practice and institution of Tithes.

Bishop Newton, in the second volume of his Works, p. 184, says, "That Tithes are first mentioned in Scripture " in the history of Abraham; the first payment being made " by him to Melchisedeck, of one-tenth of the spoils he had " acquired in conquest of his enemies." So, likewise, in various passages of the Greek and Roman Histories, we read of the Tithes of spoils acquired in war, being given to the temples. Mahomed, also, in the *Al Koran*, enjoins, that " one-fifth of the spoils shall belong to God, the " Apostle, his kindred, and the orphans, the poor, and the " traveller."* But, surely, the produce of the earth, acquired by the laudable industry of Christians, is widely distinct from increase obtained by violence and rapine.

Jacob's Vow.—The next authority quoted by Bishop Newton, for the Tithes, is that " when Jacob went to

---

* Sale's Koran, vol. 1. p. 212.

" Laban, he vowed a vow, that if God would prosper him
" in his journey, when he should return, he would surely
" give him one-tenth of his increase."

The Tithe in this case, must, by every fair interpretation
of common sense, mean the tenth of the profits resulting
from his journey. The object of Jacob's journey was
advantage, or gratification to himself, and his vow had
reference to the amount of that advantage which he might
realize on his return. So, likewise, the object of cultivation is advantage, or profit; and the amount thereof is
determined by the result, placing the expenditure for subsistence, &c., during the journey of cultivation, or the time
elapsing until the period of harvest, against the produce
derived by the harvest, to shew the increase at the end of
the journey of cultivation, from which the Tithe is to be
taken.

This interpretation is confirmed by a learned Divine, in
his History of the Bible, in the following illustration of this
very subject.*

" That if he (God) would protect and prosper him in his
" journey, provide him with common necessaries in his
" absence, and grant him an happy return to his father's
" house, to him alone he would direct his religious worship;
" in that very place where the pillar stood, upon his return,
" would he make his devout acknowledgments, and offer
" unto him the *tenth* of whatever he might *gain* in the land
" of Mesopotamia."

This interpretation of Tithe of the increase, is also fully
confirmed by the following Extract from Josephus's History
of the Antiquities of the Jews, ch. 4. book 4. written in the
first century of the Christian era.

* Stackhouse's History of the Bible, book 3. chap. 3. p. 294.

After mentioning the lands to be allotted to the tribe of Levi, it says, " Besides the imposition of a *tenth part* of " the *yearly profits* arising from the *fruits of the earth*, to " be paid as a duty on the whole people, to the Priests " and Levites, which hath been religiously observed ever " since."

The purposes of the Tithe mentioned in the 14th chap. of Deuteronomy, appear to have a strict conformity with the feasts of charity held by the primitive Christians, and mentioned in the following Extract from Mosheim's Eccles. Hist. vol. 1. p. 64.

" At the conclusion of these meetings, (celebrating the " Holy Supper,) they testified their mutual love, partly by " their liberality to the poor, and partly by sober and " friendly repasts, which, from thence, were called feasts " of charity. Among the virtues which distinguished the " rising Church in this its infancy, that of charity to the poor " and needy shone in the first rank, and with the brightest " lustre."

The distinguishing feature of Tithe, according to the present practice, is, that it dries up all the sources of charity to the poor, exciting animosity, contention, and ill-will, instead of that community of brotherly love, which is the bond of peace, of social order, and good will amongst men.

Laying aside the Levitical Law, which, as Bishop Newton justly observes, p. 185, being abolished by Christ, the divine right of Tithes ceased with it; for the reason, I suppose, assigned by Blackstone, " *Malus Usus abolendus Est.*"

The authority of this Bishop may be again quoted for the origin of Tithes, under the Christian Church. He says, p. 186, " For some ages, the voluntary contributions of " Christians supplied all the necessities and occasions of

" the Church; but this zeal cooling by degrees, and some
" offering too little, and others nothing at all, the Fathers of
" the fourth and fifth centuries were very importunate with
" their congregations to make their oblations in the pro-
" portion of the tenth of their *whole income*, as it had been
" anciently practised, first by direction of God to the
" Patriarchs, and afterwards by his express law to the
" Children of Israel."

It may be presumed as undeniable, that a tenth of the *whole income* can only mean the tenth of a man's acquisition, or the profits which he may obtain during the year.

A doubt, therefore, cannot exist of the justice and propriety of the definition of Tithe, as laid down by Mr. Justice Blackstone.

The owners and cultivators of the soil as payers of Tithes, have, therefore, a just right to claim that the Tithe be limited to the principle defined by Blackstone. The more forcibly, also, is this claim strengthened, by the consideration, that the burthens of provision for the poor, with the repairs and charges of the Church, which the Tithes were specially appropriated to provide for, have been cast as additional charges upon the Tithe contributors.

It is remarkable, that, in a Work published by Murray, 1830, intitled " The Revenues of the Church of England " not a Burden upon the Public," the Author, who has left unemployed no art of sophistry in defence of the Tithes, says, " It cannot, surely, with any appearance of justice, " be represented as inimical to the interests of the public, " that a moderate portion of the *net revenue* accruing from " land, should pass from hand to hand, and be enjoyed, " subject to the discharge of specified ecclesiastical duties."

This Author may be considered, therefore, to view the Tithe in its only defensible position, as it is placed by Blackstone; and, truly, it may be said, that it would be quite impossible to defend the Tithe on any other principle or interpretation of its quantity.

Consideration of Legal Right.—All those who have advocated the right of Tithes according to the present practice, have particularly enforced the argument, that such right does not lean for support upon enactments of the Legislature, but that it constitutes a right of property, conveyed by grant, of the ancient proprietors of the land; or that such right has been established by immemorial prescription.

Grant.—With respect to the title by grant, the law says, that, " to make such a *grant good*, the thing must be grant-" able. A man cannot grant that which he *hath not*, nor " *more* than he hath. A bare possibility of an interest which " is *uncertain*, cannot be granted to a *stranger*. Words in " grants shall be construed according to a reasonable sense."

Hence it is clear, that the owner of an estate, having a property in the rent, or natural produce arising from such estate, could convey a grant of any rent charge, or proportional part of the profits of such natural produce. But it is equally clear, that he could not extend that grant, so as to make all future owners of the estate pay one-tenth of the whole *cultivated* produce of such estate, for these reasons;—

1. Because he hath no property in the labours of posterity, by which alone the property in such produce can be obtained; therefore, he would be granting that which he hath not, and, also, more than he hath; for he neither hath the future produce, nor property in future labour.

2. Because he hath no property in the capital necessary to set that labour to work.

3. Because he would be granting an *interest* which is *uncertain*, to a stranger. For, a fixed proportion of the rent,

or natural produce, will always bear a fixed and certain proportion to the estate ; but a fixed proportion of the produce must, and will, at different times, bear a very different proportion to the estate, or to the profits arising from it.

Prescription.—By the same reasoning, Tithes, under the present practice of the law, cannot be supported by any right by prescription; for Mr. Justice Blackstone, in his Commentaries, vol. 2. p. 265. expressly lays it down as a rule of law : " A prescription cannot be for a thing which " cannot be raised by grant ; for the law allows prescription " only in supply of the loss of a grant, and, therefore, every " prescription pre-supposes a grant to have existed. Thus, " the Lord of a Manor cannot prescribe a tax, or toll, upon " strangers ; for as such claim could never have been good " by grant, it shall not be good by prescription."

Custom.—Neither can custom support the right to Tithes of the whole produce ; for Mr. Justice Blackstone, vol. 1. p. 76, 77, &c. says, " When a custom is actually proved to " exist, the next inquiry is into the legality of it : for if it " is not a good custom, it ought no longer to be used. *Ma-* " *lus Usus abolendus Est,* is an established maxim of law.

" It must have been peaceable, and acquiesced in, not " subject to contention, or dispute ; for, as customs owe " their original to common consent, their being immemo- " rially disputed, either legally, or otherwise, is a proof that " such consent was wanting.

" Customs must be reasonable, or, rather, taken nega- " tively, they must not be unreasonable."

And, in the Law Dictionary of Sir T. E. Tomlyne, it says, " A custom, contrary to the public good, or injurious " to a multitude, and beneficial only to some particular

" persons, is repugnant to the law of reason, and, con se
" quently, void."—2 Danv. 424-427.

It is evident, from the above authorities, that custom will
not support a title to the Tithe of the whole produce of cultivated land.

The limitation asked by the Petition, would, whilst protecting the pious and humane Clergyman, or Tithe-owner,
in the full and fair exercise of his rights, without any chance
or pretence for obloquy, so it would restrain the hitherto
rapacious man in those demands which inflict public injury
and private misery, by preventing the employment of the
poor, and the improvement of the land.

Whatever may be the forbearance and moderation exercised by the Tithe-owner, the present practice of the law
will ever operate, as the sword suspended over the head of
Damocles, to the terror of those who may adventure upon
the extension of cultivation, or the improvement of the land;
for though to-day they may enjoy the calm of moderation,
they are left unprotected from the storms of rapacity on the
morrow.

It is quite impossible that the present practice of the law
can ever be reconciled. There is in the human mind,
thought, and action, a repelling principle against a system
which taxes a man for the virtue of industry, which ever has
acted, ever will act, and which will daily become more
urgent, and more earnest in its manifestation, as population
will progressively be found to press upon space.

Inestimable advantages will be derived by the settlement
of the Tithe on the principles of equity and justice. The
hands of industry will become unfettered; the spirit of enterprize and improvement of the land will be released from
bondage; the odium which attaches to these very indefen-
sible laws, will be removed; religion will be disburthened
of its most exceptionable attendant; and the laws of the

country, which, on this subject, now present a lamentable memorial of darkness and ignorance, will be rendered perfectly consistent with the enlightened design and spirit of the British Constitution, and with the liberties, the rights, and the justice, due to a people, who desire to boast their perfect freedom, to be secured by just laws, under the protection of their gracious King, and of an enlightened Legislature.

CASTLEMAN'S WARGRAVE,

Feb. 9, 1831.

Tilling, Printer Chelsea.

British Labour Struggles:
Contemporary Pamphlets 1727-1850

An Arno Press/New York Times Collection

The Factory Act of 1833. 1833-1834.

Richard Oastler: King of Factory Children. 1835-1861.

The Battle for the Ten Hours Day Continues. 1837-1843.

The Factory Education Bill of 1843. 1843.

Prelude to Victory of the Ten Hours Movement. 1844.

Sunday Work. 1794-1856.

Demands for Early Closing Hours. 1843.

Conditions of Work and Living: The Reawakening of the English Conscience. 1838-1844.

Improving the Lot of the Chimney Sweeps. 1785-1840.

The Rising of the Agricultural Labourers. 1830-1831.

The Aftermath of the "Lost Labourers' Revolt". 1830-1831.